FEMINIST ECONOMICS A.. .~
PUBLIC POLICY

Professor Ailsa McKay, who was known not only for her work as a feminist economist but also her influence on Scottish social and economic policy, died in 2014 at the height of her academic career and impact on public life. Organised around the key themes of Ailsa McKay's work, this collection brings together eminent contributors to argue for the importance of making women's roles and needs more visible in economic and social policies.

Feminist Economics and Public Policy presents a uniquely coherent analysis of key issues including gender mainstreaming, universal childcare provision and universal basic income security, in the context of today's challenging economic and political environments. It draws on international perspectives to look at the economic role of women, presenting readers with interrelated sections on gender budgeting and work and childcare, before concluding with a discussion on Citizen's Basic Income and how it could contribute towards a more efficient, equitable social security system. The theoretical, empirical and practice-based contributions assembled here present recommendations for more effective public policy, working towards a world in which women's diverse roles are recognized and fully accounted for.

This book is a unique collection, which will be of great relevance to those studying gender and economics, as well as to researchers and policy makers.

Dr Jim Campbell is a Reader in Economics at Glasgow Caledonian University, Scotland, UK.

Morag Gillespie, now retired, was formerly a Senior Research Fellow at Glasgow Caledonian University and a member of Women in Scotland's Economy Research Centre, UK.

ROUTLEDGE IAFFE ADVANCES IN FEMINIST ECONOMICS

IAFFE aims to increase the visibility and range of economic research on gender; facilitate communication among scholars, policy makers and activists concerned with women's wellbeing and empowerment; promote discussions among policy makers about interventions which serve women's needs; educate economists, policy makers and the general public about feminist perspectives on economic issues; foster feminist evaluations of economics as a discipline; expose the gender blindness characteristic of much social science and the ways in which this impoverishes all research, even research that does not explicitly concern women's issues; help expand opportunities for women, especially women from underrepresented groups, within economics; and, encourage the inclusion of feminist perspectives in the teaching of economics. The IAFFE book series pursues the aims of the organisation by providing a forum in which scholars have space to develop their ideas at length and in detail. The series exemplifies the value of feminist research and the high standard of IAFFE sponsored scholarship.

1 Living Wages, Equal Wages
Gender and Labor Market Policies in the
United States
*Deborah M. Figart, Ellen Mutari and Marilyn
Power*

2 Family Time
The Social Organization of Care
Edited by Nancy Folbre and Michael Bittman

**3 Feminist Economics and the World
Bank**
History, Theory and Policy
Edited by Edith Kuiper and Drucilla K. Barker

4 Sexual Orientation Discrimination
An International Perspective
Edited by M. V. Lee Badgett and Jefferson Frank

5 The Feminist Economics of Trade
*Edited by Irene van Staveren, Diane Elson,
Caren Grown, Nilufer Catagay*

6 Sex Markets
A Denied Industry
*Marina Della Giusta, Maria Di Tommaso and
Steinar Strøm*

7 Gender and Chinese Development
Towards an Equitable Society
Lanyan Chen

**8 Gender and the Contours of
Precarious Employment**
*Leah Vosko, Martha MacDonald and Iain
Campbell*

9 Questioning Financial Governance from a Feminist Perspective
Edited by Brigitte Young, Isabella Bakker and Diane Elson

10 Challenging Knowledge, Sex and Power
Gender, Work and Engineering
Julie E. Mills, Suzanne Franzway, Judith Gill and Rhonda Sharp

11 Women and Austerity
The Economic Crisis and the Future for Gender Equality
Edited by Maria Karamessini and Jill Rubery

12 New Frontiers in Feminist Political Economy
Edited by Shirin M. Rai and Georgina Waylen

13 Gender and Climate Change Financing
Coming Out of the Margin
Mariama Williams

14 Feminist Economics and Public Policy
Reflections on the work and impact of Ailsa McKay
Edited by Jim Campbell and Morag Gillespie

FEMINIST ECONOMICS AND PUBLIC POLICY

Reflections on the work and impact of Ailsa McKay

Edited by Jim Campbell and Morag Gillespie

Routledge
Taylor & Francis Group

LONDON AND NEW YORK

First published 2016
by Routledge
2 Park Square, Milton Park, Abingdon, Oxon OX14 4RN

and by Routledge
711 Third Avenue, New York, NY 10017

Routledge is an imprint of the Taylor & Francis Group, an informa business

British Library Cataloguing in Publication Data
A catalogue record for this book is available from the British Library

Library of Congress Cataloging in Publication Data
A catalog record for this book has been requested

ISBN: 978-1-138-95085-6 (hbk)
ISBN: 978-1-138-95086-3 (pbk)
ISBN: 978-1-315-66855-0 (ebk)

Typeset in Bembo by
Servis Filmsetting Ltd, Stockport, Cheshire
Printed and bound in Great Britain by
Ashford Colour Press Ltd, Gosport, Hampshire

MIX
Paper from
responsible sources
FSC
www.fsc.org   FSC® C011748

CONTENTS

List of figures   x
List of tables   xi
Notes on contributors   xii
Acknowledgements   xvii
List of abbreviations   xviii
List of UK and international legislation   xx

PART I
Introduction and appreciation   1

1   Introduction to the themes of the book   3
    Jim Campbell and Morag Gillespie

2   Appreciation: talking to Ailsa   13
    Marilyn Waring

PART II
Gender budgeting   25

3   Gender budgeting and macroeconomic policy   27
    Diane Elson

4   Challenging the norms: gender budgeting as feminist
    policy change   38
    Angela O'Hagan

5 Gender budgeting in Scotland: seeking transformative change
through public spending   46
Angela O'Hagan and Morag Gillespie

6 Gender budgeting in the capability approach: from theory
to evidence   54
Tindara Addabbo

7 In search of a gender budget with 'actual allocation of public
monies': a wellbeing gender budget exercise   61
Gulay Gunluk-Senesen

8 The Spanish Central Government budget: comments on
recent experience   71
Paloma de Villota

PART III
Women, work and childcare   **81**

9 Childcare as an investment in infrastructure   83
Sue Himmelweit

10 Integrating economic and social policy: childcare –
a transformational policy?   94
Gary Gillespie and Uzma Khan

11 Scotland and the great recession: an analysis of the gender
impact   112
Jim Campbell, Ailsa McKay and Susanne Ross

12 Occupational segregation and Modern Apprenticeships
in Scotland   124
Emily Thomson

13 Women working together   137
Ann Henderson

PART IV
Citizen's Basic Income   **151**

14 On justifying a Citizen's Basic Income   153
Chris Pierson

15   A Citizen's Basic Income and its implications   164
     Annie Miller

16   Debating a Citizen's Basic Income: an interdisciplinary
     and cross-national perspective   177
     Caitlin McLean

17   Citizen's Basic Income: a radical and transformative idea
     for gender equality?   189
     Morag Gillespie

Conclusions   **199**

18   Concluding thoughts: building on Ailsa's legacy   201
     Jim Campbell and Morag Gillespie

Index   207

FIGURES

4.1	Key actions for feminist policy change	40
4.2	Framework of favourable conditions	43
8.1	Density function and PIT rates	76
10.1	Scottish economic strategy: framework	95
10.2	The four priorities	96
10.3	Trends in employment rate; men and women: Scotland and UK	99
10.4	Male and female employment rates by age band	100
10.5	Childcare costs as a percentage of net family income	101
10.6	Labour market status and aspirations of women with dependent children	103
10.7	Impact on the Scottish economy of increased women's labour market participation	105
10.8	Public spending on family benefits in kind, in cash and tax measures	107
10.9	Public spending on family benefits in kind as a percentage of GDP, 2009	108

TABLES

7.1   Gaziantep Municipality planned activities and budget allocations
      related to women and gender equality, 2015   67
7.2   Gaziantep Municipality budget allocations for women's capabilities,
      2015   68
8.1   Percentage of employed earners and PIT tax rates   75
10.1 Gender differences in labour market participation and employment
      March–May 2015   100
11.1 Employment in Scotland 2008–2015   113
11.2 Unemployment in Scotland 2008–2015   113
11.3 Economic inactivity in Scotland 2008–2015   114
11.4 Full-time and part-time employment in Scotland   115
11.5 Self-employment in Scotland 2008–2014   116
11.6 Underemployment in Scotland 2008–2014   118
12.1 Female participation rates by age   127
12.2 Female participation rate by SVQ level of attainment   128
12.3 Female participation in the 'top ten' occupational frameworks 2015
      and change from 2009   128

CONTRIBUTORS

Tindara Addabbo is Associate Professor of Economic Policy at the Department of Economics Marco Biagi of the University of Modena and Reggio Emilia (Italy). She is a member of CAPP (Centre for the Analysis of Public Policies), RECent (Center for Economic Research), the Scientific Committee of Fondazione Marco Biagi and the European Gender Budgeting Network. She has published in the areas of the gender impact of public and social policies, measurement of wellbeing in the capability approach, employment and wage discrimination by gender, income distribution and quality of work.

Jim Campbell is a Reader in Economics at Glasgow Caledonian University. His current research is focused on the following three areas: the impact of European Structural Funds on economic development in Scotland and in particular how changes in the level of funding and the administration of the funds will affect future economic development; occupational segregation in the context of apprenticeship training and workforce development; and the economic and social impact of the provision of childcare on local communities in areas of economic deprivation and the wider labour market implications of the expansion of childcare.

Diane Elson is Emeritus Professor of Sociology at the University of Essex, UK, and a Visiting Professor at Glasgow Caledonian University. She is a member of the UN Committee for Development Policy, and adviser to UN Women. She is a former Vice President of the International Association for Feminist Economics, and is Chair of the UK Women's Budget Group. She has published widely on gender equality, and economic policy, including articles in *World Development, Journal of International Development, Feminist Economics, Journal of Human Development and Capabilities* and *International Review of Applied Economics*. She is one of the founders of gender budget analysis with numerous publications on this issue.

Gary Gillespie was appointed Director and Scottish Government Chief Economist in 2011. He joined the civil service in 2000 from the Fraser of Allander Institute (University of Strathclyde) where his research interests included Scottish economy, regional economic modelling and foreign direct investment. His current role in providing economic advice to the First Minister is one of the most visible roles within the public sector in Scotland. He publishes regular assessments of the State of the Economy and is a regular participant in economic discussion across Scotland. He was made an Honorary Professor at Glasgow Caledonian University in January 2011 and was appointed to the role of Visiting Professor at the University of Strathclyde in 2015.

Morag Gillespie, now retired, was formerly a Senior Research Fellow at Glasgow Caledonian University and a member of Women in Scotland's Economy Research Centre. She has a long history of working with voluntary and community groups, including delivering and managing social, welfare and legal rights advice services in a variety of voluntary sector settings. She is a qualitative researcher with an interest in inclusion and involvement of groups experiencing poverty who are often excluded from research and decision making. Her writing and teaching focuses on poverty (including social security) and inequality, with particular interests in gender and women's experiences of poverty.

Gulay Gunluk-Senesen is a Professor of Public Finance at the Faculty of Political Sciences, Istanbul University, Turkey. Her publications are in the areas of gender issues (glass ceiling, women's employment and gender budgeting), input-output modelling and defence expenditures. She was a member of the Turkish delegation at the UN CSW, 52nd session on 'Financing for Gender Equality and the Empowerment of Women', New York, USA, in 2008. She is involved in The Women's Labour and Employment Initiative Platform (KEIG, www.keig.org) – Turkey. She recently led a research project on 'Public Policies, Local Governments, Gender Budgeting: Women Friendly Cities, Case of Turkey'. She is a member of the European Gender Budgeting Network.

Ann Henderson has been Assistant Secretary at the Scottish Trade Union Congress since 2007, responsible for government and parliamentary liaison. Ann has campaigned for women's equality throughout her varied working life, as a train driver, parliamentary researcher, community worker and member of the Women's National Commission. Her interests focus on improving women's working conditions, the value of women's work, women in public policy and political decision making. As a researcher early in the Scottish Parliament, Ann was instrumental in securing access for the new Scottish Women's Budget Group to promote gender analysis in the Scottish budget process. Through the STUC Women's Committee Ann organised a series of 'Economics for Equality' Weekend Schools for women trade unionists, led by Ailsa McKay.

Susan Himmelweit is Professor Emeritus in Economics at the Open University, whose research is on the economics of gender, including gender budgeting, theoretical and policy aspects of the economics of care and intra-household inequalities. She was President of the International Association for Feminist Economics, an Associate Editor of the journal *Feminist Economics* and the founding chair of the UK Women's Budget Group, whose policy advisory group she now coordinates, contributing to its reports on the gender impact of successive budgets and spending reviews (www.wbg.org.uk/RRB_Reports.htm). With Hilary Land she has written on care policy for the Equal Opportunities Commission, the Joseph Rowntree Foundation and the trade union Unison. She is a member of the EHRC's Fair Financial Decisions Advisory Group.

Uzma Khan joined the Scottish Government as a professional economist in 1999. Her experience spans a broad number of departments including providing economic advice to Scottish Ministers on education and lifelong learning, health, business and enterprise and, more recently, transport policy. Currently, Uzma heads up the Economic Policy and Strategy Unit within the Office of the Chief Economic Adviser where her key role is to develop the policy framework for the Scottish Economic Strategy and labour market economics. Uzma graduated from Glasgow University in Economics in 1999, and completed her Masters degree in Business Economics from Strathclyde University in 2002.

Caitlin McLean was the first Ailsa McKay Postdoctoral Fellow in Economics based in the WiSE Research Centre at Glasgow Caledonian University. In that post she explored the potential for a Citizen's Basic Income (CBI) to contribute to greater gender equality. She holds a PhD in Social Policy from the University of Edinburgh, where her thesis compared childcare policy and provision in the US and UK. She has also contributed to collaborative projects comparing childcare in Europe, including research for the EU-funded project 'Families & Societies' as well as an international review of childcare provision published by the Scottish Government. Caitlin is now a Workforce Research Specialist at the Center for the Study of Child Care Employment, University of California-Berkley.

Annie Miller, now retired, lectured at Heriot-Watt University, teaching mainly business economics, and maths and statistics for economists. She was a co-founder in 1984, and has been a Trustee since 1989, of The Basic Income Research Group, which became the Citizen's Income Trust in 1992. She has been Chair of CIT since 2001 and she contributes regularly to its *Citizen's Income Newsletter*. She has also given talks and presented papers on CBI both here in the UK and abroad. Annie collaborated with Ailsa to promote debate and discussion on CBI, most recently at the Scottish Parliament on 15 January 2014. Further details of Annie's publications and the work of the CIT are available at www.citizens income.org.

Angela O'Hagan is a Lecturer at Glasgow Caledonian University (GCU) and a researcher with WiSE. Angela and Ailsa met when setting up the Scottish Women's Budget Group (SWBG) and became firm friends. Convenor of SWBG since 2006, Angela is also a long-standing member of the Scottish Government Equality and Budgets Advisory Group, the UK Women's Budget Group Management Committee and the European Gender Budgeting Network. Angela completed her PhD at GCU with Ailsa McKay as her Director of Studies, comparing gender budgeting in Scotland and Spain. Angela has held a number of senior management roles in civil society and statutory organisations and has a range of current and past roles on management boards of civil society organisations.

Chris Pierson is Professor of Politics in the School of Politics and International Relations at the University of Nottingham. He is lead editor of the journal *Political Studies*. He has held visiting research posts at the University of California, Santa Barbara, the Johns Hopkins University, the Australian National University, the University of Auckland and the Hansewissenschaftskolleg in Niedersachsen, Germany. He is working on a three-volume history of justifications of private property. The first volume is published as *Just Property: A History in the Latin West*. (Oxford University Press, 2013).

Susanne Ross is a Lecturer in Business (with an interest in Public Management) at Queen Margaret University, Edinburgh. She has previously worked at the Scottish Government, Glasgow Caledonian University, Heriot-Watt University and Glasgow International College. Susanne has undertaken research into the gender impact assessment of funding decisions for, and gender-based occupational segregation within, the Scottish Modern Apprenticeship programme; gender mainstreaming within the European Structural Funds programme; as well as work on developing a system of National Accounts for Scotland. Her academic and research interests include feminist economics, women in the labour market, gender analysis and public policy. She is currently a member of the International Association for Feminist Economics and research associate for WiSE Research Centre, Glasgow Caledonian University.

Emily Thomson is a Senior Lecturer in Economics and a member of the Women in Scotland's Economy (WiSE) Research Centre at Glasgow Caledonian University. Her teaching and research interests include feminist economics, the business case for gender equality and international development. Emily is a member of the International Association for Feminist Economics, a fellow of the International Working Group on Gender, Macroeconomics and International Economics and a fellow of the Higher Education Academy.

Paloma de Villota is Professor of Applied Economy at Universidad Complutense de Madrid. She is the director and promoter of the doctorate course 'The Economic Theory from a feminist perspective' which was distinguished with 'Mención de

Calidad' by the Ministry of Education. She has worked on many studies with the European Commission and a variety of European and Latin American Universities. Her research focuses on gender incidence of taxation and public policies. She is head of the Feminist Research Institute of the Universidad Complutense, on the Board of Editorial Committee of the *Feminist Studies Magazine* (Universidad Complutense) and a leading member of the Scientific Committee of the Economía Crítica and the Spanish network Women in Science, GENET.

Marilyn Waring is Professor of Public Policy at AUT University, Auckland, New Zealand, an honorary graduate of GCU and a long-standing inspiration in the work of Ailsa McKay. Her research interests include governance and public policy, political economy, gender analysis and human rights. Marilyn received Amnesty International New Zealand's Human Rights Defender Award in 2013, and in 2014 was the Institute of Economic Research Economist of the Year, and was awarded the University Vice Chancellor's Research Medal. The film *Who's Counting? Marilyn Waring on Sex, Lies and Global Economics* forms the basis of the 'Economics for Equality' programme at GCU. Ailsa's last publication was a co-edited volume on the influence and impact of Marilyn's thinking on feminist economics in practice.

ACKNOWLEDGEMENTS

This book came about as a result of a commemorative conference held for Ailsa McKay in January 2015.

I would like to thank all of the people who attended the event, particularly the speakers who came from far and wide to celebrate Ailsa's research and impact. In particular I would like to thank Glasgow Caledonian University and the Scottish Government for providing the financial resources which enabled us to stage the conference in the first place.

Thanks to all of the contributors for responding to the various requests for changes in a timeous manner. A very special thanks to my co-editor Morag Gillespie for all her hard work in bringing this project to a successful conclusion, despite the fact that she 'retired' halfway through. Also thanks to Professor Eleanor Gordon and Professor Sara Cantillon, Director of Women in Scotland Economy Research Centre (WiSE) for providing helpful comments on some of the chapters.

The book is dedicated to the memory of Ailsa McKay and I hope that it will be a fitting testament to her impact as an academic and as an activist who made it her mission to ensure 'women counted'.

For Ailsa, 'the best thing that ever happened to me'.

Jim Campbell
September 2015

LIST OF ABBREVIATIONS

CBI	Citizen's Basic Income
CEA	Council of Economic Advisers
CIT	Citizen's Income Trust
COSLA	Convention of Scottish Local Authorities
DSS	Department of Social Security
DWP	Department for Work and Pensions
EBAG	Equality and Budgets Advisory Group
EBS	Equality Budget Statement
EGBN	European Gender Budgeting Network
EHRC	Equality and Human Rights Commission
EOC	Equal Opportunities Commission
EQF	European Qualification Framework
ESA	European System of National Accounts
EU	European Union
GDP	Gross Domestic Product
GFI	General Formal Investigation
GGEPMI	Global Gender and Economic Policy Management Initiative
HBAI	Households Below Average Incomes
HES	Household Economies of Scale
HMRC	Her Majesty's Revenue and Customs
HMSO	Her Majesty's Stationery Office
IAFFE	International Association for Feminist Economics
IMF	International Monetary Fund
JdA	Junta de Andalucía
LGBTI	Lesbian, Gay, Bi-sexual, Trans-sexual, and Intersex
LTCI	Long-Term Care Insurance
MA	Modern Apprenticeship

MDR	Marginal Deduction Rate
MSP	Member of the Scottish Parliament
MTB	Means-Tested Benefit
NHS	National Health Service
NI	National Insurance
NIC	National Insurance Contributions
NICE	National Institute for Health and Care Excellence
NLW	National Living Wage
NMW	National Minimum Wage
OECD	Organisation for Economic Co-operation and Development
ONS	Office for National Statistics
OSWG	Occupational Segregation Working Group
PIT	Personal Income Tax
R&D	Research and Development
SA	Social Assistance
SDS	Skills Development Scotland
SES	Scotland's Economic Strategy
SNA	System of National Accounts
SNP	Scottish National Party
STUC	Scottish Trades Union Congress
SVQ	Scottish Vocational Qualification
SWBG	Scottish Women's Budget Group
TL	Turkish Lira
UBI	Universal Basic Income
UK	United Kingdom
UN	United Nations
UNDP	United Nations Development Programme
UNJP	United Nations Joint Programme
UNSNA	United Nations System of National Accounts
WBG	Women's Budget Group
WiSE	Women in Scotland's Economy

LIST OF UK AND INTERNATIONAL LEGISLATION

Equality Act (2006)
Equality Act (2010)
Health and Safety at Work Act (1974)
Ley 26/2014, 27 November 2014. Madrid. BOE-A-2014-12327
Ley 39/2010, 22 December 2010. Madrid. BOE-A-2010-19703
Ley 35/2006, 28 November 2006. Madrid: BOE-A-2006-20764
Ley 30/2003, 13 October 2003. Madrid: BOE-A-2003-18920
Real Decreto Ley 20/2011, 30 December 2011. Madrid. BOE-A-2011-20638
Trade Union Act (1927)

PART I
Introduction and appreciation

1

INTRODUCTION TO THE THEMES OF THE BOOK

Jim Campbell and Morag Gillespie

> As I am an economist I could provide you with a shed load of statistics. However as I am a Feminist Economist I am going to continue to tell you stories. Not because I can't do statistics but because I think the statistics need the stories to provide a more rich understanding of their meaning. In that sense I like to follow the example of Keynes and Stiglitz – great economists of our time, who believed and continue to believe in the need to engage and persuade the public – and to tell the story in a way that we all understand and to appeal to us all to follow a path that makes sense with respect to valuing all of our assets and not just those with a market price.
>
> (McKay, 2012)

Professor Ailsa McKay told stories about women's disadvantaged position in the economy in a way that made people listen. She built a formidable international reputation as a feminist economist and had a profound influence on discussions of economic and social policy in Scotland and beyond. She died on 5 March 2014 at the height of her academic career and impact on public life.

This book is largely based on the contributions made at a two-day commemorative conference held in Ailsa's honour in January 2015. The conference themes reflected the key areas of Ailsa's research interests, namely: gender budgeting; women, work and childcare; and Citizen's Basic Income (CBI). This book follows a similar structure and is divided into three distinct but inter-related sections.

With one exception, all of the contributors to this book would regard themselves not just as colleagues of Ailsa's but friends and, in some cases, very close friends. The exception is Dr Caitlin McLean who did not know Ailsa but was appointed as the first Ailsa McKay Postdoctoral Research Fellow in Economics at Glasgow Caledonian University in January 2015. This position was created by Professor Pamela Gillies, Principal and Vice-Chancellor of Glasgow Caledonian University, in memory of Ailsa and to take her work forward.

This book encompasses a feminist analysis of a number of economic issues and policies and reflects upon the contribution of Professor Ailsa McKay to making women's roles and needs more visible. It provides a unique analysis of key economic issues concerned with addressing the changing role of women in the economy and some of the barriers and challenges they face.

Part II explores recent experiences of gender budgeting and its potential impact on the ways in which macroeconomic policy, the allocation of public sector resources through the budget process and revenue raising can reflect women's needs and roles more transparently and more effectively.

Part III on women, work and childcare discusses: the economic benefits of increased public investment in childcare for both women and the wider economy; women's position in the labour market in Scotland, including in the aftermath of the great recession; and the role of training programmes in relation to occupational gender segregation.

Part IV discusses a CBI and considers how it could contribute towards a more efficient, equitable and gender sensitive social security system and its potential to be a transformative step towards greater gender equality.

The book draws on the perspectives of internationally renowned academics including some of the leading feminist thinkers in the world, as well as public policy practitioners. It highlights some of the measures and policies necessary to move towards greater gender equality and presents a unique collection that reflects on the issues about which Ailsa McKay wrote and taught from a feminist economics view-point, always with the aim of working towards transformation in what she viewed as an overly androcentric world. Her own writing and analysis is interwoven through the book. Before describing the key themes and chapters, the next section provides a short biographical note that outlines the key stages in Ailsa McKay's career.

Ailsa McKay: a biographical note

Ailsa was born on 7 June 1963 in Falkirk, Scotland, and moved to Canada in 1965, returning to Falkirk in 1971 with her mum and three sisters. It would be fair to say that at school Ailsa was not an academic star and at seventeen she took the position as a clerical assistant in the Department of Social Security (DSS) in Falkirk. One of her roles there was to assess emergency payments for people on benefits and colleagues said that people would request her to consider their cases since she invariably found in favour of the claimant and authorised payments. She made a decision to return to education and in 1981 went to Falkirk College to do a Higher National Certificate (HNC) in Business on a part-time basis while continuing to work for the DSS. After successfully achieving the HNC in 1983 she left the DSS and became a full-time student at Stirling University in 1984, initially to do Business Studies but she switched very quickly to study economics and politics. She spent the third year of her course on exchange at the University of California, San Diego, and graduated in 1988 with a first class honours degree in Economics and Politics.

After graduation she went to work for Stirling Council housing department before becoming a welfare benefits advisor in Central Regional Council, using her knowledge of the social security system to help people obtain the benefits they were entitled to. In May 1991 she was appointed as a Lecturer in Economics at Glasgow Caledonian University, thereby beginning a highly successful academic career. She became Head of the Department of Economics and International Business in 2008 and in the following year she was made a Professor of Economics and became Vice-Dean of the Caledonian Business School.

In 2010 she established the Women in Scotland's Economy Research Centre (WiSE) at Glasgow Caledonian University. Ailsa was a member of the International Association for Feminist Economics (IAFFE) and a founding member of the Scottish Women's Budget Group (SWBG) and the European Gender Budget Network (EGBN). She was a representative of SWBG and then an academic adviser to the Scottish Government's Equality and Budgets Advisory Group as well as being a Special Adviser to the Scottish Parliament Equal Opportunities Committee in the periods 2007–2009 and 2010–2011. She was a visiting professor at the University Complutense of Madrid and regularly delivered lectures to doctoral students at the university. Ailsa was a strong advocate of knowledge exchange and passionate about making economics accessible and relevant to women; she cooperated with a variety of women across the world to deliver lectures and training and promote gender equality.

Structure of the book

Whether talking to parliamentarians, students or community groups, Ailsa McKay always challenged listeners to view mainstream economics as a useful tool for explaining how the economy works, but to recognise that it has serious limitations, particularly in its failure to reflect the reality of women's roles. She encouraged listeners both to engage with economics, but to be sceptical about and challenge mainstream economics assumptions and find ways to make economics more relevant to and reflective of women's lives. Towards this end, she often quoted Joan Robinson: 'The purpose of studying economics is not to acquire a set of ready-made answers to economic questions, but to learn how to avoid being deceived by economists' (Robinson, 1955: 75).

This mantra was one that Ailsa used to good effect in all her work. This book reflects upon and celebrates the full and varied contributions she made to making women's roles and needs more visible in economic policies. Although the chapters cover a wide range of issues, a common thread that runs through the book is the notion of 'provisioning', a term that Ailsa often used, sometimes in relation to her own and other women's caring roles but also more broadly in challenging mainstream economic analysis and assumptions. Ailsa's approach reflected the idea that 'a richer economics, whilst not excluding formal models or the study of choice, would be centred around the study of provisioning' of human life (Nelson, 1993: 33).

Nelson's definition of the economy as 'the sphere of social activities that have to do with the provisioning of the goods and services that sustain life and can promote its flourishing' (Nelson, 2006: 1061) summarises where Ailsa's key points of interest and influence lay and she challenged others to think beyond conventional assumptions about who and what count.

Whether she was discussing families and care, how work in all its forms is valued, social security or wider economic analysis, provisioning was an important central concept for Ailsa. Each of the three sections in the book connects to this interpretation of women and the economy that challenges conventional forms of analysis in order to improve the way that progress is recorded so that all needs and contributions count.

Part I Introduction and appreciation: talking to Ailsa

One of Ailsa's last publications was a co-edited volume with Margunn Bjørnholt on the influence and impact of Marilyn Waring's writing, teaching and activism for advances in feminist economics (Bjørnholt and McKay, 2014). Marilyn Waring was one of the people who most inspired Ailsa in her work and from their opposite corners of the world, they shared many conversations about work, life, family, care and more. Marilyn travelled from New Zealand to Scotland to make the keynote address at the commemorative conference for Ailsa in January 2015.

Her appreciation (Chapter 2) celebrates the characteristics of Ailsa's approach to feminist scholarship and strategy and reflects on the value of the conversations they had about the challenges facing feminist economics. With reference to key concepts of gender, care and ontological and epistemological differences in feminist economics, she discusses some issues she wanted to talk to Ailsa about: gender and the potential for 'transformative strategies and outcomes affecting third gender'; care and her concerns about the direction that debate on care is taking in feminist economics; and her fears about a mono culture developing in feminist economics.

Part II Gender budgeting

At its heart, gender budgeting aims to help to ensure that the 'provisioning' and promotion of flourishing lives through public services reflect the needs and interests of all community members. Gender budgeting is concerned with making public resource allocation and revenue raising gender aware rather than gender blind so that decisions on public spending and taxation take account of the differential needs of and impacts on women and men. In other words, the economic models that account for progress should not presume that 'rational economic woman' is the same as 'rational economic man'.

Gender budgeting is possibly the best example of how Ailsa McKay combined her academic and activist roles to create opportunities for change towards a new order for the advancement and protection of women and their rights as equal citizens. She played a central role in promoting gender budget analysis in Scotland as a key approach to making gender inequalities transparent and ensuring decision making and delivery are more responsive to and effective in tackling the causes and consequences of women's disadvantaged position.

Diane Elson was another woman who inspired Ailsa. She was also an early supporter of efforts to take gender budgeting to Scotland. She was amongst the keynote speakers at the Scottish government's first and only international conference on gender budgeting in 2002. In Chapter 3 Diane shows how macroeconomic policy decisions on whether to aim for a budget deficit or surplus are not gender neutral. She questions the rationale for viewing some aspects of spending, such as weapons systems, as suitable for public investment through borrowing, while spending on care, for example, is classified as public consumption and thus inappropriate for government borrowing. She argues that investment in social infrastructure would promote gender equality, challenges governments to design macroeconomic policy with a focus on wellbeing, not simply economic growth, and to invest in life rather than in death.

Angela O'Hagan draws on comparative analysis of experiences from Scotland, Spain and elsewhere to identify some favourable conditions that support the adoption and implementation of gender budgeting (Chapter 4). These conditions reinforce early principles proposed by the Commonwealth Secretariat – country ownership; participation; transparency; sustainability; and continuous improvement – that provided the foundation of Ailsa McKay's advocacy of gender budgeting for transformative change.

Reflecting on Ailsa McKay's distinctive approach and pivotal role in building awareness and support for gender budgeting advocacy in Scotland, Angela O'Hagan and Morag Gillespie review progress in Scotland where the Scottish government is working towards implementation of *equalities* budget analysis. However, an emphasis on process and procedural change has not yet delivered significant policy shifts. Ailsa McKay consistently highlighted how equalities mainstreaming and economic models fail to take sufficient account of women, reinforcing how crucial gender analysis is in Scottish budgetary decisions, but also that economic policy and strategy are key sites for gender budgeting and tackling women's disadvantage.

Ailsa engaged with others in Europe and beyond with an interest in gender budgeting. She told the Scottish story and used the lessons learned to help others both inside and outside government who were involved in different stages of developing gender budget initiatives. In this process, she delivered lectures, training and resources in several countries, including Spain, Turkey and Georgia, working with academics, policy makers and practitioners (Chapter 5). The approach of mutual support and learning from each other continues in a strong European network of gender budget experts and practitioners, including several examples here.

In Chapter 6 Tindara Addabbo uses examples from Italy to explore a capabilities approach to gender budgeting which argues that the methodology for applying a wellbeing lens to analysis and the implications for its use at different government levels should reflect the unequal distribution by gender of paid and unpaid work. In this way it can highlight the need for public policies able to tackle gender inequalities produced within the family that give rise to unequal development of capabilities, including addressing the impact of reductions in public spending for women.

Gulay Gunluk Senesen builds on this methodological approach in Chapter 7 and reflects on the challenges of interactions between the policy process and budget for gender budget initiatives. She discusses the experience in Turkey and uses a well-being gender audit of one municipality budget to explore policy preferences from the perspective of women's wellbeing. This analysis reveals deficiencies in policy and resource allocation and the lack of a perspective on improving gender equality.

Finally in this section, Paloma de Villota (Chapter 8) focuses on the revenue side of the budget. Reviewing the Spanish Central Government's approach to gender analysis of the budget, she argues that, while public sector transparency has improved, more research is needed to evaluate both sides of the budget from a gender perspective, particularly in relation to taxation. Her analysis of planned Personal Income Tax arrangements in Spain shows a return to tax structures similar to pre-recession levels, moving away from more progressive and redistributive tax changes introduced following the onset of the economic crisis in 2008.

Part III Women, work and childcare

Like many other feminist economists, Ailsa McKay was interested in understanding 'how public, private, and market institutions and incentives can best be designed to support both decent wages and quality care, rather than beginning with the idea that care and money are incompatible' (Meagher and Nelson, 2004: 102).

Provisioning is at the heart of discussions in this section. Ailsa was at the forefront of arguing that Scotland should have universal provision of childcare free at the point of use and that this could have a transformative impact on the wider economy as well as women and children. In August 2013, she travelled to Aberdeen, despite being very ill at the time, to make a presentation on the economic benefits of the universal provision of childcare to the Council of Economic Advisors (CEA). The CEA is a group of eminent economists, including Joseph Stiglitz and business leaders, set up by the Scottish government in 2007 to provide advice on economic policy and strategy. The Scottish government recorded that:

> Professor McKay led a wide ranging discussion which covered equality, the limitations of existing economic frameworks and the outcomes these models deliver. Improved childcare was identified as a potential lever which could have a transformational impact on the direct economy but also a positive wider indirect (and more long-term) on economic and social impacts.
>
> (Scottish Government, 2013a: 4)

That input went on to influence the Scottish Government's commitment to a transformational approach to childcare which featured in their White Paper on Independence (Scottish Government, 2013b: 193).

In Chapter 9 Sue Himmelweit outlines the economic ideas that are being harnessed in the general notion of investment in (social) infrastructure and presents Ailsa's arguments for seeing childcare specifically as such an investment. She then raises some issues about why, as campaigners for gender equality, we might want to exercise some caution in using this terminology. This is both because it can be misused, distracting attention from the case for spending on childcare as a public service, and because it can render more difficult the case for spending on some areas which are just as important but cannot so easily be seen as providing economic benefits over a period of time. She concludes with some reflections on when and where the use of arguments based on investment is helpful in promoting policies that advance gender equality.

Gary Gillespie (Chief Economic Advisor to the Scottish Government) and Uzma Khan reflect upon the influence Ailsa McKay had on the development of government policy through her interaction with the Scottish Government and Parliament and the Council of Economic Advisers (Chapter 10). Ailsa advised on equality in its widest sense, challenging policy makers to think about things differently, including the scope and relevance of economic models as they are currently constructed. She also helped specifically with the development of childcare policy. Ailsa set childcare in a wider context, arguing that it was concerned with equality, feeding into key policy areas including the labour market, occupational gender segregation and the gender pay gap. Childcare was one lever which could improve outcomes for women as part of a wider package of support. The legacy of this work is now reflected in the government's updated economic strategy.

Chapter 11 is the result of the last project which Ailsa worked on in 2013 with co-authors Jim Campbell and Suzanne Ross. It examines the impact of the recent recession and the subsequent economic recovery on the relative economic positions of men and women in Scotland. The analysis shows that women and men were affected differently, for example men's employment and unemployment levels recovered more quickly than those of women. Young people were the main victims of rising unemployment but the impact was gendered here as well. However, the great recession did not result in the massive increases in headline unemployment experienced in other less severe recessions. This can be explained, in part, by a rise in economic inactivity, part-time working and underemployment all of which are more prevalent amongst women than men.

A key theme of Ailsa McKay's research was concerned with the enduring problem of occupational gender segregation that results in women being concentrated into relatively low paid and insecure jobs. Ailsa led a number of research projects exploring the causes and consequences of gender based occupational segregation with particular reference to the Scottish Modern Apprentice programme. In Chapter 12 Emily Thomson, who worked with Ailsa on most of these projects, reviews this programme of research that shows how government funded vocational training programmes can reinforce wider patterns of occupational segregation. Where there is public investment in funding, occupational segregation by gender can also result in bias towards investment in the skills of men in training over women. However, the research has influenced positive policy changes including commitments to tackle occupational segregation in the MA programme, provision of more publicly available gender disaggregated data and a recognition of the important contribution which a feminist economics perspective brings to tackling these issues.

Ann Henderson, Assistant Secretary of the Scottish Trade Union Congress, examines some trends in women's labour market experiences in Scotland. In particular, she explores workplace improvements, legal protections and some policy outcomes, particularly concerning collective bargaining and representation. Ailsa McKay's interest in knowledge exchange and making economics accessible led to the development of 'Economics for Equality' training for women trade unionists and other groups. Joint work between academics and trade unionists is building on this legacy to support women in developing their confidence to challenge economic policy decisions that may not be in their interests.

Part IV Citizen's Basic Income

CBI is an unconditional universal income paid to all citizens. In different forms it has been debated over many years, but is a topic of heightened interest following the recession and pressure to reduce public expenditure, particularly spending on social security measures. In a very literal sense, it involves provisioning for basic needs. However, for Ailsa McKay it was a radical idea that had the potential to be not only a replacement of social security systems but also an emancipatory measure for women.

Ailsa's interest in CBI is long-standing and stretches back to her time in the Department of Social Security in Falkirk. Her PhD, awarded in 2000, was entitled 'Arguing for a Citizens' Basic Income: A Contribution From a Feminist Economics Perspective'. She was proud of her achievement and the fact that her thesis was passed with no revisions required. Her thesis formed the basis for *The Future of Social Security Policy: Women, Work and a Citizens' Basic Income*, a research monograph, published by Routledge in 2005.

In her book, Ailsa puts forward an impassioned call to promote the idea of a CBI, grounded in a feminist political economy. In her historical survey of justifications for a basic income, she tracked a series of thinkers from Tom Paine to Philippe van Parijs. Chris Pierson, Ailsa's PhD supervisor, sketches out an alternative historical route to a CBI in Chapter 14. He draws on a much older discourse which, although steeped in patriarchal values that systematically excluded women, may still be worth exploring in support of the CBI cause. He suggests that a CBI can be presented as part of the property regime that a liberal, democratic society (like the UK) should be signed up to as a token of its own core values and beliefs.

In Chapter 15, Annie Miller, Chair of the Citizen's Income Trust, demonstrates how the set of options defining the current means-tested Social Assistance system in the UK can be identified as overly complex and contributing to a series of problems, such as poverty and unemployment traps. As a consequence it often fails those who depend on it, especially women. She argues that, in contrast to this, a CBI system has the potential to result in more attractive outcomes, particularly for women, helping to reduce inequalities of income and giving them more choice and control over their lives.

A Citizen's or Universal Basic Income has gained renewed interest internationally in both academic and policy circles in recent decades. In Chapter 16, Caitlin McLean identifies key strands of recent European and international debates on the issue, covering the ethics, economics and politics of such proposals. She also summarises the existing evidence on the implementation of basic income proposals and their effects, especially on labour market outcomes and concludes with a discussion of the future of CBI research.

In the final chapter in this section Morag Gillespie explores the key arguments in Ailsa McKay's work from 'The Future of Social Security Policy: Women, Work and a Citizens' Basic Income' to the recent context of the global recession and the potential for more radical thinking before the Scottish independence referendum in 2014. Most analysis of CBI focuses on its potential as an alternative social security system, assessing its impact using a mainstream economic framework that values 'productive' activities and does not reflect the hidden and unpaid work done mainly by women. However, Ailsa argued that CBI had the potential to be an emancipatory measure for women but this requires that we rethink our assumptions about what counts as 'work' and the links between income and work.

Conclusions

In Chapter 18, we conclude by reflecting on the issues that most concerned Ailsa and consider how those interested in improving the position of women might build on her legacy, particularly in Scotland where her impact was most profound, but also more broadly.

References

Bjørnholt, M. and McKay, A. (eds) (2014). *Counting on Marilyn Waring: New Advances in Feminist Economics*. Toronto: Demeter Press.

McKay, A. (2005). *The Future of Social Security Policy: Women, Work and a Citizens' Basic Income*. Abingdon: Routledge.

McKay, A. (2012). Conference speech. *Scottish Government and STUC 1st Women and Employment Summit*, Dynamic Earth, Edinburgh 12 September 2012. [Online] Available from: www.gcu.ac.uk/gsbs/newsevents/news/article.php?id=48724 (accessed 12 August 2015).

Meagher, G. and Nelson, J.A. (2004). 'Survey article: feminism in the dismal science'. *The Journal of Political Philosophy*, 12(1): 102–126.

Nelson, J.A. (1993). 'The study of choice or the study of provisioning? Gender and the definition of economics'. In Ferber, M. and Nelson, J. *Beyond Economic Man: Feminist Theory and Economics*. Chicago: University of Chicago Press.

Nelson, J.A. (2006). 'Can we talk? Feminist economists in dialogue with social theorists'. *Journal of Women in Culture and Society*, 31(4): 1051–1074.

Robinson, J. (1955). *Marx, Marshall and Keynes*. Delhi School of Economics Occasional Paper No. 9. Delhi: University of Delhi.

Scottish Government (2013a). *Minutes of the Fourth Meeting of the Council of Economic Advisers*. Edinburgh: Scottish Government. [Online] Available from: www.gov.scot/Topics/Economy/Council-Economic-Advisers/Meetings/30-08-2013 (accessed 14 August 2015).

Scottish Government (2013b). *Scotland's Future. Your Guide to an Independent Scotland*. Edinburgh: Scottish Government.

2

APPRECIATION: TALKING TO AILSA

Marilyn Waring

Ailsa McKay was an ontological and epistemic influence of significance both in and beyond her specialist fields of gender budgeting, childcare provision and welfare reform and the Citizen's Basic Income. Ailsa was also a passionate teacher and activist, influencing changes in government practices and policies, a consultant to the Scottish Parliament, to the Scottish and Irish Government, the UK Treasury and United Nations Development Programme (UNDP). She was a networker, lobbyist and community leader, expert witness, expert adviser and well-published academic.

Ailsa never lost touch with the *political* in feminist political economy. For me a basic characteristic is to examine what transformative strategies and outcomes might result from our work. Ailsa lived what Julie Nelson called a 'process ontology' of events and experiences, where 'Scientific thought ... is both a part of our experience and a purposive seeking ... The world "becomes" rather than just is' (Nelson, 2003: 136).

Ailsa described the source of her passion for a Citizen's Basic Income (CBI) as the stories she heard while employed as a welfare rights adviser. Ailsa's CBI is a universal approach, but she clearly situates it in Scotland, and as part of the debate on devolution and issues of income maintenance and social security policies (McKay, 2005, 2007). The CBI is radical in its critique of the neo-classical framework and challenges the ontological and epistemological assumptions in the existing Western systems of social security. With Sandra Harding (2003), Ailsa understood that it takes a lot to dislodge the dominant epistemic culture. Her CBI for Scotland proposed a recurrent tax-financed transfer payable lifelong to each person, in their own right, with no means test and no work test, to satisfy their basic needs and without having to participate in paid work. There would be further allowances for age and disability. Her feminist analysis meant a CBI took account of the single largest economic sector of the community engaged in unpaid work in all its forms. Ailsa saw the CBI as a gender justice and human rights issue, which would enhance freedoms to do and be, and help sustain the social and cultural capital of unpaid work. Ailsa wrote that a CBI:

> would provide the basis for evaluating and accounting for the very different social experiences of men and women in a market based economy … [transforming the] traditional notions regarding the relationship between work and pay, and an implied notion that paid work remains the main source of economic welfare.
>
> (McKay, 2013)

A conversation about gender

Ailsa was very generous to me, with her time and her mind. I loved to have conversations with her. We had begun one about some discomforts we had about the future of gender budgeting. In 2011 I was at a Human Rights Conference in Wellington, New Zealand, listening to Phylesha Brown-Acton. The Dutch Embassy had sponsored a number of fakaleiti, fa'afafine, takutapui, and akava'ine[1] from New Zealand and the Pacific to meet independently prior to the conference. Phylesha was speaking on their behalf reporting from their meeting, a first for Pacific third gender, and spelled out quite clearly that their community were not part of a Western generic LGBTI[2] group. Third gender persons were recognised by specific nouns in their own island languages, and third gender had their own culturally traditional roles and expectations. LGBTI was arrogant in its assumption of inclusiveness, silencing other ontologies and epistemologies.

This was transformative for me – a wall of perception/deception fell down. It was a post-feminist critical analysis of gender as a dichotomy. I took this learning with me to a UNDP contract to write 12 modules on Gender and Economics for Asia Pacific as part of the Global Gender and Economic Policy Management Initiative (GEPMI) Programme.[3] One of my first decisions was to include third gender throughout the draft modules, from the following understanding I had at the time.

Gender is the social and cultural construction of what it means to be *man* or *woman* or *boy* or *girl* including roles, expectations and behaviours, and the relationships between genders. These constructions are learned through socialisation processes. They are context specific and changeable, and usually presented as a dichotomy: either male or female.

In Asia and the Pacific, there is a rich diversity of cultural and social expressions of other gender identities, for example: hijra and kothi in India, fa'afafine, fakaleiti and mahu vahine in the Pacific region, kathoeys in Thailand, lakurn-on in the Philippines and waria in Indonesia. The term *third gender* is used to describe individuals who are neither male nor female, those who have or are sexually transitioning, those who are both or neither, those who are transgender and those who cross or swap genders. The term third gender is officially recognised in India, Pakistan and Nepal. It is an option in official documents in Germany, Australia and New Zealand. The third gender is about gender identity – a person's deeply felt sense of being male or female or something other. A person's gender identity may or may not correspond with their sex (including their indeterminate sex).

Gender determines what is expected of, allowed for and valued in a woman or girl, a man or a boy, and any third gender individual, in a given context. In most societies, there are gendered differences and inequalities in responsibilities assigned, activities undertaken and access to and control over resources, as well as decision making opportunities. Third gender individuals frequently have a culturally specific role, steeped in history, which is often stigmatised by those outside the particular socio-cultural context.

Those of you as old as I am will remember the years when we had no disaggregated data by male and female, but maintained a narrative about the invisibility of women anyway. I did this for third gender throughout the modules, sometimes augmented by news items – third gender central government elected representatives (Nepal, New Zealand), mayors (Thailand, New Zealand), working as tax collectors in India, cabaret entertainers in Australia, as air crew in Thailand or in tourism services in the Pacific.

The inclusion of third gender people was discussed by me with UNDP Bangkok, who were personally supportive and agreed that UNAIDs recognised third gender and that regional ILO work was in progress on third gender and paid work. I was able to remind UNDP that my contract specified that I had to be 'accurate'. If they were going to direct me to be inaccurate and breach my contract I would have to have that in writing. But we would see what the peer reviewers thought.

The assembly of experts in the peer review was extraordinary. I learned something from every module specialist and each module was enriched with stories, critiques and feedback. There were several areas of pushback. 1) There was too much on the Pacific they said. In context this is very funny to those of us from the Pacific. In many UN documents we are mentioned once or twice, treated generically, or just subsumed by descriptions of and examples from Asia. The balance in these modules was very different. Only one peer reviewer lived in the Pacific. When I delivered the modules in the Pacific in August 2013, the participants expressed delight and surprise at the coverage of their region; 2) There was consternation that the term 'care economy', that a number of them used, seldom appeared in the modules; and 3) Third gender persons should be withdrawn from the whole course/be there as an option/ be there in the first chapter and maybe labour and that's enough/be subject to New York's approval/be removed and only introduced if there was legal recognition in the country where the course was being conducted, etc.

Anit Mukherjee, my colleague and friend, spoke about the 2009 landmark High Court case in India which had decriminalised homosexual acts and had granted equal rights to third gender persons (Mahapatra, 2014), the bi-sexuality of many Shiva images, the reality of hijra in Indian communities, and engaging third gender in his work in HIV and AIDS prevention. The Fijian head of the Women's Bureau spoke up. She said that she was very pleased to see these references here. Recently she had called a meeting for women working in the sex industry and many transgender women had attended. She had not anticipated this, but had determined she must include them and their voices: 'If I don't do this, and not just for this matter, no one else will.'

The printing of the modules included third gender persons, but countries were advised that it could be removed. It was not an issue in the regional course deliveries I took part in. As I was working on the GEPMI modules, I was wondering what might be done about the lack of data in advancing third gender rights. Where did we start? But Ailsa had that covered in the CBI: it was totally inclusive. So what implications did that have for more strategies of universality? And we'd have to talk about what it meant for the way gender budgeting had always been framed.

My own interest in gender budgets is stirred when we get to sectors such as infrastructure and energy. In 30 years of front line development work in Asia, Africa and the Pacific, for example, I have seen the multi-million dollar wastage on infrastructure for the market as opposed to wellbeing. It always reminds me of an early 'women in development' audit by USAID on a roading project, when the outcomes for women were summed up in one sentence: women walk on roads! Looking at issues of gender and infrastructure, too often the analysis is about access to paid work in such projects, of seeing prostitution and rape and pregnancy as inevitable, and the invisibility of externalities that polluted a community's drinking water, ruined footpaths, bulldozed a project's rubbish into household laundry facilities on river banks, etc. Then the floods/landslides/earthquakes/insurgents take the roads and bridges out again.

This approach always seemed to have something missing for comprehensive development of infrastructure related to the oft times largest economic sectors of subsistence agriculture or household unpaid work. Where are the single span, walking-only bridges in places where highway bridges were regularly washed away? Single span bridges would keep schools, health centres and community markets going. Where are the flying foxes fed by regular cable maintenance, the solar lit footpaths which inhibit motor bikes using them? In the Hindu Pradesh, in many regions of South America, in the Cordillera, Myanmar and Melanesia – millions of hours of time would be saved immediately. The activities of subsistence farmers, households, community, cultural and religious activities, and the foundations of social protection might be enhanced, along with an increase in informal marketing, and even in tourist access. The foot traffic only bridges could be pumped out like Lego, and the attention to raised solar lit footpaths, which exclude all motorised vehicles, would add a safer environment for women and girls. (Male violence is a major cost in all forms of development.) It seems so obvious, but we know the Cost Benefit Analysis won't add up. The largest sector, the invisible work of men and women and girls and boys, has no market value to find its way into the equation.

I have to confess I have always had an ambivalence towards 'gender analysis'. In my own experience in projects and programmes in the field, women and development approaches appeared to give me more space. In the Pacific 'gender' is synonymous with women in many central agency practices, so other than men now being able to tap into half of all 'gender' programme/project resources, nothing has changed in using the term 'gender'.

But as Kaul explained, the 'post' feminist need is to re-examine, in a multifaceted and creative way, 'what has already been accepted – (and) to highlight the tensions in the *grounds on which* it *was* accepted' (Kaul, 2003: 196, my emphasis). So I would have wanted to have a discussion with Ailsa about gender, and what our roles might be, in transformative strategies and outcomes affecting third gender.

A conversation about care

I would also have liked to talk with Ailsa about this word *care*, and some concerns I have about where feminist economics is going with this term. For 14 months in 2013–2014, I was the care manager and a primary caregiver to my 88-year-old terminally ill father, with a terminal cancer where melanoma roots slowly and methodically invaded the twelve cranial nerve tunnels on their way to the brain stem, and for my mother of 87. I took a 12-month sabbatical, gave up any consultancies and travel and only had time for reading drafts from my postgraduate research students.

Nancy Folbre wrote that caring labour is 'undertaken out of affection or a sense of responsibility for other people, with no expectation of immediate pecuniary reward' (Folbre, 1995: 75). I would have described my caring as beginning with affection and moving to obligation. Ten years later she investigated ways in which care might be defined and measured to enhance our understanding of the impact of economic development on women. She categorised care work with a focus on work done, principally by family members: cooking, cleaning, growing and preparing food, and including the subsistence activities of collecting wood and carrying water (Folbre, 2006). Folbre defined direct care services as 'paid or unpaid efforts to meet the needs of dependents, including direct care work that involves personal connection and emotional attachment to care recipients' (Folbre 2009: 112). She further noted that caring work occurs within the paid economy but that it is typically segregated, in that the paid roles in childcare, teaching, food services, elder care work, nursing, cleaning and other domestic service work is overwhelmingly performed by women (and/or migrants) and at lower rates of pay than workers in other sectors, mirroring in the market the lack of value of the work taking place unpaid in households.

Julie Nelson wrote that caring behaviour:

> does not require, and in fact forbids, that one go from the one extreme of neglect to the opposite extreme of self-sacrifice. The self-sacrificing care giver who simply reacts to any and all demands, regardless of cost, is guilty of being irresponsible to at least one human being in her care: herself.
>
> (Nelson, 1996: 71, fn. 8)

It's a lovely sentiment but it was not possible in my reality to place any part of caring for myself in front of my parents' needs. There was no individual disposable time.

I used the categories of the 2009–2010 New Zealand Time Use Survey (Statistics New Zealand, n.d.) to list the work description of my activities in my parents' home as caregiver. These were: accompanying an adult, available for care of adults, mail organisation, financial budgeting, household administration, providing accounting or advisory services, attending a meeting for unpaid work, managerial and executive work, administration secretarial or clerical work, home maintenance or improvement, purchasing health services, waiting for health services, delivery and driving services, purchasing durable and non-durable goods, food and drink preparation and cleaning, purchasing repair services, arranging, organising, running events or activities, packing away goods. My mother undertook all indoor cleaning, laundry, ironing and other clothes care, tending plants and harvesting edible produce. Think of all the different job descriptions in all those processes. This is the extent of the unpaid work that must be done to 'care' in a household. Problematically, front line 'caring' is too frequently seen as bounded by job descriptions and demarcations of professionals – paid workers – so that the range and extent of the activities necessary for one person to undertake unpaid are lost. This loss of specificity is not strategically or politically useful. Alternatively the role is seen principally as one of cooking, cleaning and shopping. These were the easy parts. Management and logistics were the cause of my months-long vice-like headache in caring for my parents.

In microcosm, I have a major issue with the use of the terms 'care', 'caregiver' or 'care economy' for all this unpaid work. These terms do not describe the management, logistics, administration, resource mobilisation, transportation, food production, increasingly specialised food preparation, coordination that are necessary.

In much of the world, it is also important to remember that, in addition to work directly related to assisting dependants, household work – the daily maintenance of wellbeing – must continue. Household access to water, hygienic practices, transportation and a clean environment, along with the management and logistics of all expectations, are daily chores that cannot be neglected. When someone is gravely ill, needs don't happen according to a daily timetable. The work is very complex and difficult and the list of things to do is very long.

In 2010 I worked with colleagues on research with the carers of those living with HIV and AIDs in Bangladesh, Botswana, Canada, Guyana, India, Jamaica, Namibia, New Zealand, Nigeria, Papua New Guinea and Uganda (Waring et al., 2011). In addition to all the unpaid work involved in precarious caring situations, they told us stories of stigma and discrimination, of violence, of poverty and despair, hunger, poor health, social exclusion, losing income, withdrawal from education. Many were abandoned by traditional networks of church or extended family. The required policy responses could not be encompassed by a care work economic analysis.

These carers worked for rights in their socio/political environment, then did work that is part of the management of caring, then all the household work, then they did the so called 'care' work. I have a colleague writing a case study in New Zealand of a mother of a teenage girl with multiple complex, severe health issues. In the last two years, her mother has had to deal with 22 personnel from 18 different agencies. Imagine that work – the forms, the phone calls, the frustration, the time. There's an important insight here. If the work would have to be done in institutions caring for dependent residents, then it has to be done in microcosm in the household for a dependant, with no possibilities of economies of scale.

Let's look at this another way. Armstrong (2013) describes Canadian long-term residential care interests as including governments at multiple levels, national and international level for-profit and not-for-profit organisations, professions, unions and organised as well as unorganised workers, residents, families and volunteers, community organisations and other groups representing various publics. While the coinage and use of care economy is found in feminist economics, demographic projections in my lifetime showed that the care economy was a growing sector that would involve the households, communities, the private and public sectors. It would involve globalisation, migration, multinationals running facilities and a large low paid work force. The care economy is a vibrant, growing, significant economic sector, subject to market forces, and subject to all the rules of the United Nations System of National Accounts (United Nations, 2008).

I 'get' South Korea and Long-Term Care Insurance as the care economy. I was well briefed on this in 2011 during my GEPMI consultancy. Long-Term Care Insurance (LTCI) was implemented on 1 August 2008 to reduce the burden of care on family members and to provide for a rapidly expanding older demographic. The South Korean Government faced a choice between the provision of services, and the payment of a benefit to those in need to purchase those services. A country-wide feminist response from women was that elderly men would just spend any money on gambling, smoking, drinking and their social life, and women would still be expected to do the unpaid caring. 'We won't do it' was the loud message for the government. Hence, LTCI was introduced.

Elderly recipients' eligibility is dependent on the certification of LTCI. Based on their individual needs, care is then (mainly) delivered in kind according to the wishes of the client. The client has the freedom to choose their service provider. Long term care benefits consist of community-based home care, institutional care and cash benefits.

Before the introduction of LTCI healthcare spending, welfare expenditure and pension spending were rapidly rising. Since LTCI has been meeting the needs of the elderly there has been a rise in LTCI spending. However, 'healthy aging' of the aging population has resulted in a decrease in healthcare spending, and a decrease in hospitalisation for the elderly from 15.7 days to 11 days (Waring, n.d.).

The increase in healthy elderly means more elderly are remaining in the working population and 95.8 per cent of families of the elderly have reported that LTCI insurance has helped them participate in economic activity, all of which benefits tax revenue.

In comparison with other sectors where employment levels decreased or were stable because of the economic recession, health and social work, which includes the LTCI industry, are the exception. Workers at LTCI facilities have increased by more than 190,000. Increased workers in other sectors include more than 40,000 in the field of technological innovation and manufacturing in elder care support (Waring, n.d.). That's a very economic transformation of the care economy. The LTCI will also establish a significant central investment fund, creating a form of compulsory savings.

I'd like to discuss all this with Ailsa. From my geography, region, cultural influences, for me, the 'care economy' is one element of all unpaid work and is not a replacement for all the characteristics of unpaid work. I hope we are not heading for a 'boundary of reproduction' which declares what is and is not 'care', in mimicry of the barren 'boundary of production' about what is and is not work, that is found in the UNSNA. For example, I plant roses for informal marketing (not care), I plant tomatoes for household (care?), I plant garlic to keep aphids off the roses (not care), and to use medicinally and in meals in the home (care then?) and marigolds also as companion plants and because they are perennials (not care?) but I can use them in salads and to make tea (care?).

With Sabine O'Hara (2013) I am in the camp where everything needs care: our planet and our eco-systems, where climate change is having severe, widespread and irreversible impacts; our transparent democratic practices, indigenous languages and cultures; human rights, our neighbourhoods and communities. Ailsa thought a starting point for feminist economic theories was that they fully acknowledged care for each other and care for the planet (Bjørnholt and McKay, 2014: 16–17). Ecological care is primary – nothing else can exist without it. It seems very strange to exclude such a fundamental reality from any operative concept of 'care' in any discipline.

Certainly the 'care economy' illustrates the space which most challenges the Chicago man busy self-actualising and acting in his own self–interest. The 'care economy' is a contradiction to this framing. The needs of the *other* come first and are the starting point for the carer, not maximising their own rational self-interest (Jochimsen 2003: 239). It is the needs of the *other*, the person being cared for which is the focus of the transactional behaviour, especially in caring situations for young children, the frail, elderly, sick, disabled. This is a most useful theoretical insight in exposing the 'Chicago School' man. This exposure also resonates with many indigenous economic approaches, and by much of the work on the 'commons' led by Elinor Ostrom (1990). But when I was taking unpaid care of my father, there is no suggestion that I was more imbued with selfless motivations which would improve his quality of care, compared with the young male Filipina nurse who took over in the last five weeks, with more skills, experience, expertise and patience than I could ever muster. I would not wish to argue that the nurse's only motivation was the market income he would receive, and it was my observation that 'care' was a professional characteristic that he practised in all his waged work.

At other times reading another essay on 'care', I wonder to myself: 'but if my care is for the eco system, does that rule me out of the "care economy" parameters?' of this or that particular author. What about the delayed reciprocity and communal transactions that are a part of male and female cultural exchanges in many non-Western communities, which meet the Folbre parameters of responsibility for others with no expectation of intrinsic reward (Zein-Elabdin, 2003)? I think it's time for some post-feminist reflection on 'care', and it's another conversation I would love to have with Ailsa.

Resisting a mono cultural feminist economics

I have always been in some trepidation when addressing European and US audiences. I grew up in a community where there were quite clearly different claims to knowledge and culturally embedded beliefs, where indigenous ways of being, a familiarity with and practice of subsistence economics, and a life of work for and with the ecology of New Zealand are my roots. Standards were established in a childhood, where dualities were a constant. This was of enormous influence in my political life, and in my research and writing. It has been my experience that I hear and read a different way. Let me give you an example.

In 2006, Vanuatu discovered it had been given the number one ranking in the Happy Planet Index (Campbell, 2006). But far from celebrating, this announcement was the impetus for a different survey of wellbeing. Vanuatu leaders were surprised that people who had never asked them what they valued, never visited and knew little of the Pacific, could impose their ideas in this way. In general in Vanuatu, the collection of, and comparison with, Western-framed economic data, are of little value to developing community strategies. The project to track Melanesian wellbeing began in June 2010 with participation from Fiji, Solomon Islands, Kanaky New Caledonia, Papua New Guinea, Bougainville and Vanuatu. The pilot led to the development of twelve national minimum development indicators for culture (Prism, n.d.).

The Vanuatu indicators in the 'access' field showed 79 per cent of the population with access to customary lands. Ninety per cent were certain of these boundaries, 88 per cent felt their accessible lands met their basic needs, 64 per cent had full access to forest resources and 59 per cent full access to marine resources. Seventy-seven per cent never missed or reduced meals for lack of food. The foundation of social protection in the Pacific is traditional economy where environmental protection, livelihoods, social equity and nutrition, for example, are safeguarded (Waring et al., 2013: 46).

Into this context came a request to me from a UN agency for a paper on gender and social protection in the Pacific. It said:

> The report will include a conceptual framework, and chapters on labour markets, macroeconomics and gender, and social policies. In order *to reflect the experience of the Pacific* in the report, we are commissioning two papers on the region – one will be a data driven paper, using micro data *from labour force*

surveys, to obtain a picture of how women are faring within labour markets (formal and informal employment).

(UN, 2013; my italics)

At this I sigh and say to myself – if you were remotely interested in 'reflecting the experience of the Pacific in the report', you wouldn't look for it in labour force surveys.

A Labour Force Survey is supposed to measure the number of citizens between 15 and 74 years, who have worked for at least one hour for pay during the reference week or have 'worked without pay for one hour or more in work which contributed directly to the operation of a farm, business, or professional practice owned or operated by a relative' (OECD, 2000: 65). For a start, the work of large numbers in the Pacific and of hundreds of millions of men, women and children in the informal and subsistence economy is not counted as work or counted in the UNSNA, both because of the ideological bias in the accounting framework, and because of technical, logistical and budget resource capabilities (Rizzo et al., 2015). The countries with the largest subsistence economies frequently need development assistance to carry out national statistical surveys. The domination of market interests, both national and international, means that scarce resources measure what the World Bank, IMF, regional banks, donors and all the private sector wants – market data. Just shifting the rules about what qualifies as work has made no difference to visibility and policy responses. In Nigeria, Liberia and Zimbabwe for example, the base years for calculating GDP are 1990, 1992 and 1994 respectively. These statistics have not included the 1993 or 2008 UNSNA revisions. Forty-one sub-Saharan countries had base years more than 20 years old, so all this data is unreliable (Jerven et al., 2015). Think of all the thought and time going into the exercise to determine what the data categories should be for the Sustainable Development Goals to follow the Millennium Development Goals. Whose ontological and epistemological positions determine what these might be?

There was another element to the UN agency request.

> The second paper will examine the extent to which Pacific countries have been able to introduce *progressive social policies* – both social protection (cash transfers, child benefits, pensions etc.) and universal social services (health and education) – and the challenges that they have faced in doing so. This paper will also set these social policies within the broader macroeconomic framework.
>
> (UN, 2013)

In 2015 the universalising continues. A polite response may have been Fabienne Peter's approach: that the challenge lies in rethinking the legitimacy of knowledge claims in ways that make obvious the inherent political and ethical aspects of knowledge production (Peter, 2003: 112). We may have much better intersectionality practice in feminist economics, but are we still framing inside the Western paradigm?

So Ailsa, I would like to talk with you about this problem of Euro-centric discourse. Ailsa constantly examined her political and ethical standards in knowledge production. Ailsa knew Scotland and the timing and opportunity to argue the case for the CBI in her place at her time. She understood where her expertise lay and where it could most usefully be shared. She understood culture and difference as lived experience – as many Scots do.

Funny, insightful, wicked, tactical, evidenced and passionate – Ailsa, these are just a few of the conversations I would like to have with you.

Notes

1 Terms used to describe third gender persons from Tonga, Samoa, Maori and Cook Islands languages.
2 An international acronym for Lesbian, Gay, Bi-sexual, Trans-sexual, and Intersex persons.
3 UNDP programme, overview. [Online] Available from: www.undp.org/content/undp/en/home/ourwork/povertyreduction/focus_areas/focus_gender_and_poverty/gepmi.html (accessed 28 July 2015).

References

Armstrong, P. (2013). 'Puzzling skills: feminist political economy approaches'. *Canadian Review of Sociology/Revue Canadienne de Sociologie*, 50: 256–283.

Bjørnholt, M. and McKay, A. (2014). 'Advances in feminist economics in times of economic crisis'. In Bjørnholt, M. and McKay, A. (eds) *Counting on Marilyn Waring: New Advances in Feminist Economics*. Toronto: Demeter Press, 7–20.

Brown Acton, P. (2011). *Human Rights Conference Address*. [Online] Available from: www.pridenz.com/apog_phylesha_brown_acton_keynote.html (accessed 6 January 2015).

Campbell, D. (2006). 'Vanuatu tops wellbeing and environment index'. *Guardian*, 12 July 2006. [Online] Available from: www.theguardian.com/world/2006/jul/12/healthandwellbeing.lifeandhealth (accessed 12 July 2015).

Folbre, N. (1995). '"Holding hands at midnight": the paradox of caring labor'. *Feminist Economics*, 1(1): 73–92.

Folbre, N. (2006). 'Measuring care: gender, empowerment, and the care economy'. *Journal of Human Development*, 7(2): 183–199.

Folbre, N. (2009). 'Reforming care'. In Gornick, J.C. and Meyers, Marcia K. (eds) *Gender Equality: Transforming Family Divisions of Labor*. New York: Verso.

Harding, S. (2003). 'After objectivism and realism'. In Baxter, D. K. and Kuiper, E. (eds) *Toward a Feminist Philosophy of Economics*. London: Routledge, pp. 122–124.

Jerven, M., Kale, Y., Ebo Duncan, M. and Nyoni, M. (2015). 'GDP revisions and updating statistical systems in sub-Saharan Africa: reports from the Statistical Offices in Nigeria, Liberia and Zimbabwe'. *The Journal of Development Studies*, 51(2): 194–207.

Jochimsen, M.A. (2003). 'Integrating vulnerability: on the impact of caring on economic theorizing'. In Baxter, D.K. and Kuiper, E. (eds) *Toward a Feminist Philosophy of Economics*. London: Routledge, pp. 231–246.

Kaul, N. (2003). 'The anxious identities we inhibit; Post'isms and economic understanding'. In Baxter, D.K. and Kuiper, E. (eds) *Toward a Feminist Philosophy of Economics*. London: Routledge, pp. 196–197.

Mahapatra, D. (2014). 'Supreme Court recognizes transgenders as "third gender"'. *The Times of India*, 15 April 2014. [Online] Available from: http://timesofindia.indiatimes.com/india/Supreme-Court-recognizes-transgenders-as-third-gender/articleshow/33767900.cms (accessed 29 July 2015).

McKay, A. (2005). *The Future of Social Security Policy: Women, Work and a Citizen's Basic Income*. London: Routledge.

McKay, A. (2007). 'Why a Citizen's Basic Income? A question of gender equality or gender bias'. *Work, Employment and Society*, 21(2): 337–348.

McKay, A. (2013). *Being Radical – Arguing for a Citizens Basic Income in the New Scotland*. Blog post, 21 February, University of Edinburgh. [Online] Available from: www.referendum.ed.ac.uk/being-radical-arguing-for-a-citizens-basic-income-in-the-new-Scotland (accessed 5 January 2015).

Nelson, J.A. (1996). *Feminism, Objectivity and Economics*. London and New York: Routledge.

Nelson, J.A. (2003). 'How did "the moral" get split from "the economic"?' In Baxter, D.K. and Kuiper, E. (eds) *Toward a Feminist Philosophy of Economics*. London: Routledge, pp. 134–137.

OECD (2000). *Main Economic Indicators: Sources and Definitions*. Paris: OECD Publishing.

O'Hara, S. (2013). 'Everything needs care: towards a context based economy'. In Bjørnholt, M. and McKay, A. (eds), *Counting on Marilyn Waring: New Advances in Economics*. Toronto: Demeter Press, pp. 37–56.

Ostrom, E. (1990). *Governing the Commons: The Evolution of Institutions for Collective Action*. Cambridge: Cambridge University Press.

Peter, F. (2003). 'Foregrounding practices – feminist philosophy of economics beyond rhetoric and realism'. In Baxter, D.K. and Kuiper, E. (eds) *Toward a Feminist Philosophy of Economics*. London: Routledge, pp. 105–121.

Prism (n.d.). *Vanuatu Pacific Living Conditions Factsheets Available*. [Online] Available from: www.spc.int/prism/vanuatu-hybrid (accessed 29 July 2015).

Rizzo, M., Kilama, B. and Wuyts, M. (2015). 'The invisibility of wage employment in statistics on the informal economy in Africa: causes and consequences'. *The Journal of Development Studies*, 51(2): 149–161.

Statistics New Zealand (n.d.). *Activity Classification for the Time Use Survey*. [Online] Available from: www.stats.govt.nz/methods/classifications-and-standards/classification-related-stats-standards/activity-time-use-survey.aspx (accessed 29 July 2015).

United Nations (2008). *System of National Accounts 2008 – 2008 SNA*. [Online] Available from: http://unstats.un.org/unsd/nationalaccount/sna2008.asp (accessed 29 July 2015).

United Nations (2013). Personal communication with the author, 8 November, unpublished.

Waring, M. (n.d.) Fieldnotes and meeting notes. Various dates, unpublished.

Waring, M., Carr, R., Mukherjee, A. and Shivdas, M. (2011). *Who Cares? The Economics of Dignity: A Case Study of HIV and AIDS Care-Giving*. London: Commonwealth Secretariat.

Waring, M., Carr, R., Mukherjee, A., Reid, E. and Shivdas, M. (2013). *Anticipatory Social Protection: Claiming Dignity and Rights*. London: Commonwealth Secretariat.

Zein-Elabdin, E. (2003). 'The difficulty of a feminist economics'. In Baxter, D.K. and Kuiper, E. (eds) *Toward a Feminist Philosophy of Economics*. London: Routledge, pp. 331–333.

PART II
Gender budgeting

3

GENDER BUDGETING AND MACROECONOMIC POLICY

Diane Elson

Introduction

This chapter takes up some of the concerns that Ailsa McKay had about macroeconomic policy and the extent to which it is supportive of public investment that reduces gender inequality, improves women's wellbeing and contributes to a more just and productive economy. Ailsa knew that gender budgeting has to look at the big picture, as well as scrutinise each tax and expenditure measure. She argued that we need a fundamental shift in thinking about macroeconomic policy that requires an acceptance of the centrality, and indeed the superiority, of public sector expenditure and the care sector in supporting economic and human development. She argued that we must improve upon our economic models in ways that incorporate care work and caring activities as investment (McKay, 2013: 20–21). This chapter explores that challenge in relation to macroeconomic policy, in the context of UK fiscal policy since 2010.

Macroeconomic analysis and policy: gender neutral or gender biased?

Macroeconomic analysis focuses on national output, income and expenditure, savings, investment, imports and exports. It is concerned with market flows of money, labour, goods and services, and stocks of available means of production-labour, equipment, buildings, physical infrastructure like roads, ports and power supplies, and natural resources, like land. For most purposes, macroeconomic analysis considers labour and natural resources to be non-produced means of production, whereas the rest are considered produced means of production, i.e. capital assets. Spending to create capital assets is considered to be investment.

Macroeconomic policy is concerned with the level and growth of national output and income, employment and unemployment, and inflation. These are influenced by monetary policy and fiscal policy. A key aspect of fiscal policy is whether the overall government budget is in deficit or surplus, and whether government borrowing is expanding or falling. There is no mention of men or women, except perhaps in relation to employment and unemployment. The analysis and policy appears to be gender-neutral but feminist economists have argued that if you look more closely this is not so (Cagatay et al., 1995; Elson, 1991).

In particular, feminist economists have argued that labour is a produced means of production that requires investment of resources for it to be available for production on a daily and intergenerational basis. Some of that investment requires spending money – on food, shelter, clothing, education, care and health services, for instance; and some of that investment requires spending unpaid time to shop, turn food into meals, keep shelter and clothing clean and in good repair, supervise homework and provide care for family and community. This unpaid work is disproportionately done by women and girls (Picchio, 1992; Folbre, 1994; Elson, 1998).

Public spending as well as private spending is needed to reduce the burden on women and girls and to reap the benefits of economies of scale in provision of clean water and sanitation, energy, housing, education, care and health. Underinvestment in public services and infrastructure will reduce the productivity of the current and future labour force (UN Women 2015: ch. 3).

Feminist economists also argue that macroeconomic policy needs to look beyond the level and growth of national output and income, employment and unemployment, and inflation to address directly the wellbeing and human rights of people (Balakrishnan and Elson, 2011; Seguino, 2011; Elson et al., 2012; Bjørnholt and McKay, 2014).

If we consider the unpaid economy as well as the paid economy, it becomes clear that many macroeconomic policies are not gender-neutral in their impact. For instance, attempts to reduce a government budget deficit by cutting public expenditure in a country like the UK are likely to impact more on women than on men. This is because women tend to make greater use of public services than men, linked to greater care responsibilities and greater use of care services; and a higher proportion of women's employment is in public sector than men's. Moreover, social security payments make up a greater share of women's incomes than men's, because women earn less in the labour market (UK Women's Budget Group, 2010: 2).

The Coalition government that came to power in the UK in May 2010 tried to reduce the budget deficit primarily by cutting expenditure, with much less focus on increasing taxation. The independent Institute for Fiscal Studies reports that deficit reduction between 2010 and 2015 has comprised 82 per cent expenditure cuts, and only 18 per cent tax revenue increases (Institute for Fiscal Studies, 2015). Since June 2010, the UK government has made £26bn 'savings' through cuts to spending on social security and changes to direct taxes, of which £22bn have come from women – 85 per cent of the total, with only 15 per cent coming from men (Grice, 2014).

Ailsa McKay and her co-authors (McKay et al., 2013) examine the gendered impacts of the first phase of these cuts, showing how the UK government ignored the provisions of the UK Equality Act (2006) in designing the cuts to public expenditure, and abolished the independent (but publically funded) National Women's Commission.

The UK Women's Budget Group in partnership with researcher Howard Reed has examined the impacts on different kinds of household, taking into account changes to indirect taxes and cuts to public services as well as changes in direct taxes and cuts to social security (UK Women's Budget Group, 2013). The losses in total income in cash, and in kind (from public services), as a percentage of household income are estimated as follows:

- Among families with children, single mothers lose the most: 15.6 per cent, compared to single fathers who lose 11.7 per cent and couples with children who lose 9.7 per cent.
- Among working age families with no children, single women lose 10.9 per cent, single men lose 9.0 per cent and couples lose 4.1 per cent.
- Among pensioners, single women pensioners lose most: 12.5 per cent, compared to single male pensioners who lose 9.5 per cent and couple pensioners, who lose 8.6 per cent.

These losses, which are disproportionately borne by women, could be reduced and even avoided if a different fiscal policy were adopted, as we now discuss.

Macroeconomics of the budget: is there any alternative to austerity?

The current UK Chancellor of the Exchequer (i.e. Minister of Finance) claimed that the high budget deficit he found when he came to office in May 2010 was evidence that the previous Chancellor of the Exchequer had 'maxed out' the national credit card. He claimed that the ratio of public debt to GDP of around 70 per cent was proof that the previous government had overspent; and that therefore cuts to public spending were inevitable so that the nation could 'live within its means'. He was appealing to the 'common sense' view based on the situation of individuals: if you had 'maxed out' your credit card, what would you have to do? (New Economics Foundation, 2013). It seems obvious that you should cut your spending. If you obtain additional credit cards and/or borrow from 'pay-day lenders' this just postpones the problem, and you end up with higher and higher monthly interest payments.

However, the situation of a government is not the same as for an individual. If a person cuts their spending, this does not lead to a fall in their income. But if a government cuts spending, it can lead to a fall in the income that the government gets through tax revenue. This happens because the cuts in public spending lead to a fall in incomes for those who supply the public sector with goods and services, and for public sector employees (some of whom may lose their jobs). It also leads to a fall in income for recipients of social security benefits. All these people tend to reduce what they spend, which in turn reduces the incomes of other people and the profits of businesses. This means they will pay less in taxes and government tax revenue falls. The budget deficit and the debt to GDP ratio can worsen rather than improve. The Chancellor anticipated that his cuts to public spending would reduce the budget deficit to around £40 billion in 2014, but in fact it was expected to be £90 billion, largely because tax revenues had fallen (UK Women's Budget Group, 2014). In the context of a recession, it makes sense to run a budget deficit and let debt rise until the economy has recovered. Sustaining public spending compensates for falls in spending by households and businesses and enables employment and output to rise to pre-recession levels.

In particular it makes sense to promote recovery by public investment. Cutting public investment often seems the politically easiest way of reducing the budget deficit. The share of public investment in GDP has fallen in the UK and in the Eurozone since the 2008 financial crisis (Truger, 2015: fig. 3 p. 15). Restoring public investment levels creates jobs and public assets that have the capacity to improve productivity, economic growth and wellbeing in the future. As Sen (2015) points out, when the UK Labour government invested in creating the National Health Service in 1948, the ratio of debt to GDP was over 200 per cent. In July 1957 when a Conservative government was presiding over a large programme of construction of social housing, the debt ratio was more than 120 per cent. High debt ratios did not prompt cuts to public investment in the 1940s, 1950s and 1960s, and investment in the welfare state and public services supported economic growth, bringing down the debt to GDP ratio, as well as reducing inequality and increasing wellbeing.

Once the economy has recovered to pre-recession levels of output, employment and income, improvements in wellbeing could be sustained through public investment if governments adopted the 'golden rule' to guide the management of the budget, rather than simply aiming to reduce the budget deficit and public debt.

The 'golden rule' for budgets: borrow to invest but not for day-to-day spending

The 'golden rule' allows governments to finance net public investment through budget deficits, i.e. by borrowing. The rationale is that net public investment increases the stock of assets and provides benefits for people in the future. Therefore, it is justified that future generations contribute to financing those investments via taxation to pay debt service. Future generations inherit the obligation to service public debt, but in exchange they receive a corresponding stock of assets. The 'golden rule' has been a widely accepted concept in mainstream economics of public finance for decades (see Musgrave, 1939 and 1959: 556–575).

Although the general idea behind the 'golden rule' is easy to understand, the question of how to define public investment is more complex. Theoretically, any government action that creates benefits – in the widest sense – for more than one period may qualify for this. However, the public finance literature usually focusses on future economic benefits in terms of higher productivity and growth. The question is posed whether an individual potential investment project has economic returns that are higher than or at least equal to its costs in terms of interest payments. Ideally, if the returns are high enough, debt sustainability would automatically be satisfied as the additional growth would decrease or at least stabilise the debt to GDP ratio (IMF, 2014: 110).

In practice, rather than a focus on individual investments, economists have focussed on whether general categories of public spending can be identified that are usually associated with sufficiently higher growth and productivity. This runs the risk of including types of public spending that should not be classified as investment as well as excluding types of public spending that should be classified as investment in terms of future benefits. In the past, public spending on physical infrastructure like transport facilities (roads, railways, ports, airports), communication systems and power generation and other utilities, and on equipment and buildings for public services has been defined as public investment. This corresponds to the traditional definition of public investment in the system of national accounts, and has been used by governments that have operationalised the 'golden rule'. The limitations of this are discussed in the next section.

The 'golden rule' was introduced in the UK under the Labour government in 1997 and was adhered to until the March 2008 budget. The rule stated that the government, over the economic cycle, would borrow in order to invest in infrastructure projects that produce assets (the capital account of the budget) but not to fund on-going day-to-day spending required to operate public services and provide social security (the current account of the budget). However, the financial crisis made it impossible to balance the current account of the budget, as tax revenues collapsed. Huge cuts in current spending would have been necessary in order to stick to the 'golden rule' and it was judged by the Institute of Fiscal Studies that these would have been irresponsibly high (Chote et al., 2009). The 'golden rule' was suspended by the Labour government in the April 2009 budget to allow for a fiscal stimulus to offset the recessionary impact of the crisis. The Coalition government that came to power in May 2010 reversed that policy and instead introduced austerity policies that prioritised reduction of the budget deficit and government debt, cutting both current and capital spending.

The next attempt to introduce a budget rule in the UK was the Charter for Budget Responsibility passed by House of Commons on 13 January 2015, supported by Conservative, Liberal Democrat and Labour parties (HM Treasury, 2014). It included a commitment to eliminate the deficit in the current account of the budget by 2017/2018, implying continued and massive cuts in public expenditure on services and social security, but left open the possibility of borrowing to finance a deficit in the capital account, which covers public investment. The benefits to women of this possibility are however limited by official definitions of public investment.

Problems with official definitions of public investment: both too wide and too narrow

The way that public investment is defined in the European System of National Accounts (ESA) has been changed to include expenditures that do *not* support future increases in productivity, output and human wellbeing, but the expanded definition still excludes important categories of expenditure that *do* support such increases. ESA 2010 now counts military expenditure on weapons systems (comprising vehicles and other equipment such as warships, submarines, military aircrafts, tanks, missile carriers and launchers, etc.) as investment (Eurostat, 2013: 74 and 443). Weapons systems are potentially destructive and if really used they destroy productive assets instead of enhancing them, which was the reason why spending on them was previously recorded as public consumption (i.e. current spending) under ESA 1995.

An implication of this change is that a UK government could borrow to build a new Trident submarine and nuclear missile system without breaching the 'golden rule' or the January 2015 Charter for Budget Responsibility. In the context of the Eurozone this change, by enabling a government of a Eurozone country to count public spending on weapons systems as public investment, makes it easier for them to comply with the highly restrictive fiscal rules established for the Eurozone, the Stability and Growth Pact (Truger, 2015).

At the same times as spending on military systems is included in public investment, spending on the on-going delivery of services that does enhance future productivity, output and human wellbeing is excluded from public investment. For instance, public spending on education services is classified as current expenditure in the existing system of national accounts and is part of the current account of the budget (though building new schools is public investment and counts as capital spending). The application of the 'golden rule' would allow a government to borrow to build new schools, but not to borrow to enable them to be used for education. This ignores the fact that the future returns, in terms of wellbeing and in terms of enhanced productivity and economic growth, are not produced by the buildings but by the teaching and learning that goes on within them. Indeed, mainstream economic analysis sees education as investment in human capital, with both private and public returns (see for instance Psacharopoulos and Patrinos, 2004). Public finance and the system of national accounts has not caught up with this, and instead defines investment principally in terms of acquisition of fixed assets, though ESA 2010 does also include 'certain additions to the value of non-produced assets realised by the productive activity of producer or institutional units' such as major improvements of land (Eurostat, 2013: 73–74). In addition ESA 2010 for the first time includes expenditure on research and development, which is an intangible asset, with a caveat that 'Expenditure on R&D will only be treated as fixed capital formation when a high level of reliability and comparability of the estimates by member states has been achieved' (Eurostat, 2013: 74).

Both the creation of fixed assets and the delivery of services require the employment of labour, but the ESA definitions, and those used in the budget accounts, treat labour engaged in the two types of activity differently. When a government enters into a contract for the construction of a school, the price it pays to the construction company covers not only the building materials but also the wages of the construction workers. In effect the wages of construction workers counts as public investment (although in the accounts of the construction company they are current expenditure). However when a government staffs the school to provide education, the wages of the teachers are not counted as investment expenditure but as current expenditure. This means that, if the ESA definition of investment is used in operating the 'golden rule', it is permitted to borrow to pay construction workers but not teachers. But the future benefits produced by building schools depend on teachers as well as construction workers. The benefits produced by teachers are not just 'day to day' immediate benefits, but benefits that accrue over the years both to the people who have been educated and to the wider economy and society.

The same argument applies to some other types of expenditure besides educational expenditure. Health expenditures contribute to more healthy people and a more productive workforce in years to come. Spending on childcare and early years education can substantially increase both parents' labour force participation, and the learning abilities of children, with gains to future output and productivity and wellbeing (Campbell et al., 2013).

If ESA 2010 definitions are used as the basis for the 'golden rule' it encourages governments to invest in death more than in life. Feminists might want to challenge the ways in which investment is defined in the ESA 2010, in the way that they have challenged the exclusion of unpaid production of household services from the definition of GDP. However, that challenge has met with only limited success – the ESA 2010 does not include unpaid production of household services as part of GDP, though it does include a satellite account covering this production. The UK Office of National Statistics did produce a household satellite account in 2002 (Holloway et al., 2002) but such satellite accounts are not produced on a regular basis. An alternative approach is to modify the interpretation of the 'golden rule', so that the spending that it covers excludes expenditure on military weapons systems and includes spending on education, health, and childcare and early years education. This is the approach suggested by Truger (2015).

From a feminist point of view, there is also a problem with the ways in which returns to public investment are defined only in terms of the market economy: productivity, output and income. This makes it more difficult to justify spending on services for those who will never be future workers in the market economy as investment – people with severe disabilities, frail elderly people. To some extent, an economic justification can be provided in terms of releasing able-bodied working age adults from unpaid care duties and enabling them to participate in paid work, similar to the argument that investing in childcare and early years education releases parents to participate in paid work. But such a focus tends to underplay the importance of the quality of care services to the people receiving them. In the case of children, a focus on investing in quality can be given an economic rationale by arguing it increases their future productivity as workers. This rationale is not available for investments in the quality of the care for those who will not be future workers. To include such spending as investment we have to look at the returns as measured by increases in future wellbeing, not just economic returns, and also talk of investment in the social fabric, in the creation of a decent society in which all can live in dignity.

Ailsa McKay and other feminist economists have embraced this approach, arguing that care services are a form of *social* infrastructure, for which borrowing should be permitted, like physical infrastructure (UK Women's Budget Group and Scottish Women's Budget Group, 2015). At least one key decision maker has listened: Nicola Sturgeon, First Minister of Scotland said on 15 November 2014:

> Our flagship infrastructure project in this parliament has been the new Forth Bridge – the Queensferry Crossing … I want to make one of our biggest infrastructure projects for the next parliament a different kind of bridge. I want it to be comprehensive childcare, giving our young people the best start in life and a bridge to a better future.
>
> (Sturgeon, 2014)

But the introduction of a new budget rule in UK will make this harder, especially in England and Wales. This new rule is discussed in the next section.

The UK Fiscal Charter: budget must be in surplus in 'normal' times

A much more restrictive rule than the 'golden rule' was introduced by the UK Chancellor of the Exchequer in the first budget of the Conservative government in July 2015. He published a Fiscal Charter, alongside the budget, committing government to keeping debt falling as a share of GDP every year and to achieve an overall budget surplus by 2019/2020 (HM Treasury, 2015). After that, the Fiscal Charter requires governments to maintain a budget surplus in 'normal' times, i.e. when there is not a recession or a marked slowdown in economic growth. This means no borrowing, not even to finance investment. A surplus will not be required if the independent Office for Budget Responsibility judges that real GDP growth is less than 1 per cent a year, measured on a rolling four-quarter basis. The argument in the Chancellor's budget speech was that if a government does not commit to the Fiscal Charter, it is acting irresponsibly. He claimed that only an overall budget surplus will give business the confidence to invest and create jobs; and that only an overall budget surplus will provide the necessary reserves to safeguard jobs and incomes in future economic difficulties. By 2019/2020, the Chancellor implied, we will be able to withstand any future economic crisis because 'Britain will be back in the black.'

The economic forecasts produced by the Office for Budget Responsibility show that this is not true. The OBR forecasts that by 2019/2020 the private sector will be running a large financial deficit and household debt will soar to levels last seen before the 2008 financial crisis, rising to more than 167 per cent of GDP by 2020 (Office for Budget Responsibility, 2015: 63). This is the only way that there will be enough demand to support job creation if the public sector is cutting net spending.

What the Fiscal Charter implies is that while public debt is bad, private debt of businesses and households is good. But it was the unsustainable build-up of risky business and household debt that was a key factor leading to the 2008 financial crisis. Running a budget surplus in normal times will not guarantee economic security for people in the UK. It will instead severely limit the pooling and sharing of risk through public investment in social and physical infrastructure. Underpinning the Fiscal Charter is the message that you are on your own. You should be able to meet most of your own lifetime needs, not only through earning but also through borrowing.

The policies of the Conservative government specifically require people to take on debt to fund their higher education and encourage people to take on debt to buy houses. But as the July 2015 budget also cut £12 billion annually from social security spending, there is little safety net for those of working age who are unable, for whatever reason, to earn. People will have to take on debt, not only to buy a house, and an education, but also, quite possibly, to buy food and heating if for any reason they are unable to earn enough. This is particularly likely to hit women hard because of their caring responsibilities. At the heart of the welfare state is the recognition that caring responsibilities need to be shared though public investment. This recognition was shared by successive UK governments from the late 1940s to the 2000s. The budget deficit has averaged just over 2.5 per cent of GDP, and there have been only seven occasions since 1950 when the budget has been in surplus (Sawyer, 2015).

The highly restrictive Fiscal Charter does not acknowledge that the UK government can borrow to finance public investment in ways that are less costly and less risky than the opportunities open to individuals and even businesses. The UK government borrows in sterling, a currency that it controls; and less than a quarter of its debts are owed to overseas investors – most of the debts are to UK citizens, such as pension holders via their pension funds; the UK can borrow cheaply and does not run the risk of being excluded from capital markets (Stewart, 2015). Adoption of the Fiscal Charter will severely limit the extent to which public investment is possible. It will not reduce but will increase insecurity for women, and will mean that opportunities to reduce gender inequality and to increase productivity, output and wellbeing are wasted.

Conclusions

Ailsa McKay was a passionate and fearless feminist economist who would have rejected the Fiscal Charter, and would have called for a macroeconomic policy that does not fetishise debt and deficit reduction but instead focuses on equality and wellbeing. Adoption of the 'golden rule', that borrowing is permitted to finance public investment, would do more to realise her vision, but only if the scope of investment is widened to include spending on social infrastructure as well as physical infrastructure.

References

Balakrishnan, R. and Elson, D. (eds) (2011). *Economic Policy and Human Rights Obligations*. London: Zed Press.

Bjørnholt, M. and McKay, A. (eds) (2014). *Counting on Marilyn Waring: New Advances in Feminist Economics*. Bradford, Ontario: Demeter Press.

Cagatay, N., Elson, D. and Grown, C. (1995). 'Introduction: gender, adjustment and macroeconomics'. *World Development*, 23(11): 1827–1836.

Campbell, J., Elson, D. and McKay, A. (2013). *The Economic Case for Investing in High Quality Childcare and Early Years Education*. WISE Briefing Sheet. Glasgow: Women in Scotland's Economy Research Centre, Glasgow Caledonian University.

Chote, R., Emmerson, C. and Tetlow, G. (2009). 'The fiscal rules and policy framework'. In Chote, R., Emmerson, C., Miles, D. and Shaw, J. (eds) *The IFS Green Budget*. London: Institute of Fiscal Studies, pp. 81–112.

Elson, D. (1991).'Male bias in macro-economics: the case of structural adjustment'. In Elson, D. (ed.) *Male Bias in the Development Process*. Manchester: Manchester University Press, pp. 164–190.

Elson, D. (1998). 'The economic, the political and the domestic: businesses, states and households in the organisation of production'. *New Political Economy*, 3(2): 189–208.

Elson, D., Fukuda-Parr, S. and Vizard, P. (eds) (2012). *Human Rights and the Capabilities Approach: An Interdisciplinary Dialogue*. London: Routledge.

Eurostat (2013). *European System of Accounts ESA2010*. Luxembourg: Publications Office of the European Union.

Folbre, N. (1994). *Who Pays for the Kids? Gender and the Structures of Constraint*. London: Routledge.

Grice, A. (2014). 'Women bear 85 per cent of burden after Coalition's tax and benefit tweaks'. *Independent*, 6 December. [Online] Available from: www.independent.co.uk/news/uk/politics/women-bear-85-of-burden-after-coalitions-tax-and-benefit-tweaks-9907143.html (accessed 18 July 2015).

HM Treasury (2014). *Charter for Budget Responsibility: Autumn Statement 2014 Update*. [Online] Available from: www.gov.uk/government/publications/charter-for-budget-responsibility-autumn-statement-2014-update (accessed 1 September 2015).

HM Treasury (2015). *Charter for Budget Responsibility: Summer Budget 2015 Update*. [Online] Available fromwww.gov.uk/government/publications/charter-for-budget-responsibility-summer-budget-2015-update (accessed 1 September 2015).

Holloway, S., Short, S. and Tamplin, S. (2002). *Household Satellite Account*. London: Office of National Statistics.

IMF (2014). *World Economic Outlook October 2014*. Washington D.C.: International Monetary Fund.

Institute for Fiscal Studies (2015). *Green Budget 2015*. [Online] Available from: www.ifs.org.uk/publications/7530 (accessed 18 July 2015).

McKay, A. (2013). *International Women's Day Lecture*. EIS. Edinburgh. [Online] Available from: www.gcu.ac.uk/wise/whatwedo/resources/ (accessed 18 July 2015).

McKay, A., Campbell, J., Thomson, E. and Ross, S. (2013). 'Economic recession and recovery in the UK: what's gender got to do with it?' *Feminist Economics*, 19(3): 108–123.

Musgrave, R.A. (1939). 'The nature of budgetary balance and the case for a capital-budget'. *American Economic Review*, 29: 260–271.

Musgrave R.A. (1959). *The Theory of Public Finance. A Study in Public Economy*. New York: McGraw-Hill.

New Economics Foundation (2013). *Mythbusters*: 'Britain is broke – we can't afford to invest'. Blog posted 4 April 2013. [Online] Available from: www.neweconomics. org/blog/entry/mythbusters-britain-is-broke-we-cant-afford-to-invest (accessed   1 September 2015).

Office for Budget Responsibility (2015). *Economic and Fiscal Outlook July 2015* [Online] Available from http://budgetresponsibility.org.uk/economic-fiscal-outlook-july-2015-2/ (accessed 23 August 2015).

Picchio, A. (1992). *Social Reproduction: The Political Economy of the Labour Market*. Cambridge: Cambridge University Press.

Psacharopoulos, G. and Patrinos, H.A. (2004). 'Returns to investment in education. A further update'. *Education Economics*, 12(2): 111–134.

Sawyer, M. (2015). *Budget 2015: The Budget Surplus Rule Scam*. London: CLASS (Centre for Labour and Social Studies). [Online] Available from: http://classonline.org.uk/pubs/ item/the-budget-surplus-rule-scam (accessed 18 July 2015).

Seguino, S. (2011). 'Rebooting is not an option: toward equitable social and economic development'. In Jain, D. and Elson, D. (eds) *Harvesting Feminist Knowledge for Public Policy*. Delhi: Sage, pp. 21–47.

Sen, A. (2015). 'The economic consequences of austerity'. *New Statesman*. London, 4 June.

Stewart, H. (2015). 'This isn't "good housekeeping": it's dogmatic, risky and unjust'. *The Observer*, June 7. [Online] Available from: www.theguardian.com/business/2015/ jun/07/austerity-isnt-good-housekeeping-dogmatic-risky-unjust (accessed   18   July 2015).

Sturgeon, N. (2014). *Nicola Sturgeon Address to SNP Conference*. [Online] Available at: www.snp.org/media-centre/news/2014/nov/nicola-sturgeon-address-snp-conference (accessed 22 June 2015).

Truger, A. (2015). *Implementing the Golden Rule for Public Investment in Europe: Safeguarding Public Investment and Supporting the Recovery*. Materialien zu Wirtschaftund Gesellschaft Nr. 138. Working Paper-Reihe der AK Wien, Herausgegeben von der Abteilung Wirtschaftswissenschaft und Statistik der Kammer für Arbeiter und Angestellte für Wien.

UK Women's Budget Group (2010). *Report on Budget Proposals in Party Manifestos*. [Online] Available from http://wbg.org.uk/RRB_Reports_12_3556891183.pdf (accessed 23 August 2015).

UK Women's Budget Group (2013). *To Ensure Economic Recovery For Women, We Need Plan F*. [Online] Available from: http://wbg.org.uk/wp-content/uploads/2013/10/Plan-F_ WBG-Parties-briefing_Sept-2013_final.pdf (accessed 18 July 2015).

UK Women's Budget Group (2014). *Response to the Autumn Financial Statement 2014*. [Online] Available from: http://wbg.org.uk/wp-content/uploads/2015/01/WBG-AFS-final.pdf (accessed 18 July 2015).

UK Women's Budget Group and Scottish Women's Budget Group (2015). *Plan F. A Feminist Economic Strategy for a Caring and Sustainable Economy*. [Online] Available from: http://wbg.org.uk/wp-content/uploads/2015/02/PLAN-F-2015.pdf (accessed 18 July 2015).

UN Women (2015). *Progress of the World's Women 2015–2016. Transforming Economies, Realizing Rights*. New York: UN Women.

4

CHALLENGING THE NORMS

Gender budgeting as feminist policy change

Angela O'Hagan

Introduction

This chapter discusses the idea of gender budgeting as feminist policy change. This approach is consistent with Ailsa McKay's desire for change for women and the ultimate intention of feminism – the transformation of the status quo whereby the gender order is recast into more equal relations between women and men and improved economic, social and political status for women is secured.

Political institutions, access to them from outsider interests and the responses of formal institutions to alternative processes and new opportunities are central to the story of gender budgeting in Scotland and elsewhere. This chapter draws on a comparative assessment of experiences in Scotland and in Autonomous Communities in Spain to adopt and implement gender budgeting and the favourable conditions necessary to support that process.

Introducing gender budgeting

First developed in Australia and South Africa in the 1980s as 'women's budgets', the concept of gender budgeting has since gained purchase as a potentially transformative approach to gender equality policy globally (Addabbo et al., 2015). Gender budgeting – also known as gender budget analysis or gender responsive budgeting – is essentially concerned with embedding gender analysis in the budget process of governments and public administration. According to Diane Elson, 'the way governments raise and spend money has the potential to reduce the inequalities that occur in families, communities, markets and businesses; or to amplify them' (Scottish Government, 2010: 3).

This perspective confirms the centrality of the budget in the policy process and in decision making on policy priorities and resource allocation.

Following the premise that political institutions are inherently biased, that men have traditionally dominated in decision making and the male norm is held as universal, policy and resource decisions are blind to gender differences (Elson, 1995). Gender budgeting seeks to remedy the assumption that budgets are purely technical gender neutral exercises. Furthermore, as a feminist gender equality policy, gender budgeting incorporates what Ailsa McKay consistently framed as a 'question of values', as expressed by Pregs Govender MP, in the first women's budgets in South Africa: 'the budget reflects the values of a country – who it values, whose work it values and who it rewards ... and who and what and whose work it doesn't' (Govender, 1996: 7).

Gender budgeting has also been characterised as part of a strategy of mainstreaming gender analysis through the public policy process as it requires an examination of policy decisions across the range of government spending and revenue generation to identify and eliminate outcomes that would maintain or worsen women's disadvantage. Arguably it goes further than gender mainstreaming. Gender budgeting *activates* gender mainstreaming by implicating all aspects of policy and programmes, revenue generation and expenditure by locating gender in the principal expression of a government's priorities – the budget.

The goals of gender budgeting include different kinds of policy making where gender analysis is mainstreamed throughout policy and leads to budgetary processes that improve government accountability (Sharp, 2002: 88). Using a range of tools to assess the gender impact, alternative decisions can result in a redistribution of resources to remedy an imbalance or to produce more progressive decisions on social security spending or taxation regimes than is currently the norm. Gender budgeting is not about setting separate budgets for spending on women or men, but rather ensuring that the allocation of public resources and how they are generated actively advances equality between women and men.

Gender budgeting renders gender visible in economic and other policy domains (Himmelweit, 2002). This focus on making women count and making women visible in economic policy is at the heart of gender budget analysis as feminist policy change. Making women and men, boys and girls visible in the policy and therefore budget process and acknowledging their differences and the different ways in which they access and use public services lead to different policy and budgetary decisions. In Ailsa McKay's own words this meant: 'taking account of these differences, [so that] policy-makers can ensure better policy targeting, more effective delivery and greater equality' (McKay, 2004: 13).

Gender budgeting combines feminist economics and gender mainstreaming in a 'fundamental reconsideration of the foundations of economic theory and policy making ... that creates the potential for feminist economics and gender mainstreaming to be "transformatory" in their impact' (Rubery, 2005: 2).

This potential to transform the status quo through alternative, feminist, economic analysis held great appeal for Ailsa McKay in seeking to challenge established economic norms and the policy institutions that support them.

Gender budgeting as feminist policy change

Feminist economists, including Ailsa McKay, are interested in the potential of gender budgeting to 'chang[e] policies, programs and resource allocation so that they promote gender equality and the empowerment of women' (Sharp and Vas Dev, 2004: 1).

Feminist political science scholars have debated over many years the presence and significance of a range of factors in securing feminist policy change, as set out in Figure 4.1. Policy venues and the relationships between critical actors, issues and political agendas and how feminist organisations engage with state reconfiguration and wider political and discursive opportunity structures are particularly relevant.

Amy Mazur proposed a set of key characteristics of feminist policy that seeks the improvement of women's rights, status or situation relative to men's; reduces gender-based hierarchies; distinguishes between public and private spheres; addresses the status of women and men; and responds to demands from recognised feminist movements (Mazur, 2002: 30–31). While gender budgeting clearly meets these criteria, it also fits a more challenging concept of gender equality policies as presented by Htun and Weldon (2010). Their categorisation of gender equality policies as 'gender status' or 'class-based' supports the proposition that gender budgeting as a gender equality policy is both. It is a 'gender status' policy because it seeks to remedy disadvantage and discrimination against women as *women* (original emphasis), and a 'class-based' policy as it targets the unequal distribution of resources and sexual division of labour (Htun and Weldon, 2010: 209).

In seeking to remedy exclusion and marginalisation from political, democratic and constitutional processes and encourage greater acknowledgement of women and participation by women in the budget process, it is a 'gender status' policy. By rendering visible the sexual division of labour and the economic and social inequalities that flow from this, gender budgeting is also a 'class-based' policy as it seeks

---

- Raise awareness with all relevant actors (women, politicians, parliamentarians)
- Engage and involve stakeholders and actors inside and outside government
- Engage government officials and technical [finance] officials
- Secure political will
- Access budget documents and processes;
- Use research and gender-disaggregated data to inform advocacy
- Ensure relevant data is available and accessible (disaggregated by sex and sensitive to gender dynamics) to actors inside and outside government
- Train officials and other actors in gender analysis
- Maximise windows of opportunity presented by political change
- Ensure clear objectives and expectations of what can be achieved from gender budgeting analysis
- Ensure a strategy for continuity

FIGURE 4.1 Key actions for feminist policy change

Source: O'Hagan (2015a)

a more equitable distribution of resources between women and men. Specifically, gender budgeting aims to equalise the status of all women by extending economic resources and civic rights to ensure that access to publicly funded services and the increasingly marketed provision of alternative forms of care is not restricted to women with higher incomes or greater access to financial resources.

On the basis of these criteria, gender budgeting is a feminist policy for the advancement of gender equality. Characterising gender budgeting in this way responds to its intrinsic ambition for the re-orientation of public resources, increased participation and visibility of women in decision making, and a more equitable distribution of resources between women and men.

A matter of principle

In the early 2000s the Commonwealth Secretariat set out a series of principles for gender budgeting in guidance by Budlender and Hewitt (2002). Country ownership; participation; transparency; sustainability; and continuous improvement have served in many different contexts and remained a guiding structure for Ailsa McKay's framing of gender budgeting, shaping her activism and engagement on gender budgeting in Scotland and internationally.

Every country or sub-national level of government has its own political and economic context. There are also variances in the level of feminist activism, especially in relation to economic equality and variable possibilities for accessing political institutions and the appropriate venue and level of decision making. Attempting feminist political change within a fast changing political environment, such as Scotland's increasing autonomy and expanding political momentum over the last 20 years, has been an exciting opportunity.

In the early 2000s gender responsive budgeting was heavily promoted by international bodies such as the United Nations and the Commonwealth Secretariat. Links with international feminist scholars and activists were pivotal in the learning and development of activists in Scotland seeking to create opportunities and gain access to the political processes of the new institutions in Scotland. As the Scottish Women's Budget Group (SWBG) developed and advocacy and influence with the new Scottish political institutions increased, international links expanded (O'Hagan and Gillespie, 2016). This in part created a feedback loop of practice development between emerging approaches to gender budgeting from which advocates and practitioners were learning in bi-lateral exchanges and through the development of the European Gender Budgeting Network (EGBN).

Early examples of this learning and transfer include the attempts to introduce gender budgeting to the government of the Basque Country in Spain from 2000. When EMAKUNDE, the women's policy agency funded by the Basque government, were looking for examples of gender budgeting at sub-national government within developed economies, Scotland was the obvious choice. Ailsa McKay and Rona Fitzgerald were selected as the key researchers to deliver a manual for EMAKUNDE based on international experience and the early learning from political and institutional engagement in Scotland (McKay and Fitzgerald, 2003). Later, when the Junta de Andalucía (JdA), the regional government of the Autonomous Community of Andalucía, had embarked on its gender budgeting journey, Ailsa McKay was invited to address the second international conference organised by the JdA in 2009.

Making it happen: favourable conditions for gender budgeting

My friendship and professional association with Ailsa are intertwined with the developments of gender budgeting in Scotland as we first met in the early days of establishing the Scottish Women's Budget Group. As well as sisters-in-arms we became academic colleagues when Ailsa became Director of Studies for my PhD on which the research discussed below is based.

Engaging with politicians, policy officials and activists (inside and outside government) in Scotland, the Basque Country and Andalucía, I sought to build on relationships established during the overlapping experiences of introducing gender budgeting and to deepen our understanding of what conditions support or inhibit the adoption and implementation of gender budgeting. Close analysis of the early attempts to introduce gender budgeting over the sub-national and autonomous government sites of Scotland (2000–2009), the Basque Country (2000–2005) and Andalusia (2005–2009) reveals a range of factors in relation to political and economic structures, civil society presence and engagement, the openness and responsiveness of policy actors, and the political will and institutional arrangements in place that affect the initial adoption of gender budgeting and its progression to implementation. These factors are presented as a *Framework of Favourable Conditions*, set out in Figure 4.2 (O'Hagan, 2015a).

These conditions vary in the extent to which they are present or have influence on the adoption or implementation of gender budgeting. Arguably two of the essential conditions for the successful adoption and sustained implementation of gender budgeting are political will and leadership at the appropriate level(s) of government; and a clear conceptual analysis and framing of gender budgeting as a gender equality policy.

Exemplifying 'feminist politics in action' (Sharp, 2003), gender budgeting is rooted in feminist analysis and engagement with the state, indicating a significant shift in feminist perception of political institutions and relationships with state structures. In the three sub-national contexts that informed the *Framework of Favourable Conditions*, there are significant differences in the strength of local feminist advocacy for gender budgeting and the comparative ease of access to political institutions. In Scotland, SWBG has been distinctive as an outside government initiative which secured early access to government and parliamentary institutions. This contrasts with the experiences in the Spanish Autonomous Communities of Andalusia and the Basque Country. Here the principal critical actors were largely inside government or government agencies drawing upon the influence of external feminist academics and activists as a significant part of early agenda-setting.

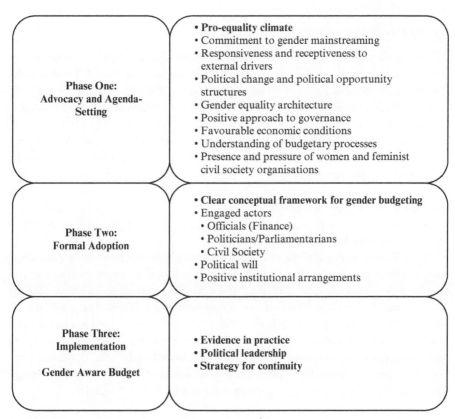

Phase One: Advocacy and Agenda- Setting	• **Pro-equality climate** • Commitment to gender mainstreaming • Responsiveness and receptiveness to external drivers • Political change and political opportunity structures • Gender equality architecture • Positive approach to governance • Favourable economic conditions • Understanding of budgetary processes • Presence and pressure of women and feminist civil society organisations

Phase Two:
Formal Adoption
	• **Clear conceptual framework for gender budgeting**
	• Engaged actors
	    • Officials (Finance)
	    • Politicians/Parliamentarians
	    • Civil Society
	• Political will
	• Positive institutional arrangements

Phase Three: Implementation Gender Aware Budget	• **Evidence in practice** • **Political leadership** • **Strategy for continuity**

FIGURE 4.2 Framework of favourable conditions
Source: O'Hagan (2015a)

The political will of elected members to commit to gender equality as a political priority is essential in developing a robust analysis and framing of gender equality, and in establishing effective institutional arrangements to drive the necessary analysis. In Scotland, early access to newly established institutions proved relatively easy in the first instance given the personal, professional and political relationships that exist in a small country where activists often have multiple roles and identities. A more political route was potentially a path of lesser resistance than that encountered by the officials in EMAKUNDE who found less cooperation in their dealings with the finance department at that time. In contrast to both these experiences, early developments in the case of Andalucía were supported by the finance ministry who led the gender budgeting initiative, carefully guided and influenced by key femocrats within the administration. Securing the engagement of financial officials and ministers has been documented across the gender budgeting literature as a regular sticking point in advancing the change in practice and budget process that is necessary to develop gender budgeting.

From advocacy to gender budgets

Clarity of purpose and a clear articulation of gender equality and how gender budgeting as a process contributes to achieving that vision are essential. Furthermore, there is a greater chance of securing policy change if there is resonance with the dominant government frames. In Scotland gender budgeting was first framed as supporting economic efficiency and more effective and targeted policy making, in line with arguments from the new administration (see also O'Hagan and Gillespie, 2016). In Andalucía at the outset there was a more visibly feminist thread to the arguments on the need to create social as well as economic change, framed as a more pronounced response to the context of European Union policy. In the early attempt by the Basque government a mix of frames were in play, principally economic development and gender equality, conceptualised as equal opportunities and gender mainstreaming policy.

It is clear from the analysis of these cases that a range of potentially competing frames are in play in the dominant government discourses on economic growth, social justice, effective policy making and efficient government. Gender equality can be stretched and bent to fit these (Lombardo et al., 2009), but it can also be identifiable as a priority focus of government policy. To be adopted as a component and approach of a government's commitment to gender equality, the concept of gender budgeting needs both to be clearly articulated within the dominant government frames *and* gender equality must be understood conceptually and through data analysis and promoted as a government priority (O'Hagan, 2015b).

Conclusion

Conceptualising gender budgeting as feminist policy change brings together feminist economics and feminist policy analysis, strengthening the concept and its practice through its powerful rationale and potential as a transformative gender equality policy. Securing the adoption and implementation of gender budgeting requires the presence and interaction of a range of *Favourable Conditions* that exist to greater and lesser degrees at different moments in time and in different political contexts – and even then can remain elusive as the experience of the EGBN and other epistemic or practitioner communities can testify.

Ailsa McKay sought to create and consolidate these conditions in Scotland and, as an international advocate for gender budgeting, challenged the established ways of thinking and doing in budgetary processes, by opening them up to make women and their lives visible in the process. While rooted in Scotland culturally and politically, Ailsa grew in knowledge and status as an academic and researcher through her increasing international activity and profile. Both as an engaged activist and as part of an epistemic community, exchange of experience and knowledge underscored Ailsa's approach and is a key characteristic of how gender budgeting has travelled as feminist policy change.

References

Addabbo, T., Gunluk-Senesen, G. and O'Hagan, A. (2015). 'Gender budgeting: insights from current methodologies and experiences in Europe'. *Politica Economica/Journal of Economic Policy*, XXXI(2), 125–132.

Budlender, D. and Hewitt, G. (eds.) (2002). *Gender Budgets Make Cents*. London: Commonwealth Secretariat.

Elson, D. (1995). *Male Bias in the Development Process*. Manchester: Manchester University Press.

Govender, P. (1996). 'Foreword'. In Budlender, D. *The Women's Budget*. Cape Town: Idasa.

Himmelweit, S. (2002). 'Making visible the hidden economy: the case for gender-impact analysis of economic policy'. *Feminist Economics*, 8(1): 49–70.

Htun, M. and Weldon, S.L. (2010). 'When do governments promote women's rights? A framework for the comparative analysis of sex equality policy'. *Perspectives on Politics*, 8(1): 207–216.

Lombardo, E., Meier, P. and Verloo, M. (eds) (2009). *The Discursive Politics of Gender Equality: Stretching, Bending and Policymaking*. London: Routledge.

Mazur, A. (2002). *Theorizing Feminist Policy*. Oxford: Oxford University Press.

McKay, A. (2004). 'Practical application – focus on process or policy? Case studies from Scotland, the Basque Country and the UK Treasury'. *Gender Budgeting Initiative (GBI) in CEE/NIS region*. Sopot, Poland, 14–18 April 2004: 10–23.

McKay, A. and Fitzgerald, R. (2003). *Manual: Gender Sensitive Budgeting in the Autonomous Community of the Basque Country*. Vitoria-Gasteiz: EMAKUNDE. [Online] Available from: www.presupuestoygenero.net/media/fitzgeraldmcKay.pdf (accessed 26 August 2015).

O'Hagan, A. (2015a). 'Favourable conditions for the adoption and implementation of gender budgeting: insights from comparative analysis', Special Issue *Journal of Economic Policy/Politica Economica*, XXXI(2), 233–252.

O'Hagan, A. (2015b). 'Implementing gender budgeting in Scotland and Spain: a comparative feminist analysis'. In Korkut, U., Mahendran, K., Bucken-Knapp, G. and Henry Cox, R. (eds) *Discursive Governance in Politics, Policy, and the Public Sphere*. New York: Palgrave Macmillan, pp. 109–125.

O'Hagan, A. and Gillespie M. (2016). 'Gender budgeting in Scotland: seeking transformative change through public spending'. In Campbell, J. and Gillespie, M. (eds.) *Feminist Economics and Public Policy: Reflections on the Work and Impact of Ailsa McKay*. Abingdon: Routledge, pp. 46–53.

Rubery, J. (2005). 'Reflections on gender mainstreaming: an example of feminist economics in action?' *Feminist Economics*, 11(3): 1–26.

Scottish Government (2010). *Equality Statement Scotland's Budget 2011–2012*. Edinburgh: Scottish Government.

Sharp, R. (2002). 'Moving forward: multiple strategies and guiding goals'. *Gender Budget Initiatives: Strategies, Concepts and Experiences*. New York, UNIFEM (UN): 86–98.

Sharp, R. (2003). *Budgeting for Equity: Gender Budget Initiatives Within a Framework of Performance Oriented Budgeting*. New York: United Nations Development Fund for Women (UNIFEM).

Sharp, R. and Vas Dev, S. (2004). *Bridging the Gap Between Gender Analysis and Gender-Responsive Budgets: Key Lessons From a Pilot Project in the Republic of the Marshall Islands*. University of South Australia: Hawke Research Institute.

5

GENDER BUDGETING IN SCOTLAND

Seeking transformative change through public spending

Angela O'Hagan and Morag Gillespie

Introduction

The Scottish Parliament was created in 1999 with powers devolved from the Westminster Parliament on a range of social and economic policy issues. Founded on key principles of power sharing, accountability, access, participation and equal opportunities, it presented an opportunity for new ideas and a 'new politics' to flourish (McKay and O'Hagan, 2009). The work of women campaigners contributed to a range of features that made the new parliament more 'women friendly'. Combined with more women parliamentarians, this created an environment that facilitated women's wider participation in policy making processes (Mackay et al., 2005; Mackay, 2009). Buoyed by the wave of anticipation and opportunism that existed at the time, gender budgeting came to Scotland.

Ailsa McKay was passionate about advancing and protecting women's rights to secure income, economic independence and social security. This chapter summarises key developments in gender budgeting and equalities budget analysis in Scotland and Ailsa McKay's distinctive approach and pivotal role in the progress to date.

Gender budgeting in Scotland: early developments

Feminist activists seized upon the opportunity of political change as a chance to act on the relatively novel concept of gender budgeting that the 1995 Beijing Platforms for Action and experiences elsewhere, for example in Australia and South Africa (Sharp, 2003), had brought to their attention. Ailsa McKay played a central role in promoting gender budget analysis as a key approach to making gender inequality transparent in Scotland and decision making responsive to its causes and consequences.

A small group of women formed the Scottish Women's Budget Group (SWBG) around Ailsa's kitchen table in 2000. SWBG aimed to ensure that gender impact analysis was embedded within the Scottish public policy and resource allocation processes. For most of its existence, the group has been unfunded, relying on the voluntary efforts of its members to convince key players in the Scottish policy-making community why gender matters in the budget process. As both the Scottish budgetary process and SWBG's engagement around it matured, the focus grew from understanding how the budget was determined in Scotland, and its points of engagement and influence, to the development of new structures to tighten the connections between aspirations on equality and public expenditure decisions in Scotland.

In seeking to make women visible as contributors, actors and beneficiaries of public resource allocations, SWBG engaged with government ministers, parliamentarians, government and parliamentary officials and researchers in a complex and far-reaching 'wiring circuit' of influence (Mackay et al., 2005). Through written submissions, oral evidence to parliamentary committees and informal engagement, SWBG argued that because the budget reflects the social and economic priorities of a government, taking greater account of the different needs and resources of women and men would result in better policy, more efficient delivery and less inequality. In the case of Scotland, this work has focused on government spending: although the Scottish Parliament has always had some limited tax raising powers, these have not been used to date, hence the focus on expenditure that consists mostly of the allocation of funds from the UK government.

SWBG quickly earned its reputation as a credible and authoritative voice, a 'formidable lobby that is not going to go away' (Mackay et al., 2005: 31). This early impact was reinforced when the Scottish Government commissioned key group members to undertake research on gender impact assessment in the Scottish budgetary process (McKay and Fitzgerald, 2002) as part of building a wider understanding of the budgetary process, as much for the benefit of civil servants in the new institutions as civil society activists. An advisory group established to take this work forward – now called the Equality and Budgets Advisory Group (EBAG) – included representatives of SWBG and key government officials with an interest in equalities and budgets. To reflect wider equality interests, membership has expanded over time to include organisations such as the Equality and Human Rights Commission (EHRC) and the Convention of Scottish Local Authorities (COSLA).[1] These voices strengthened arguments for focusing on the budget as a key site for the advancement of equality, including gender equality.

EBAG is an inside government group of officials and external interests whose remit is to advise the Scottish Government on the technical process of integrating equality analysis into the Scottish Budget process. It does not advise on policy priorities but rather retains a focus on promoting links between the policy process and resource allocation. Its most significant achievement to date has been to secure the production of an Equality Budget Statement attached to the annual Draft Budget since 2009. This is the only approach of its kind within the UK countries and is a serious attempt to expose the value of resources allocated for the advancement of equality and the process by which such decisions are made. As an accompaniment to the budget proposals it is by its nature partisan and partial, but it is also work in progress and something of a barometer of political engagement on equality.

Gender budgeting and the economy

Over the first two sessions of the Scottish Parliament (1999–2007) the government expressed commitments to improving women's economic and social status, but policy was framed as 'tackling inequality', 'promoting social justice' or 'social inclusion', advanced through a dominant 'equalities mainstreaming' approach. SWBG cautioned against the conflation of a broad social justice discourse with a focus on inequality as a proxy for equality analysis that is necessary for effective gender equality policy (SWBG, 2015). SWBG argued instead for analysis to recognise the links that structural inequality and discrimination have with economic disadvantage and social deprivation in order to develop a more complete understanding of the causes and consequences of social exclusion, more effective targeting of resources, more easily identifiable and transparent resource allocation and better policy outcomes.

The government's first Equality Strategy expressed commitments to mainstream equality and to develop tools for equality impact assessment of the budget process (Scottish Executive, 2000). As an approach to policy making, equalities mainstreaming has resulted in activity to implement analysis of the budget, taking a wider view across a range of 'equalities' groups and issues rather than having a core focus on gender equality. SWBG has challenged the persistence of a 'conceptual fuzziness' (Beveridge and Nott, 2002) around gender equality as undermining progress on gender budgeting in Scotland (McKay and Gillespie, 2007; O'Hagan, 2015) and argued that this has resulted in ineffective targeting of policy measures to promote gender equality and a dilution of impact.

In 2007, the Scottish National Party (SNP) formed a minority government and became a majority government after the Scottish parliament elections in 2011. Since then the dominant political narrative has shifted as the first Government Economic Strategy declared the overarching purpose of government to be: 'creating a more successful country, with opportunities for all of Scotland to flourish, through increasing sustainable economic growth' (Scottish Government, 2007: 8).

This shift in political emphasis and character of government created new opportunities to reframe the discourse on gender budgeting as central to economic policy. An early sign of this was when the Parliament's Equal Opportunities Committee appointed a Special Adviser on the Budget for the first time in 2007. That Adviser was Ailsa McKay: she supported the committee's analysis of three Draft Budgets in the parliamentary session 2007–2011. This was a key opportunity to strengthen the focus on gender equality, specifically the relationship between policy decisions expressed in the budget and the implications for women's economic status in Scotland. Committee reports and the commentary in both Equality Budget Statements and Draft Budgets reflect this sharpened vision (see for example: Scottish Parliament, 2011; Scottish Government, 2010, 2012, 2015).

In 2008 a refreshed EBAG was expanded to include the Office of the Chief Economic Adviser. The first Equality Budget Statement (EBS) reflected this step-change in government engagement. Consecutive EBS reveal a growing influence on the Scottish Government through the annual meeting of EBAG with the Cabinet Secretary for Finance and Sustainable Growth, as evidenced in commentary in the EBS 2010: 'In particular the discussion focused on issues relating to women's role and participation in the labour market, the formal and informal economy and the challenge of measurement and economic modelling' (Scottish Government, 2010: 9).

Similarly, changes in phrasing and tone are evident in parliamentary as well as government documents. Ailsa's influence can be seen in the Equal Opportunities Committee's final report on the Draft Budget for 2011–2012 demanding that future spending plans are informed by a framework of economic analysis that incorporates:

> equality considerations, *thus embedding equality within the mainstream budgetary process* … with a view to the Scottish Government applying equality impact analysis to the framework of economic modelling employed in determining the relevant range of the economic forecasts that in turn inform its future economic strategy.
>
> (Scottish Parliament, 2011: para. 68; our emphasis)

Particularly in the second term of the SNP administration, government rhetoric gave increasing prominence to equality as a driver of growth, reflecting that inequality:

> detracts from our economic performance and our social wellbeing. We make clear in our Economic Strategy, the importance of increasing participation in the labour market, removing the structural and long standing barriers which limit opportunities and harnessing diversity and wealth of talent we have available to us as a nation.
>
> (Scottish Government, 2011: 10)

While the emphasis was on labour market participation and economic growth, a constant refrain of Ailsa's was to highlight and challenge the 'limitations of economic models', as acknowledged in the EBS for 2013–2014, (Scottish Government, 2012: 6). This developing understanding arguably laid the foundations for a refreshed Economic Strategy in 2015 (Scottish Government, 2015) with twin pillars of tackling inequality and increasing Scotland's economic competitiveness. Only time will tell how well this victory of ideas will translate into practice, but it represents a significant and hard-won policy shift.

Add women and stir?

A favourite phrase of Ailsa McKay, widely used and first attributed to Charlotte Bunch (1990), to describe the default position of policymakers towards gender analysis, was simply that they 'add women and stir' rather than engaging in rigorous analysis of the gender relations and gendered norms that result in women's unequal economic and social status.

Robust gender disaggregated data, analysed effectively, are central to the promotion of gender budgeting and analysis of social and economic policies. This has been a key area of concern for Ailsa McKay and SWBG members through EBAG and in successive responses to Draft Budgets and other consultations. It is central to the focus of Women in Scotland's Economy Research Centre (WiSE) at Glasgow Caledonian University, established by Ailsa in 2010.

One example of this was a WiSE knowledge exchange programme that she led, to develop a gender impact analysis 'tool' for gender budget analysis. This work was funded by the Economic and Social Research Council and conducted in partnership with Close the Gap, an organisation funded by the Scottish Government to encourage and enable action to address the gender pay gap (Close the Gap, 2015). Using the Scottish Modern Apprenticeship programme as an example and working with key agencies involved in delivering the Modern Apprenticeship programme, the project assessed the tool's usefulness for understanding the nature of gender inequalities in the programme and informing decision making (McKay et al., 2014).

Sharing knowledge at home and abroad

There is an essential part of the Scottish political character that considers itself internationalist and outward looking. Ailsa McKay's work and SWBG, from its inception, reflected this and the ideal of 'feminist politics in action' (Sharp, 2003).

SWBG drew heavily on experiences from elsewhere, including the Commonwealth Secretariat principles that have helped to shape the approach in Scotland (O'Hagan, 2016). Ailsa and other SWBG activists in Scotland developed strong links with international feminist scholars and activists on gender budgeting as part of strategies to create opportunities and gain leverage with the political processes of the new institutions in Scotland. The first international event on gender budgeting hosted by the Scottish Government (and the only one to date) was in 2002. Following this, Ailsa seized an opportunity to share practical knowledge of the early activity in Scotland and tie in the Scottish Executive on commitments to integrate gender analysis in the Scottish Budget process by contributing a case study along with other SWBG members to the second Commonwealth Secretariat publication on gender budgeting (McKay et al., 2002). She built on the Commonwealth framework in her international work that included presentations and training, for example in Poland in 2004, Istanbul in 2006, as visiting Chair in Gender Studies at the Complutense University in Madrid from 2006–2012 and elsewhere.

At home and abroad, Ailsa McKay regularly exhorted policy makers to 'get underneath the data'. But, in working towards a more inclusive polity in Scotland, she was equally keen to ensure that 'ordinary' women connected with formal economics, despite the apparent remoteness from their lives, and developed a range of approaches to building awareness and engagement that remain key strategies of SWBG.

One example is a series of training programmes under the banner 'Economics for Equality' (E4E), initiated by SWBG member Anne Meikle and piloted in 2006. A follow-on Oxfam-funded programme for community activists and policy makers aimed to show how public money is allocated, the links with equality in policy and practice and why economics and its influence on resource allocation processes and decisions are matters of interest for us all. It explored key issues of significance for gender equality, including poverty and social justice, built awareness of gender budget analysis and its relevance for equality policy and practice in Scotland and helped community participants to engage in the budgetary decisions that affect their lives. Participants clearly valued the training as it boosted their confidence to engage on spending decisions at local, workplace and national level in the language of economics (McKay et al., 2010).

Subsequently E4E has evolved into a formal module at Glasgow Caledonian University and a series of weekend schools developed for women trade unionists and activists by Ailsa McKay with the Scottish Trade Unions Congress Women's Committee. Indeed her last public appearance was participating and presenting at a school in March 2014 to women from across Scotland, inspiring them to see economics as important to women's lives, and encouraging them to make women visible in formal policy and budgetary decision making.

Conclusions

In 2005, Mackay et al. (2005) questioned whether SWBG would be able to stay the course. SWBG has evolved, grown and matured, nurtured by mutual support and learning within Scotland from feminist communities and shared global learning of experiences in gender budgeting projects. Ailsa McKay's work, individually and as a group member, has provided the cornerstone for this development. Commitments from successive Scottish governments demonstrate political will to advance gender equality policy in Scotland. Institutional arrangements such as EBAG and the active scrutiny of the parliamentary Equal Opportunities and Finance Committees are evidence of political interest in progressing equality analysis of the Scottish Budget process, with an increased focus on gender analysis and women's equality.

These developments are potentially optimistic signs that the arguments are having some influence on policy development in Scotland. Evidence of the impact of advocacy on childcare (Campbell et al., 2013) is one example. It helped to shape the White Paper on independence (Scottish Government, 2013) and the refreshed economic strategy (Gillespie and Khan, 2016).

However, despite the influence and impact of Ailsa McKay (and others), a definitive shift in economic decision-making with gender equality as a starting point remains an incomplete but ongoing project. SWBG continues to advance a long-term strategy for feminist policy change structured around a gender-sensitive budget process and for gender analysis to be at the heart of government policy and clearly articulated in the budgetary process because:

> We need to develop a better understanding of how the structures and processes associated with our economic systems can better serve the needs of all citizens across all of our communities. Women *are* the heart of our local communities and are *at* the heart of local communities.
>
> (McKay, 2013)

Note

1 COSLA is the representative voice of local authorities in Scotland and acts as their employers' association (see: www.cosla.gov.uk). The EHRC is funded by the UK government and exists to challenge discrimination, and protect and promote human rights (see: http://www.equalityhumanrights.com/about-us).

References

Beveridge, F. and Nott, S. (2002). 'Mainstreaming: a case for optimism and cynicism'. *Feminist Legal Studies*, 10(3): 299–311.

Bunch, C. (1990). 'Women's rights as human rights: toward a re-vision of human rights'. *Human Rights Quarterly*, 12(4): 486–498.

Campbell, J., Elson, D. and McKay, A. (2013). *The Economic Case for Investing in High-Quality Childcare and Early Years Education*. WiSE Briefing Sheet, November. Glasgow: Glasgow Caledonian University. [Online] Available from: www.gcu.ac.uk/media/WiSEBriefingPaperNov13.pdf (accessed 6 July 2015).

Close the Gap (2015). *Close the Gap: Our Aims* [Online]. Available from: www.closethegap.org.uk/content/about-aims/ (accessed 30 July 2015).

Gillespie, G. and Khan, U. (2016). 'Integrating economic and social policy: childcare – a transformational policy?' In Campbell, J. and Gillespie, M. (eds) *Feminist Economics and Public Policy: Reflections on the Work and Impact of Ailsa McKay*. Abingdon: Routledge, pp. 94–111.

Mackay, F., Kenny, M. and Pollot-Thomson, E. (2005). *Access, Voice … and Influence? Women's Organisations in Post-Devolution Scotland*. Edinburgh: Engender.

Mackay, F. (2009). 'Travelling the distance? Equal opportunities and the Scottish Parliament'. In Jeffery, C. and Mitchell, J. (eds) *The Scottish Parliament 1999–2009: The First Decade*. Edinburgh: Luath Press, pp. 49–55.

McKay, A. (2013). 'Hope'. Speech delivered at Radical Independence Conference, 23 November 2013. [Online] Available from: www.youtube.com/watch?v=cEZBat3H-Rmw (accessed 10 August 2015).

McKay, A and Fitzgerald, R. (2002). *Exploring the Role of Gender Impact Assessment in the Scottish Budgetary Process: Understanding the Scottish Budgetary Process*. Edinburgh: Scottish Executive, Equality Unit.

McKay, A. and Gillespie, M. (2007). 'Gender mainstreaming or "mainstreaming gender"? A question of delivering on gender equality in the new Scotland'. In Keating, M. (ed.)

Scottish Social Democracy: Progressive Ideas for Public Policy, Brussels: P.I.E. Peter Lang, pp. 191–212.

McKay, A. and O'Hagan, A. (2009). 'Promoting gender equality in the new Scotland: rhetoric not reality'. *British Politics Review*, 2: 13–14.

McKay, A., Campbell, J., Gillespie, M., Ross, S. and Thomson, E. (2014). *Accounting for Gender in the Modern Apprenticeship Programme in Scotland*. ESRC End of Award Report, ES/K005685/1. ESRC: Swindon. [Online] Available from: www.esrc.ac.uk/my-esrc/grants/ES.K005685.1/outputs/Read/cbfffe63-1742-4e51-923d-5e8518ea7886 (accessed 11 August 2015).

McKay, A., Fitzgerald, R., O'Hagan, A., Gillespie, M. (2002). 'Scotland: using political change to advance gender issues'. In Budlender, D. and Hewitt, G. (eds) *Gender Budgets Make More Cents*. London: Commonwealth Secretariat, pp. 133–151.

McKay, A., Gillespie, M., Meikle, A., Fitzgerald, R. and O'Hagan, A. (2010). *Economics for Gender Equality: Why Public Spending Matters*. Unpublished report to Oxfam. Glasgow: Glasgow Caledonian University.

O'Hagan (2016). 'Challenging the norms: gender budgeting as feminist policy change'. In Campbell, J. and Gillespie, M. (eds) *Feminist Economics and Public Policy: Reflections on the Work and Impact of Ailsa McKay*. Abingdon: Routledge, pp. 38–45.

O'Hagan, A. (2015). 'Implementing gender budgeting in Scotland and Spain: a comparative feminist analysis'. In Korkut, U., Mahendran, K., Bucken-Knapp, G. and Cox, R.H. (eds) *Discursive Governance in Politics, Policy, and the Public Sphere*. New York: Palgrave Macmillan, pp.109–125.

Scottish Executive (2000). *Equality Strategy: Working Together for Equality*. Edinburgh: Scottish Executive.

Scottish Government (2007). *The Government Economic Strategy*. Edinburgh: Scottish Government. [Online] Available from: www.gov.scot/Resource/Doc/202993/0054092. pdf (accessed 31 July 2015).

Scottish Government (2010). *Equality Statement Scottish Budget 2011/12*. Edinburgh: Scottish Government. [Online] Available from: www.gov.scot/resource/doc/331 780/0107965.pdf (accessed 31 July 2015).

Scottish Government (2011). *Equality Statement on Scottish Spending Review 2011 and Draft Budget 2012–13*. Edinburgh: Scottish Government. [Online] Available from: www.gov. scot/resource/doc/358418/0121145.pdf (accessed 30 July 2015).

Scottish Government (2012). *Equality Statement: Scottish Draft Budget 2013–14*. [Online] Edinburgh: Scottish Government. Available from: www.gov.scot/Resource/0040/ 00402326.pdf (accessed 31 July 2015).

Scottish Government (2013). *Scotland's Future: Your Guide to an Independent Scotland*. Edinburgh: Scottish Government.

Scottish Government (2015). *Scotland's Economic Strategy*. Edinburgh: Scottish Government.

Scottish Parliament (2011). *Equal Opportunities Committee Report on the Draft Budget 2011–12*. [Online] Available from: http://archive.scottish.parliament.uk/s3/committees/finance/ reports-11/fir11-02-vol2-01.htm#ANNF (accessed 30 July 2015).

SWBG (2015). *Publications*. [Online] Available from: www.swbg.org.uk/content/publica tions/ (accessed 25 August 2015).

Sharp, R. (2003). *Budgeting for Equity: Gender Budget Initiatives Within a Framework of Performance Oriented Budgeting*. New York: United Nations Development Fund for Women (UNIFEM).

6

GENDER BUDGETING IN THE CAPABILITY APPROACH

From theory to evidence

Tindara Addabbo

Critical reviews of gender auditing and gender budgeting (for example Sharp and Broomhill, 2002; Stotsky, 2006) document developments using different models reflecting: the level of government involvement in the process (inside and outside government or both); government accountability on gender issues; government and community awareness of gender budgeting; and changes in public policy design or the budgeting process itself. This chapter focuses on the application of Sen and Nussbaum's capabilities approach to gender budgeting as proposed by Addabbo et al. (2010). The aims are to explain it and to reflect upon its first applications at different levels of government in Italy (see Addabbo et al., 2011 for an assessment of the different experiences), where the approach has been applied at regional level (Emilia Romagna, Piedmont and Lazio), district level (Modena, Bologna and Rome) and municipal level (Modena, Forlì and Vicenza).

The use of Amartya Sen and Martha Nussbaum's capability approach extends the focus of gender budgeting to the impact of policies on wellbeing, with its multiple dimensions and complexity, departing from an evaluation based exclusively on income or commodities. Wellbeing is defined at the individual level, and this, also according to feminist economics, requires investigating what happens inside the family and recognising the possibility of conflicts amongst its members on the construction of wellbeing. Individual wellbeing is measured in terms of capabilities that are defined as a set of opportunities that can be converted into functionings (Sen, 1985, 1995, 1999). Sen defined capabilities as: 'the various combinations of functionings (beings and doings) that the person can achieve. Capability is, thus, a set of vectors of functionings, reflecting the person's freedom to lead one type of life or another' (Sen, 1995: 40).

Regarding the freedom to choose, Sen stated: 'the achieved functionings constitute a person's wellbeing, then the capability to achieve functionings (i.e. all the alternative combinations of functionings a person can choose to have) will constitute the person's freedom – the real opportunities – to have wellbeing' (Sen, 1995: 40).

For instance we can observe the functioning of being employed as a conversion of the capability of working. In the conversion into functionings personal, social or environmental factors play a crucial role (Robeyns, 2005). Institutions can be important in that they affect conversion factors and the bundle of income, commodities and services available to the individual to develop her capabilities and/or to convert them into observable functionings. For instance, by providing schools, the State can directly affect social factors that enable the capability of being educated to be converted into achieved education. Or by setting standards to reduce pollution, the State can affect the conversion of the capability to live a healthy life into not being ill or suffering from respiratory diseases. Governments should 'think from the start about what obstacles there are to full and effective empowerment for all citizens, and devise measures that address these obstacles' (Nussbaum, 2003: 39).

In the capability approach adopting a gender perspective entails knowledge about the different roles played by men and women in the definition of wellbeing. If account is taken of the centrality of social reproduction, as recognised, amongst others, by Picchio (1992), Elson (1998) and Himmelweit (2002), women's role in the production of wellbeing for other members of the family is made explicit and the effect of this contribution on the development of women's capabilities is revealed. By devoting time to unpaid housework to a greater extent than their partners, women develop more than them the capability of caring for others, but they will be left with less time to devote to other roles that could allow them to develop other capabilities, for instance the capability of work and access to resources or the capability of caring for oneself.

This unequal distribution of household labour is bound to produce differentiated effects of public policies and, if ignored, may produce inefficiency in the policies enacted and/or may fail to recognise who will pay the costs of changes in public expenditure. For example, in the field of public finance, Elson (1998) highlights the centrality of the interaction between public policy and the distribution of unpaid work by gender and the implications of public expenditure cutbacks in terms of their consequences for women: for example, an increase in women's unpaid work and depletion of women's human resources due to their overwork which in turn is likely to impact on the sustainability of budget cutbacks in the long run.

By neglecting the changes in unpaid work inside the family that can occur after a reduction in the provision of public services, the shifts from public services to private (and mainly women's) unpaid work are hidden as are the costs in terms of the human resources employed in the process and the unequal distribution of work by gender. This is also highlighted by McKay et al. (2013) with regards to the impact of public spending cuts in the UK after the global financial crisis.

The effects that have been recognised and stressed in the literature and in the application of gender auditing of public policies will reproduce long-lasting differences when these effects are seen in the capability approach to gender budgeting.

The unequal distribution of total work by gender that makes women mainly responsible for the unpaid activities of childcare and care of the elderly, in a context where the public provision of such services is rationed (as in Italy), can have negative effects on the development of other capabilities for the main carers. As a result they face time constraints and discrimination in their access to the labour market. If women, owing to their total (paid and unpaid) work load, are less likely to engage in life-long learning, this may also hamper the development of their capabilities of being educated and of accessing resources which enable career progression.

The effects of this unequal time distribution are apparent not only on the main carer's capabilities but also on those of other family members. The unequal distribution of care work within the family reproduces differences in the intra-household development of the capability to care for others and it induces fathers to make less use of parental leave. In Italy, where there is a legal right to take parental leave, the business culture tends to discourage fathers from doing so (Addabbo, 2005). Also, analysis of parental leave in Italy shows that the take-up of parental leave by fathers is much lower than mothers, and fathers continue to play a weaker role in their children's education and growth, with costs in terms of children's wellbeing (Fine-Davis et al., 2004; Addabbo et al., 2014).

When applying the capability approach to gender budgeting or in any evaluation of wellbeing, a methodological problem to be addressed is how to define the list of capabilities to be used (Nussbaum, 2003; Robeyns, 2003; Sen, 2004). One can employ the universal list of capabilities defined in Nussbaum (2000, 2003), or follow the procedural approach described by Robeyns (2003) or, as suggested in Addabbo et al. (2010), construct a list on the basis of the functions of the institution involved in gender budgeting. The process leading to the definition of a list of capabilities can involve the participation of citizens, civil society or the specific group of analysis (as in Biggeri et al., 2006). A participatory definition of the list can increase community participation in the budgeting process and awareness of gender differences; it can also lead to governmental commitment to a given list.

When a list of capabilities has been drawn up, the next step in the capability approach to gender budgeting is to conduct context analysis and devise indicators that can be used for policy evaluation. However, when capabilities are used as the referents for gender budgeting, difficulties arise in their measurement. Primary data sources on capabilities are not readily available and one is often forced to use secondary data sources, thus encountering difficulties in the measurement of capabilities (see Anand et al., 2005; Kuklys, 2005; Chiappero-Martinetti, 2008; and Addabbo et al., 2004, on the operationalisation of the capabilities approach). The available secondary data provide measures of the achieved functionings and on conversion factors that affect the achievement of functionings. During the context analysis, since public policies can affect the capabilities by creating the social environment for their development, exploratory analysis on the possible constraints inducing the unequal development of capabilities by gender, and therefore unequal gender wellbeing, should be performed as the basis for the subsequent capability approach to gender budgeting analysis.

Once the list of capabilities has been defined and the context analysis has been performed on the measurement of wellbeing and the limits in its development by gender, the next step is to state, on the basis of each level of government responsibility, whether that institution affects the development of a given capability. This assessment can be represented by means of a matrix representation of capabilities by different items of public budgets. The rows of this matrix are the capabilities, and the columns (whose choice defines a different matrix) can be:

- different institutions;
- departments within a given institution;
- budget-responsible units and/or elementary cost units of an institution;
- the institution's targets as defined in the mandate budget or in other institutional programmes.

Having analysed the possible direct and indirect impact exerted on the development of the capabilities by each unit and by each programme related to that cost unit, one can use the indicators collected in the context analysis with regard to that specific capability to assess the impact of the programmes and to provide policy suggestions.

Assessing the possible impact of expenditures on human wellbeing can lead to changes in the definition of public expenditure from current to capital. For example, current expenditure on childcare and schools is bound to have long-term effects on children and parents affected, such that it could be considered as investment spending rather than current expenditure (Himmelweit, 2016).

The same policy may have contrasting effects on different capabilities. Consider for instance the introduction of limiting car access to town centres. This will have a positive effect on the capability to live a healthy life if it reduces pollution and a positive effect on the capability of enjoying cultural events and infrastructures. However, it may also have a negative effect on both the physical mobility and feeling safe capabilities. Consequently countervailing policies are required, for example this could range from reduced and publicly subsidised taxi fares for unaccompanied women in places that are unsafe for them, to places reserved for women in car parks served by 'park and ride' facilities, or the increased policing of town centres.

A complete gender budgeting analysis using the capability approach would require analysis of the contribution of different sectors to structural support for the different capabilities and can lead to the allocation of budget expenditures by capabilities. Examples of funding allocations analysed by gender and capability can be found in Addabbo and Saltini (2009) for the Modena municipality in Italy and in Gunluk-Senesen (2016) for a specific programme in Turkey. Further, the contribution of different levels of government to capabilities can be analysed, making the interaction and the responsibility of each level of government visible. The analysis can also be extended to other social actors operating in the area; these may interact with public bodies in the structural support for wellbeing and capabilities development. In this regard, a recent analysis of the application of wellbeing gender budgets to tertiary education institutions in Italy and Spain has shown the impact of public sector cuts and pay freezes on employees' working conditions as having a relevant gender impact connected to the size of female employment in those institutions (Addabbo et al., 2015). This can be considered as an example of the direct impact of decisions taken at the national level on the local context of wellbeing.

Conclusions

By focusing on the gender impact of public policies in the development of wellbeing this approach to gender budgeting can unveil the role of the analysed institution in the construction of wellbeing. This awareness should better guide public actors in their policies and in the allocation of resources. In the capability approach to public policies, as has been stressed in the literature (Bonvin, 2014), not only is the content of the policy relevant but also how it is implemented in terms of the effect on the ability to express one's opinion and make it count in public discussion (the capability for voice). In this regard a participatory wellbeing gender budgeting can achieve this aim through the definition of the list of capabilities, and in the identification of those factors that prevent their development, by giving voice to those who are not usually heard. This is in line with the application of the capability approach to social policies as discussed in Bonvin (2014). The attention to the capability for voice can be found in the application of wellbeing gender budgeting, for instance in gender budgeting of the Modena municipality (Addabbo and Saltini, 2009). In this case each programme included in the auditing was analysed also in terms of its participatory dimension, evaluating the extent of inclusion of subjects interested (directly or indirectly) in the action and usually neglected by participation (for instance migrant women living in an area that has been subjected to major urban renewals). Providing indicators to allow for the evaluation of this aspect appears to be very relevant in the application of the capability approach to gender budgeting.

In the classification of public policies for wellbeing gender budgeting, as stated above, can not only suggest re-classification of expenditures that have an impact on the development of capabilities as investment rather than current spending, but can detect multiplier effects of the same policy on more than one capability. In so doing it provides a multifaceted vision of the public budget, bringing insight to the complexity of the construction of wellbeing and detecting gender inequalities in each dimension.

Acknowledgements

Previous versions of this chapter were presented to other international conferences on gender budgeting. I thank the participants to these conferences for the inspiring exchange of ideas and stimulating comments that lead to this new version that is also informed by further applications of the wellbeing gender budgeting.

References

Addabbo, T. (ed.) (2005). *Genitorialità, lavoro e qualità della vita: una conciliazione possibile? Riflessioni da un'indagine in provincia di Modena*. Milan: Angeli.

Addabbo, T. and Saltini, S. (2009). *Gender Auditing del Bilancio del Comune di Modena Secondo l'Approccio dello Sviluppo Umano*. Research report, Modena and Reggio Emilia: Comune di Modena and Gender CAPP.

Addabbo, T., Badalassi, G., Corrado, F. and Picchio, A. (2011). 'A social-reproduction and well-being approach to gender budgets: experiments at local government level in Italy'. In Addis, E., de Villota, P., Degavre, F. and Eriksen, J. (eds) *Gender and Well-being: The Role of Institutions*. Aldershot, UK and Burlington, VT (USA): Ashgate, pp. 105–124.

Addabbo, T., Di Tommaso, M.L. and Facchinetti, G. (2004). 'To what extent fuzzy set theory and structural equation modelling can measure functionings? An application to child well being'. *Materiali di Discussione del Dipartimento di Economia Politica* 468, September.

Addabbo, T., Di Tommaso, M.L. and Maccagnan, A. (2014). 'Gender differences in Italian children's capabilities'. *Feminist Economics*, 20(2): 90–121.

Addabbo, T., Gálvez-Muñoz, L. and Rodríguez-Modroño, P. (2015). 'Gender budgeting in education from a well-being approach: an application to Italy and Spain'. *Journal of Economic Policy*, XXXI(2): 195–212.

Addabbo, T., Lanzi, D. and Picchio, A. (2010). 'Gender budgets: a capability approach'. *Journal of Human Development and Capabilities: A Multi-Disciplinary Journal for People-Centered Development*, 11(4): 479–501.

Anand, P., Hunter, G. and Smith, R. (2005). 'Capabilities and well-being: evidence based on the Sen–Nussbaum approach to welfare'. *Social Indicators Research*, 74(1): 9–55.

Biggeri, M., Libanora, R., Mariani, S. and Menchini, L. (2006). 'Children conceptualizing their capabilities: results of the survey during the first children's world congress on child labour'. *Journal of Human Development*, 7(1): 59–83.

Bonvin, J.M. (2014). 'Towards a more critical appraisal of social policies – the contribution of the capability approach'. In Otto, H. and Ziegler, H. (eds) *Critical Social Policy and the Capability Approach*. Berlin: Barbara Budrich Publishers, pp. 231–248.

Chiappero-Martinetti, E. (2008). 'Complexity and vagueness in the capability approach: strengths or weaknesses?' In Alkire S., Comim F. and Qizilbash M. (eds) *The Capability Approach: Concepts, Applications and Measurement*. Cambridge: Cambridge University Press, pp. 268–309.

Elson, D. (1998). 'Integrating gender issues into national budgetary policies and procedures: some policy options'. *Journal of International Development* 10(7): 929–941.

Fine-Davis, M., Fagnani, J., Giovannini, D., Hojgaard, L. and Clarke, H. (2004). *Fathers and Mothers: Dilemmas of the Work-Life Balance: A Comparative Study on Four European Countries*. Social Indicators Research Series, 21. Dordrecht: Kluwer Academic.

Gunluk-Senesen, G. (2016). 'In search of a gender budget with "actual allocation of public monies": a wellbeing gender budget exercise'. In Campbell, J. and Gillespie, M. (eds) *Feminist Economics and Public Policy: Reflections on the Work and Impact of Ailsa McKay*. Abingdon: Routledge, pp. 61–70.

Himmelweit, S. (2002). 'Making visible the hidden economy: the case for gender-impact analysis of economic policy'. *Feminist Economics*, 8(1): 49–70.

Himmelweit, S. (2016). 'Childcare as an investment in infrastructure'. In Campbell, J. and Gillespie, M. (eds) *Feminist Economics and Public Policy: Reflections on the Work and Impact of Ailsa McKay*. Abingdon: Routledge, pp. 83–93.

Kuklys, W. (2005). *Amartya Sen's Capability Approach: Theoretical Insights and Empirical Applications*. Berlin: Springer Verlag.

McKay, A., Campbell, J., Thomson, E. and Ross, S. (2013). 'Economic recession and recovery in the UK: what's gender got to do with it?'. *Feminist Economics*, 19(3): 108–123.

Nussbaum, M. (2000). *Women and Human Development. The Capabilities Approach.* Cambridge: Cambridge University Press.

Nussbaum, M. (2003). 'Capabilities as fundamental entitlements: Sen and social justice'. *Feminist Economics*, 9(2–3): 33–59.

Picchio, A. (1992). *Social Reproduction: The Political Economy of the Labour Market.* Cambridge: Cambridge University Press.

Robeyns I. (2003). 'Sen's capability approach and gender inequality: selecting relevant capabilities'. *Feminist Economics*, 9(2–3): 61–92.

Robeyns, I. (2005). 'The capability approach: a theoretical survey'. *Journal Of Human Development*, 6(1): 93–114.

Sen A.K. (1985). *Commodities and Capabilities*. Amsterdam: North Holland.

Sen A.K. (1995). *Inequality Re-Examined*. Cambridge, MA.: Harvard University Press.

Sen, A.K. (1999). *Development as Freedom*. New York: Alfred Knopf.

Sen, A.K. (2004). 'Capabilities, lists and public reason: continuing the conversation'. *Feminist Economics*, 10(3): 77–80.

Sharp, R. and Broomhill, R. (2002). 'Budgeting for equality: the Australian experience'. *Feminist Economics*, 8(1): 25–47.

Stotsky, J.G. (2006). *Gender Budgeting*. International Monetary Fund Working Paper, WP/06/232. Washington: International Monetary Fund.

7

IN SEARCH OF A GENDER BUDGET WITH 'ACTUAL ALLOCATION OF PUBLIC MONIES'

A wellbeing gender budget exercise

Gulay Gunluk-Senesen

Introduction

An extensive literature has grown up in the last two decades concerning the theoretical and practical aspects of gender budgeting, manuals inclusive. Most practical cases are pilot projects at local small-scale level and are usually referred to as 'gender budget initiatives' (e.g. see Hadziahmetovic et al., 2013). The 'initiative' experiences provide a very valuable base for feminist criticism of public policy and resource allocation; are reflected in policy agendas of inter-governmental entities like the United Nations (UN), the European Union (EU), the Inter-Parliamentary Union and the International Monetary Fund (IMF); and have raised gender awareness in target communities and public administrations. However, the 'initiative' reference also implies an uncertain future and content.

Institutionalisation of gender budgeting requires penetration of the political rhetoric into public finance practice. There appears to be as yet no continuous and standardised local or central government budget documentation (at least in English), which has 'introduced a gender perspective into all levels of the public budgeting process' as recommended by the Council of Europe Parliamentary Assembly (2006).

The analytical framework adopted in this chapter is based on several premises. Firstly, gender budgeting is a reflection of public policy, of the political process shaped by all sorts of power relations:

> Embarking upon a gender budget initiative then, initially involves developing an understanding of the relationship between policy and the actual allocation of public monies and to locate the budget within the policy process as opposed to viewing the two as distinct.
>
> (McKay, 2004a: 2)

The interrelatedness between the budget and the policy process requires budget literacy and familiarity with budget and policy documents (McKay, 2008; Gunluk-Senesen and McKay, 2012).

Secondly, gender budgeting is not solely or inherently a local or national issue. Promotion of gender budgeting by international institutions and civil society organisations has served more as an entry point for gender mainstreaming in the developing world.

Thirdly, and in connection to the above premise, gender budgeting is not solely concerned with development issues or poverty alleviation, although these could be the focus. Most pilot projects of gender budgeting address women's poverty only and reflect marginal concern for gender equality in overall public resource allocation (e.g. see Woestman, 2009; UNIFEM, 2010).

Finally, gender budgeting is an instrument for constructing a new gender contract for women and men (McKay, 2006). The usual practice is identification of gender budgeting with women-specific funding allocations, an approach criticised by the Scottish Women's Budget Group (SWBG) who promote 'gender analysis of spending plans to highlight any gaps between policy statements and the resources committed to their implementation' which 'ensures that any evidence of gender-bias in the promotion of social justice is accounted for and, where appropriate, offset' (McKay, 2004b: 15).

The above principles comply with some gender budgeting experiences, but deviate from others, although the overarching problem is common. The shared concern with the shortage of actual shifts in budget allocations that reflect gendered analysis implies the presence of unbalanced pillars on which the gender budgeting 'tripod' rests (Gunluk-Senesen et al., 2015). The three main pillars are: gender mainstreaming in public policy design; its reflections in budget documents; and implementation practice with sustainable balance in the interaction and support between the legs of the tripod, i.e. national, regional and/or local government levels. Obviously the public administration structure of the particular country will determine the entry points for gender budgeting.

This chapter assesses the present situation of these interactions for gender budgeting in Turkey within this analytic framework and discusses an exercise of gender auditing of the Gaziantep municipality budget from a wellbeing perspective. A brief overview of the gender budgeting agenda in Turkey leads to a discussion on the gender wellbeing approach and the Gaziantep budget allocation structure based on a classification with respect to women's capabilities. An overall assessment is given in the final section.

The gender budgeting agenda in Turkey: central and local government levels

Gender budgeting has been on the agenda at all levels of government and civil society organisations in Turkey since 2006. There have been commitments for gender budgeting by the central government with the potential for policy transfer (from the EU and UN) in due course. The rhetoric of gender mainstreaming and related reforms owes much to the EU pre-accession programmes. Gender budgeting related activities, all of which were projects funded by international agencies, were mainly limited to one- or two-day training sessions, workshops and conferences led by international experts, including Ailsa McKay in 2008. These activities contributed to raising awareness of gender issues and adoption of the rhetoric in political circles at both central and local government levels (Gunluk-Senesen, 2013).

Gender budgeting at central government level

The 10th Development Plan (2014–2018), which is the main policy document of the road map and vision for macroeconomic and social policies, states: 'Awareness will be generated about gender budgeting and pilot implementations will be run' (Republic of Turkey, 2014: 41). An issue of concern is the way the present plan addresses gender, since it reduces gender equality between men and women to *empowerment of women*. The targets of empowerment of women in education, employability, decision making and protection from domestic violence would not be problematic from a feminist perspective had this not appeared as: 'In the context of gender equality, the main objectives are to empower women in all aspects of social, economic and cultural life, *to improve the status of family while preserving the institution* and to strengthen social integration' (Republic of Turkey, 2014: 40; emphasis added). This is consistent with repeated prioritisation of the family and women's traditional roles at home in policy design in the last decade.

The Minister of Finance's statement in October 2011, 'We are gender sensitizing our budget for 2012', the first and only one so far, had stirred hopes for a prospective holistic budget approach, but what was actually inferred was a fund allocation of an undisclosed amount for several specific women empowerment schemes: promotion of girls' education (rural and poor), women's employment (compensation of employer social security premium payments), women's shelters and training women in agriculture (rural and poor).

Though rather weak at central government level, the Ministry of Interior led cooperation with the UN agencies to develop local administration reforms which encompass gender mainstreaming and budgeting. Finance ministry staff involvement in gender budgeting activities has been negligible.

Gender budgeting at local government level: international involvement

Gender perspectives in policy making at the municipal level in Turkey were introduced through projects initiated by the UN agencies in collaboration with central and local governments, with expanding coverage over time (UNDP, 2009; and United Nations Joint Programme (UNJP) projects like UNJP 2006a, 2006b, 2011 and 2012). The umbrella concept in these is gender mainstreaming at local level, including small-scale training sessions on gender budgeting for local administrators and members of women's organisations. These contributed towards awareness of gender budgeting but had little impact on transforming the budget with actual monetary allocation (Gunluk-Senesen et al., 2015). One main component of the latest project is gendering the budgets in 11 pilot provinces (UNJP, 2012). This project is undertaken by a consortium including UNDP, UN Women and several government ministries.

The local governments' strategic plans for 2015–2019 and the performance programmes for 2015 were issued after local elections in 2014. The extent of gender coverage in these documents is determined by local power relations along with the social and economic structures which shape the priorities of policy makers. Common to all is poor gender statistics, particularly with respect to beneficiaries. We chose Gaziantep from among the pilot cities for our exercise mainly because the municipal performance programme for 2015 offered a relatively detailed documentation of budget allocation intentions for women. The key factors for this are that the mayor elected in 2014 was the former Minister of Family and Social Policies and Gaziantep was included both in UNJP (2011) and UNJP (2012) projects, so it was a province apparently with promising prospects.

A wellbeing gender auditing exercise: the Gaziantep budget

While auditing of policy documents and the budget using a gender lens provides useful information on gender gaps to the disadvantage of women, integrating this with wellbeing analysis links this with a set of desired outcomes specified on the basis of gender equality.

Adopting the wellbeing gender budgeting approach, elaborated in Addabbo (2016), Gunluk-Senesen et al. (2014) developed a set of women's capabilities to map with the functions delivered by the Turkish municipalities. Infrastructure upgrading like gentrification and regeneration, social housing, construction of roads, transport (buses) and sport and recreation facilities are the main tasks of the municipalities and the leading budget expenditure items. The first three in our list of capabilities below are identified on the basis of access to these functions, the rest relate to the social policy domain:

1. adequate and secure living spaces;
2. adequate mobility and environmental planning;
3. leisure time and sports activities;
4. adequate care services;
5. social and political participation;
6. paid employment and decent working conditions;
7. cash and in-kind income (for the needy);
8. health;
9. education and training;
10. ability to lead a life without violence.

The Gaziantep performance programme includes the goal entitled 'Equal and Able City', the first component of which stipulates 'equal treatment of all citizens indiscriminating with respect to gender', with a budget of 790,000 Turkish Lira (TL) (equivalent to around $280,000 or €260,000) in 2015. Yet the planned activities are women specific, and so are the budget allocations. We relate the activities (and the budget 5,660,000 TL) of the second goal component 'Able City' also to women's wellbeing since facilities for people with disabilities benefit women who are the major caregivers. Inspection of all other policy items and inclusion of those which would improve women's capabilities, along with the funds and departments, form the main procedure underlying our wellbeing gender budget exercise.

The output of our search for a gender budget with 'actual allocation of public monies' is shown in Table 7.1. Apart from the department responsible for construction, all other planned activities specifically for women are assigned to the Health and Social Services Department in the performance programme. An overarching cooperation among departments is lacking and there is no involvement of the finance department.

While investments in services such as transport, recreation areas, sport facilities, housing and street lights improve the wellbeing of all citizens, their implications for women's capabilities are not clear as there are no statistics with a gender breakdown. The only beneficiary data is for literacy courses for women, which amounts to only 100 in a city with around 60,000 illiterate women (around 8 per cent of women over age 6), a very low level of activity.

Our mapping of activities and capabilities is mostly self-explanatory. However note the item 9.1.6 which serves gender equality in general and offers girls opportunities other than marriage, yet contradictorily with the focus on 'family priority' could act as a restricting environment for girls and women to realise their potential outside the home.

Table 7.2 summarises funding for women's capabilities which in total take less than 2 per cent of the total municipality budget and few planned outputs. The most significant (around 75 per cent) allocation is for care services, which lies at the core of gender inequalities. Domestic violence is a hot topic in Turkey and is the next most significant item in our gender-wellbeing budget. Health services in Turkey are mainly the central government's responsibility, but the Gaziantep municipality also assigns local action, mainly for maternity services, as detailed in Table 7.1. The support for women's entrepreneurship is also interesting and we associate this (4.2.2) and vocational courses (9.1.4) with the employability capability. Promotion of business start-ups for women has its roots in past microcredit projects, but supporting women's skill formation for the job market has much less significance in Gaziantep.

Our exercise also illustrates that capacity building in the administration not only has an administrative relevance but its performance is conditional upon specific budget funding to advance implementation of gender budgeting.

TABLE 7.1 Gaziantep Municipality planned activities and budget allocations related to women and gender equality, 2015

Code	TASK	OUTPUT	DEPARTMENT	CAPABILITY	BUDGET 1,000 TL
4.1.4	Care centres for children, aged and disabled	5	Technical Works	Access to adequate care services	50
4.2.1	Furnishing and operating childcare and mother centres		Health and Social Services	Access to adequate care services	1,000
4.2.2	Consultancy centre for women entrepreneurs (operation)	1	Health and Social Services	Access to paid employment and decent working conditions	500
4.2.3	Family Consultancy Centre (operation)		Health and Social Services	Ability to lead a life without violence	500
4.2.4	Women's shelters (operation)		Health and Social Services	Ability to lead a life without violence	100
4.7.4	Women's shelters (service)		Health And Social Services	Ability to lead life without violence	500
4.5.3	Public laundrette	1	Health and Social Services	Ability to lead a life without violence	500
4.6.1	Social organisations for the aged	1	Health and Social Services	Access to adequate care services	50
4.7.3	Consultancy for women for child development		Health and Social Services	Access to adequate care services	100
6.16.4	Pre-birth mother hotel	1	Health and Social Services	Access to health	150
6.16.6	Pregnant training centre	1	Health and Social Services	Access to health	100
6.16.7	In-house care and health centre for the needy	1	Health and Social Services	Access to adequate care services	3,000
6.16.8	Mobile mammography vehicle	1	Health and Social Services	Access to health	100
6.21.1	Equipment for the day care centre for the aged		Health and Social Services	Access to adequate care services	50
9.1.1	Local Equality Action Plan Preparation		Health and Social Services	CAPACITY BUILDING OF THE MUNICIPALITY	10
9.1.2	Literacy courses for women	100 women	Health and Social Services	Access to education and training	20
9.1.3	Social and cultural activities for women	3	Health and Social Services	Access to leisure time and sports activities	100

Code	TASK	OUTPUT	DEPARTMENT	CAPABILITY	BUDGET 1,000 TL
9.1.4	Vocational courses for women	3	Health and Social Services	Access to paid employment and decent working conditions	50
9.1.5	Training of the staff of the Department of Health and Social Services on gender equality and gender budgeting		Health and Social Services	CAPACITY BUILDING OF THE DEPARTMENT OF HEALTH AND SOCIAL SERVICES	50
9.1.6	Awareness-raising activities for elimination of gender discrimination, prevention of early marriages and promotion of family integrity	1	Health and Social Services	Social and political participation	200
9.1.7	Materials for 9.1.6		Health and Social Services	Social and political participation	100
9.1.8	Activities for Women Friendly City status		Health and Social Services	Social and political participation	100
9.1.9	Activities for prevention of violence against women	1	Health and Social Services	Ability to lead a life without violence	160
9.2	Social inclusion activities for people with disabilities: Training, consultancy, equipment, prosthesis, home support		Disabilities	Access to adequate care services	5,660
	BUDGET FOR WOMEN'S CAPABILITIES				13,090
	BUDGET FOR ADMINISTRATIVE CAPACITY				60

Source: Compiled from *2015 Mali Yıtı Performans Programı*: www.gantep.bel.tr/files/2015-performans-programi.pdf (accessed 18 June 2015)
Note: The codes in the first column relate to the specific activities under the main goals in the performance programme. Goal 4 is Efficient Social Services, Goal 6 is Life Quality Improvement, Goal 9 is "Equal (9.1) and Able (9.2) City". The activity and funds items listed in this table are those we associate with women's capabilities from the comprehensive set of items in the programme.

TABLE 7.2 Gaziantep Municipality budget allocations for women's capabilities, 2015

No.	CAPABILITY	BUDGET, 1,000 TL
1	Access to adequate and secure living spaces	
2	Access to adequate mobility and environmental planning	
3	Access to leisure time and sports activities	100
4	Access to adequate care services	10,410
5	Social and political participation	400
6	Access to paid employment and decent working conditions	550
7	Access to cash and in-kind income (social transfers)	
8	Access to health	350
9	Access to education and training	20
10	Ability to lead a life without violence	1,260
	WOMEN'S CAPABILITIES TOTAL	13,090
	ADMINISTRATIVE CAPACITY BUILDING	60
	TOTAL	13,150
	TOTAL BUDGET	**773,320**

Source: extract from Table 7.1

Conclusions

Gender auditing is a second-best but realistic approach to 'holding governments to account' (Bjørnholt and McKay, 2014: 16) for gender equality since the ideal of gender budgeting is usually lacking. Impact or incidence analysis is not yet possible in Turkey as gender issues are only very recently integrated. Nonetheless, the reconciled wellbeing approach enables us to audit both the policy and budget allocations and expose the extent to which these support gender equality.

Though limited in scope, the Gaziantep performance programme for 2015 provides a detailed documentation of a municipal budget which presents a case beyond a gender budget initiative. This outcome owes much to a suitable political climate under which societal and governmental stakeholders could collaborate with international actors, the efficiency and efficacy of which depends on the domestic/local climate for change (Rubin and Bartle, 2005).

As the Turkish public administration system is highly centralised, local administration policy design is shaped by central government, including how gender inequalities are addressed. For example, integrity of the family as the priority for a conservative government is reflected at the local level (in our case, Gaziantep). Although a focus on (and expenditures for) women could serve women's empowerment, the impact would be limited in comparison to a focus on (and expenditures for) eliminating gender imbalances for which gender-disaggregated data is a pre-condition.

Nevertheless our exercise with the Gaziantep budget reveals several innovations which could contribute to gender budgeting practice. Firstly, even if restricted to spending for women, developing a profile of women's wellbeing in terms of their capabilities reveals policy areas where action is needed. Foremost in our case is access to care services followed by access to a safe life. These would also improve access to (and coincide with) a gender friendly public sphere (decent employability, mobility, leisure, secure living spaces, safe transport and social and political participation). Hence establishing links between various capabilities and related monetary allocations poses a challenge to research and practice in gender budgeting.

Secondly, monetary allocations reveal the priority rankings of the policy makers in their approach to gender wellbeing. This also serves as a basis for contesting the 'gender performance' of the administrations which can be pressurised to develop operational indicators.

Last but not least, institutionalisation and hence sustainability of gender budgeting is conditional upon capacity building within the administration in charge, which also requires monetary allocation. This point has had little attention in the gender budgeting literature.

Acknowledgements

I thank Aysegul Yakar Onal and Yelda Yucel for constructive comments, and Metehan Gultasli and Ebru Ozberk for the inspiration to work on the Gaziantep case. I acknowledge the support of the Scientific Research Projects Coordination Unit of Istanbul University: BYP-11976.

References

Addabbo T. (2016). 'Gender budgeting in the capability approach: from theory to evidence'. In Campbell, J. and Gillespie, M. (eds) *Feminist Economics and Public Policy: Reflections on the Work and Impact of Ailsa McKay*. Abingdon: Routledge, pp. 54–60.

Bjornhølt, M. and McKay, A. (2014). 'Advances in feminist economics in times of economic crisis'. In Bjornhølt, M. and McKay, A. (eds) *Counting on Marilyn Waring: New Advances in Feminist Economics*. Canada: Demeter, pp. 7–20.

Council of Europe Parliamentary Assembly (2006). *Recommendation 1739 (2006) 'Gender budgeting'*. [Online] Available from:http://assembly.coe.int/nw/xml/XRef/Xref-XML2HTML-en.asp?fileid=17420&lang=en (accessed 27 June 2015).

Gunluk-Senesen, G. (2013). 'Toplumsal cinsiyete duyarli butceleme: kapsam, ornekler ve Turkiye icin oneriler'. In Altug, F., Kesik, A. and Seker, M. (eds) *Kamu Butcesinde Yeni Yaklasimlar*. Seckin: Ankara, pp. 97–128.

Gunluk-Senesen, G. and McKay, A. (2012). 'Opportunities and challenges for gender budgeting: comparing the Scottish and Turkish stories'. Presentation, *2012 IAFFE Annual Conference*. Barcelona, Spain, 27–29 June, 2012. Unpublished.

Gunluk-Senesen, G., Ergunes, N., Yakar Onal, A., Yakut Cakar, B. and Yucel, Y. (2014). *Kamu Politikalari, Yerel Yonetimler, Toplumsal Cinsiyete Duyarli Butceleme: Kadin Dostu Kentler, Turkiye Ornegi*. Project no. 112K481 funded by TUBİTAK (The Scientific and Technological Research Council of Turkey). [Online] Available from: https://drive.google.com/file/d/0B24iuzmrzn5RM2VwNkhzV3NFWms/view?usp=sharing (accessed 27 June 2015).

Gunluk-Senesen, G., Yucel, Y., Yakar-Onal, A., Yakut-Cakar, B. and Ergunes, N. (2015). 'Gender budgeting in Turkey: an assessment of local practices from the well-being perspective'. *Politica Economica-Journal of Economic Policy*, XXXI(2):175–194.

Hadziahmetovic, A., Duric-Kuzmanovic, T., Klatzer, E.M. and Risteska, M. (2013). *Gender Responsive Budgeting-Textbook for Universities*. Sarajevo: UNWOMEN-University Press (Izdanja magistrat).

McKay, A. (2004a). *Developing a Gender Budget Initiative: A Question of Process or Policy? Lessons from Scotland*. [Online] Available from: www.gender-budgets.org/index. php?option=com_joomdoc&view=documents&path=resources/by-region-country/europe-cee-and-cis-documents/developing-a-gender-budget-initiative-a-question-of-process-or-policy-lessons-from-scotland&Itemid=542 (accessed 15 December 2014).

McKay, A. (2004b). 'Practical application – focus on process or policy? Case studies from Scotland, the Basque Country and the UK Treasury'. *Gender Budgeting Initiative (GBI) in CEE/NIS region – Strategic Planning Meeting Report*, 14–16 April, Sopot, Poland. [Online] Available from: www.neww.org.pl/download/Gender_Budgeting_Initiative.pdf (accessed 27 June 2015).

McKay, A. (2006). 'Promoting gender sensitive budgeting: a case of applied feminist economics'. Presentation, *Turkish Economic Association International Conference*. Ankara, 11–13 September. Unpublished.

McKay, A. (2008). 'Using political change to promote gender sensitive budgeting in Scotland, the experience of the Scottish Women's Budget Group'. Presentation, *KEIG Workshop on Gender Budgeting in Turkey*, Istanbul, 3 November. Unpublished.

Republic of Turkey (2014). *The Tenth Development Plan, 2014–2018*. [Online] Available from: www.mod.gov.tr/Lists/DevelopmentPlans/Attachments/5/The%20Tenth%20Development%20Plan%20(2014-2018).pdf (accessed 24 July 2015).

Rubin, M.M. and Bartle J.R. (2005). 'Integrating gender into government budgets: a new perspective'. *Public Administration Review*, 65(3): 259–272.

UNDP (2009). *Support to Further Implementation of Local Administration Reform in Turkey*. (Lar Phase 2) (Version 5: 1 April 2009). [Online] Available from: www.tg.undp.org/content/brussels/en/home/ourwork/democraticgovernance/successstories/support-to-the-further-implementation-of-local-administration-re.html (accessed 26 July 2015).

UNIFEM (2010). *Gender-Responsive Budgeting in South Eastern Europe: UNIFEM Experiences*. [Online] Available from www.unwomen.org/en/digital-library/publications/2010/1/gender-responsive-budgeting-in-south-eastern-europe-unifem-experiences (accessed 26 June 2015).

UNJP (2006a). *UN Joint Programme 'To Protect and Promote the Human Rights of Women and Girls'*. [Online] Available from: www.kadindostukentler.org/content/docs/outputs/women-friendly-cities-2010.pdf (accessed 29 July 2015).

UNJP (2006b). *Women Friendly Cities*. Phase 1. [Online] Available from www.kadindostukentler.org/project.php (accessed 26 June 2015).

UNJP (2011). *Women Friendly Cities*. Phase 2. [Online] Available from: www.kadindostukentler.org/project.php (accessed 26 June 2015).

UNJP (2012). *Promoting the Human Rights of Women*. [Online] Available from: www.tr.undp.org/content/turkey/en/home/operations/projects/democratic_governance/UN_joint_program_for_promoting_the_human_rights_of_women.html (accessed 26 June 2015).

Woestman, L. (2009). *Engendering EU General Budget Support: GRB as a Tool for Fostering Gender Equality in EU Partner Countries*. [Online] Available from: http://gender-financing.unwomen.org/en/resources/e/n/g/engendering-eu-general-budget-support-grb-as-a-tool-for-fostering-gender-equality (accessed 20 June 2015).

8

THE SPANISH CENTRAL GOVERNMENT BUDGET

Comments on recent experience

Paloma de Villota

Introduction

In Spain gender budget analysis has mainly concentrated on expenditure. However, expenditure alone is insufficient for understanding the gender impact of budgets, and the tax system and taxation changes are also important. This chapter assesses the impact of recent changes to taxation in Spain and shows that, while fewer women will pay tax other issues, including a VAT increase, offset these gains for low-paid women.

At the beginning of the twenty-first century two Autonomous Communities (AC) in Spain started gender budgeting analysis: the Basque Country and Andalusia. The Central Government of Spain did not join the process until 2009. In this process Ailsa McKay made great contributions towards the improvement at all levels of gender budget analysis in Spain through participation over several years in doctoral and masters level courses and seminars in the University Complutense of Madrid and other parts of the country. We are grateful for the opportunity to share her considerable knowledge and experience.

The Spanish Parliament established the obligation in 2003 that gender impact analysis should accompany every Bill presented for discussion and approval in the Spanish Parliament or any of the 17 Autonomous Parliaments corresponding to each Autonomous Community (Boletín Oficial del Estado (BOE), 2003). However, the Finance Minister did not consider himself affected by this legal requirement in the case of the presentation of the State Budget to the Spanish Parliament. Clearly, this situation was anomalous: on the one hand the Finance Minister did not consider his Ministry affected by this commitment and, on the other hand, some feminist associations were applying pressure through a public campaign for a gender impact report on the draft State Budget. The feminist NGOs involved took the Socialist Government to court for failing to fulfil the Law of 2003. Following this, the

Socialist Government added gender impact analysis to the 2009 and all subsequent State Budgets presented to the Spanish Parliament (Morán, 2008).

The Constitution of 1978, Article 9.2, obliges all public institutions to promote liberty and equality and diminish social discrimination. Has gender budgeting analysis been an adequate tool for improving Spaniards' gender equality? There are several reasons for scepticism about this which cannot be enlarged upon here, but one crucial issue is that gender impact analysis takes little consideration of the revenue side of the budget, which is essential for comprehensive analysis. In Spain in 2015, gender impact analysis of the State budget is limited to the expenditure side, suggesting that taxes and other public revenues have little or no gender impact. Furthermore, this situation continues despite strong pressure from the Women's Institute to include both sides of the budget, including recommendations to change the annual Ministerial regulation which is the starting point of the budget process and gives general instructions to all Ministries and other Public Institutions (Villota et al., 2009).

The latest Ministerial Regulation, in May 2014, was unchanged, assessing only expenditure in the gender report (Ministerio de Hacienda, 2014). However, the revenue side is included in the gender impact of the budget for 2015; some aspects related to Personal Income Tax (PIT) are considered briefly. For example, the gender report includes the number of joint or individual tax returns as well as the mean value of their income in 2012, disaggregated by sex. The Ministry has also expanded upon the recommendations that Fitzgerald et al. made to the Scottish Government for gender analysis of public expenditure to be done comprehensively to 'ensure that sex disaggregated data is available across all policy areas. It should be standard practice to provide this information' (Fitzgerald et al., 2006: 16).

In Spain, however, further and deeper analysis on taxation incidence is required and studies external to the government have tried to fill this vacuum (for example, see Villota and Ferrari, 2003; Carbajo, 2005; Alarcón, 2014).

The new Income Tax Law 26/2014 from a gender perspective

This chapter examines the gender impact of new tariffs on wages arising from the recently published Law of Personal Income Tax 26/2014 (BOE, 2014) in comparison with the previous Law 35/2006 (BOE, 2006).

The general decline in the progressive nature of income tax has led the OECD to voice concerns over the reduction in the redistributive capacity of fiscal systems, highlighting that three decades ago maximum marginal tax rates on personal income tax in the EU were higher than at present by more than 20 percentage points (OECD, 2011). In the EU-28 there has been a fall in tax rates of 9 percentage points on average between 1995 and 2012, with several countries adopting a flat rate of tax (proportional) and at a lower rate, for example Bulgaria, Estonia, Hungary, Lithuania and Rumania (European Commission, 2013).

Spain has been no exception to this trend since the highest tax rate was reduced from 53 per cent, to 43 per cent between 2007 and 2010. Adiego et al. (2013)

show that the Personal Income Tax (PIT) has been losing its redistributive capacity, with clear stagnation prior to the recent economic crisis. Over 2005 to 2010 the fall in the Gini inequality index after tax was only 0.04 points. Tax rises in 2010 and 2011 as a result of the crisis had a limited effect, affecting less than 1 per cent of those filing returns. However, they did result in a partial recovery of the redistributive capacity of PIT. Consequently, from 2011 to 2012 the Gini index showed a fall of 0.04 points, a similar reduction in inequality, in just one year (Adiego et al., 2013).

The response following the economic crisis should lead to a trend change, with more progressive tax levels because the Law of the State General Budgets for 2011 (Ley 39/2010) increases the previous maximum tax rate from 43 per cent to 44 per cent for taxable income over €120,000 and a new higher 45 per cent rate for taxable income over €175,000. However, this does not signal a return to previous levels of progressive taxation since a 45 per cent tax rate applied to taxable income above €60,000 prior to the 2006 reform.

Soon after being formed following the 2011 election, the new government contradicted the promise in the Party's electoral program and campaign and imposed a 0.75 to 7 percentage point *temporary* surcharge on PIT, increasing the tax range from a minimum of 24.75 per cent to a maximum of 52 per cent, affecting mainly tax payers on average and high wage incomes. The justification for the surcharge was the need to cut the budget deficit (BOE, 2011).

The reform of Personal Income Tax, 2015

The optimistic view argues that the austerity measures taken over recent years have produced the desired effect as shown by 'the improved macroeconomic indicators, and, especially, the effective fall in the public deficit' (BOE, 2014: 1) and considers that consequently the time has come to keep one's promises and, thus, reduce PIT. Previously, a Commission of Experts for the Reform of the Spanish tax system, consisting exclusively of men, was constituted in 2013 with the aim of: 'reviewing the tax system as a whole and drawing up a plan for reform which might contribute to a fiscal consolidation in the country, as well as contributing to the economic recovery of Spain and, especially, to creating employment' (MINAP, 2014: 1–2).

The conclusions of this Commission served to deepen and consolidate further the neoliberal bias that the Spanish fiscal system had adopted during recent years. With the last published Law 26/2014 the Government aims to reduce the tax burden on taxpayers, particularly those on low incomes and also for those with 'greater family pressure, particularly large families or disabled members, with the benefits accruing for several economic variables' and 'strengthen the fight against fiscal fraud' (BOE, 2014: 2).

The announced tax reduction returns Spanish tax payers to a situation similar to the pre-crisis tax levels in force from 2007 to 2011. From a gender viewpoint, it means there is still no modification of those aspects which have been repeatedly criticised by specialists (Villota et al., 2008) and feminist associations, including that couples continue to have the option of a joint tax return rather than compulsory individual taxation that would achieve more (gender) neutral taxation.

Thanks to the existence of a sample of taxpayers, it is possible to develop a microsimulation model which reproduces the changes in Spanish PIT for different levels of income. Table 8.1 shows the distribution of taxable income in 2009 of the Common Fiscal Territory (CFT) that comprises all Autonomous Communities, except the Basque Country and Navarre which have different fiscal regimes. Note that Spanish income tax applies to earned income from wages and sources including contributory pensions, unemployment benefits etc.

This analysis indicates a return to the parameters in force before the crisis hit Spain with an almost identical structure except for the splitting of the lowest tax bracket. This will improve the position of those on very low incomes (up to €12,550 taxable income) levied with a 24 per cent tax rate. This modification means the bracket from zero to €17,707.20 taxable income is slightly extended and split into two: the first, up to €12,550, has a 19 per cent tax rate and the second from €12,550.01 to €20,200 is at 24 per cent. At the other extreme the rate is fixed at 45 per cent for taxable income over €60,000. These tax rates come into force from 2016 onwards. The tax free allowance is maintained at a similar amount, €5,550 against €5,050 in 2007.

It must be remembered that the tax rate and the tax free allowance define the progressiveness of total tax liability. In the case of the Spanish PIT the tax exemption cut-off consists of personal and family exemptions and a reduction for work. The latter does not show any significant variation following reform since it is fixed at €4,000 compared to €3,700 in 2007.

In order to evaluate the effect of these new parameters on people the effect of these modifications (new rate and personal minimum) is compared with their earned income. This is done by taking the distribution of those contributing through PIT in 2009, the last sample provided by the Agencia Estatal de Administración Tributaria (AEAT), the Spanish Revenue Service. The values of the parameters established in Ley 35/2006 are applied and the ones envisaged to apply in 2016. The results are shown in Figure 8.1 and Table 8.1.

Table 8.1 shows that an estimated 36.9 per cent of female and 22.2 per cent of male workers are in the zero rate tax bracket in the new structure in 2016. For women, this represents an increase from 27.8 per cent in the year 2007. Furthermore, a proportion (29.6 per cent) will have a higher disposable income as a consequence of the fall in the marginal tax rate from 24 per cent to 19 per cent. The new regulation introduces a slight modification to the taxation of working people, with the following changes:

1. Reduced amount in the tax allowance for obtaining earnings from work.
2. Elimination of €400 tax credit for workers with income below €12,000.
3. A €2,000 deductible allowance for employment income (this applies for all earners).

TABLE 8.1 Percentage of employed earners and PIT tax rates

2007				
Tax rate %	Women	% Women	Men	% Men
0.0	2,025,736	27.8	1,532,223	15.0
24.0	3,592,254	49.3	5,317,504	52.2
28.0	1,211,181	16.6	2,197,849	21.6
37.0	336,887	4.6	727,871	7.1
43.0	119,914	1.6	413,585	4.1
Total	7,285,972	100.0	10,189,031	100.0
2016				
Tax rate %	Women	% Women	Men	% Men
0.0	2,687,624	36.9	2,260,364	22.2
19.0	2,157,157	29.6	3,206,880	31.5
24.0	1,063,274	14.6	1,950,503	19.1
30.0	1,031,840	14.2	1,806,406	17.7
37.0	268,477	3.7	664,192	6.5
45.0	77,600	1.1	300,686	3.0
Total	7,285,972	100.0	10,189,031	100.0

Source: Authors own microsimulation estimates based on Muestra IRPF 2009 IRPF-AEAT declarants

These changes, in particular the new tax rate and the extension of the personal minimum, produce a fall of 661,888 in the number of women obliged to file a return compared with 728,141 men. Further, when the lowest tax rate, previously 24 per cent, is split into two rates (19 per cent and 24 per cent) there are tax reductions for 1,495,268 female workers and 2,468,739 male workers. It is worth stressing the existing gender inequalities in earnings mean that, for example, only 110,724 women against 176,577 men benefit from the reduction in marginal tax rate from 37 per cent to 30 per cent (for gross earnings between €42,300 and €45,300). Finally, we should also note that those receiving higher incomes (between €62,400 and €70,200) also get favourable treatment since their marginal tax rate will fall from 43 per cent to 37 per cent. These estimates, based on data obtained from the microsimulation carried out with the sample of IEF-AEAT taxpayers, suggest this will affect a much higher number of men than women (112,899 compared to 42,312).

Splitting the lowest bracket is significant because it will undoubtedly favour those with the lowest taxable incomes. This will affect a similar percentage of women and men (29.9 per cent and 31.5 per cent respectively) as a result of the drastic reduction in male wages due to the impact of the economic crisis and a corresponding increase in the number of men in the lower income brackets.

Finally, this analysis shows that the 2015 PIT design returns partially to the outline of Ley 35/2006, of which it can be considered a continuation of lower rates of taxation but with a less progressive profile. But it cannot be stated that

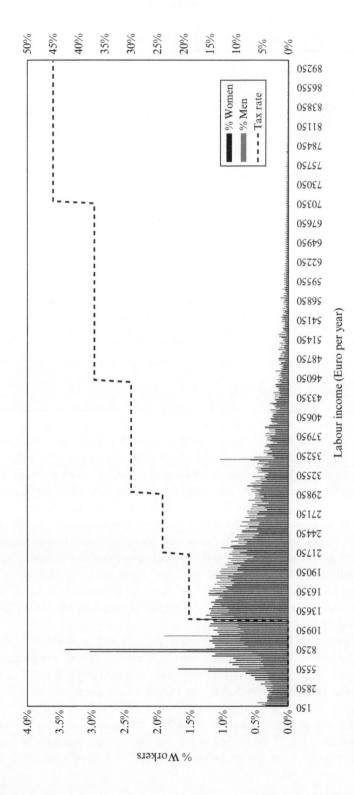

FIGURE 8.1 Density function and PIT rates

Source: own microsimulation estimates based on Muestra IRPF 2009 IRPF–AEAT declarants

the gender discrimination of the past has been eliminated, particularly when we still have the optional joint declaration, discrimination against the second wage earner and fiscal penalisation of one-parent families (Villota and Ferrari, 2004). As before, in 2015, PIT tax expenditure (income foregone through tax allowances) is estimated to exceed €30 billion in the Common Fiscal Territory which represents 37.8 per cent of the whole amount of tax generated by PIT, a proportion similar to previous years. However, deductions benefiting large families are increased so that family allowances are set at €2,400 annually for the first child, €2,700 for the second, €4,000 for third and €4,500 for the fourth and above. What is more, taxpayers, with large families who work outside the home could reduce the total tax liability with an additional €1,200 tax credit refundable for each descendant or adult dependent with a liability. Nonetheless, the reduction in the lower marginal tax rate in the new Law has partially improved the situation of women workers, since the minimum tax rate was fixed at 24 per cent in 2006.

Conclusion

Government claims of increased incomes across the board are misleading. While it is true that the new PIT reduces taxes in 2015 compared to the previous three years when surcharges were imposed, the situation remains very similar to 2011, because only one in three taxpayers shows a slight increase in disposable income. Furthermore, people lose out from the new PIT design, in comparison with the situation in 2007, if they have taxable income between €29,700 and €42,300 (12.6 per cent women and 16.0 per cent men) as do those with taxable incomes over €70,200 who face a rise in the maximum tax rate from 43 per cent in 2007 to 45 per cent in 2016 (1.1 per cent women and 3.0 per cent men). Thus, the impact of reductions in the fiscal burden is not homogeneous, it is not consistently progressive, nor does everyone who gains benefit equally.

Although the gender impact of the latest modifications in other taxes is not discussed here in detail, there is a negative impact of indirect tax increases during the last few years in both Value Added Tax (VAT) and Special Taxes. This aspect is important for a comprehensive evaluation of the fiscal modifications made in recent years, because there is evidence that those on low and average incomes have suffered the consequences of this more than most. From 2010 the standard and reduced rates of VAT have increased twice, generating a negative impact on families with dependent children (Gómez de la Torre and López, 2010; López and Gómez de la Torre, 2012). They bear a heavier burden than other family types because, in Spain, on the one hand, not all families with dependent children have access to tax allowances' especially when their incomes are below €12,250, but on the other their children's food and clothes are VAT taxed, unlike countries such as Britain (De Henau et al., 2010). This highlights the need for further research on the combined effects of changes in PIT and VAT on families with dependent children. It also reinforces that no tax alteration is gender neutral and, therefore, each year gender budgeting analysis should also assess the impact of the revenue side of the public budget (Villota et al., 2009).

References

Adiego, M., Cantó, O., Paniagua, M. and Pérez Barrasa, T. (2013). *The Redistributive Effects of Changes in the Personal Income Tax during the Great Recession in Spain*. Ponencia presentada en XX Encuentro de Economía Pública. Sevilla: Universidad de Sevilla. [Online] Available from: http://dialnet.unirioja.es/servlet/articulo?codigo=4800901 (accessed 22 August 2015).

AEAT (various years). *Mercado de Trabajo y Pensiones en las Fuentes Tributarias*. Madrid: AEAT. [Online] Available from: www.agenciatributaria.es/AEAT.internet/datosabiertos/catalogo/hacienda/Mercado_de_Trabajo_y_Pensiones_en_las_Fuentes_Tributarias.shtml (accessed 15 July 2015).

AEAT (2014). *Estadísticas de los declarantes del Impuesto sobre la Renta de las Personas Físicas*. Madrid: AEAT. [Online] Available from: www.agenciatributaria.es/AEAT.internet/datosabiertos/catalogo/hacienda/Estadistica_de_los_declarantes_del_IRPF.shtml (accessed 22 August 2015).

Alarcón, G., (2014). 'El tratamiento fiscal de la familia y, en particular, de la monoparental. Pasado, presente y futuro'. In *Fiscalidad, elecciones, violencia de género*. XXIV Taller Forum de Política Feminista. [Online] Madrid: Forum de Política Feminista. Available from: www.forumpoliticafeminista.org /?q=publicaciones (accessed 22 August 2015).

BOE (2003). *Ley 30/2003, Madrid*: BOE-A-2003-18920. Madrid: BOE. [Online] Available from: www.boe.es/buscar/doc.php?id=BOE-A-2003-18920 (accessed 22 August 2015).

BOE (2006). *Ley 35/2006*, Madrid. BOE-A-2006-20764 Madrid: BOE. [Online] Available from: www.boe.es/buscar/act.php?id=BOE-A-2006-20764 (accessed 22 August 2015).

BOE (2011). *Real Decreto Ley 20/2011*, BOE-A-2011-20638. Madrid: BOE. [Online] Available from: www.boe.es/boe/dias/2011/12/31/pdfs/BOE-A-2011-20638.pdf (accessed 22 August 2015).

BOE (2014). *Ley 26/2014*, Madrid. BOE-A-2014-12327 Madrid: BOE. [Online] Available from: www.boe.es/diario_boe/txt.php?id=BOE-A-2014-12327 (accessed 22 August 2015).

Carbajo, D. (2005). 'La tributación conjunta en el impuesto sobre la renta y la igualdad de género'. In Pazos, M. (ed.) *Política Fiscal y Género*. Madrid: Instituto de Estudios Fiscales, pp. 83–96.

De Henau, J., Himmelweit, S. and Santos, C., (2010). 'Gender equality and taxation. A UK case study'. In Grown, C. and Valodia, I., *Taxation and Gender Equity*. London. Routledge, pp. 261–298.

European Commission (2013). *Tax Reforms in EU Member States 2013. Tax Policy Challenges for Economic Growth and Fiscal Sustainability*. European Economy 5|2013.

Fitzgerald, R., McKay, A. and Simpson, K. (2006). *Gender Impact Analysis and the Scottish Budget. Sports and Health Pilots*. Report prepared for the Equality Unit. Edinburgh: Scottish Executive. [Online] Available from: www.gov.scot/Resource/Doc/1032/0041301.doc (accessed 29 July 2015).

Gómez de la Torre, M. and Lopez, T. (2010). *IVA y familia en los PGE para 2010*. Fundación Acción Familiar. Documento de Trabajo 01/2010. Madrid. ISSN 1989-2527.

MINAP (2014). *Informe de la Comisión de Expertos para la Reforma del Sistema Tributario Español* (2014). Madrid: Ministerio de Hacienda y Administraciones Públicas. [Online]

Available from: www.abc.es/gestordocumental/uploads/economia/fe007a24af859ec-8ce790387ba6b7755.pdf (accessed 29 July 2015).

Ministerio de Hacienda (2014). *Orden HAP/988/2014, de 12 de junio, por la que se dictan las normas para la elaboración de los Presupuestos Generales del Estado para 2015.* Madrid: Ministerio de Hacienda y Administraciones Públicas. [Online] Available from: www.minhap.gob.es/Documentacion/Publico/NormativaDoctrina/Presupuestos/OM%20Elaboraci%C3%B3n%20PGE%202015.pdf (accessed 28 July 2015).

Morán, Carmen (2008). 'Aído arranca a Solbes un informe de género en los Presupuestos. Economía encarga estudios para cumplir la Ley de Igualdad'. *El País* 15/10/2008. Madrid. [Online] Available from: http://elpais.com/diario/2008/10/15/sociedad/122 4021606_850215.html (accessed 22 August 2015).

OECD (2011). *Divided We Stand. Why Inequality Keeps Rising.* Paris: OECD. [Online] Available from: www.oecd.org/els/soc/49170768.pdf (accessed 12 March 2015).

Pérez López, C., Burgos Prieto, M. J. Huete, S. and Gallego, C. (2012). *La muestra de IRPF de 2009: descripción general y principales magnitudes.* Documento de Trabajo 11/12. Madrid: Instituto de Estudios Fiscales.

Real Decreto Ley 20/2011 de medidas urgentes en materia presupuestaria, tributaria y financiera para la corrección del déficit público. 30 December 2011. Madrid. BOE-A-2011-20638 [Online] Madrid: BOE. Available from: www.boe.es/boe/dias/2011/12/31/pdfs/BOE-A-2011-20638.pdf (accessed 22 August 2015).

Villota, P. and Ferrari, I. (2003). *Aproximación al análisis de las figuras impositivas del sistema fiscal español desde una perspectiva de género.* Instituto de la Mujer (Serie Estudios no. 80). Madrid: Ministerio de Trabajo y Asuntos Sociales.

Villota, P. and Ferrari, I. (2004). *Reflexiones sobre el IRPF desde la perspectiva de género: la discriminación fiscal del/de la segundo/a perceptor/a.* Documento de Trabajo 9/04. Madrid: Instituto de Estudios Fiscales. [Online] Available from: www.ief.es/documentos/recursos/publicaciones/libros/Investigaciones/Inves2004_09.pdf (accessed 12 March 2015).

Villota, P., Ferrari, I. and Jubeto, Y. (2009). *Diseño de la estrategia que permita la integración de la perspectiva de género en los presupuestos públicos.* Madrid: Instituto de la Mujer, Ministerio de Igualdad. [Online] Available from: www.inmujer.gob.es/observatorios/observIgualdad/estudiosInformes/docs/disenno.pdf (accessed 22 August 2015).

Villota, P., Ferrari, I. and Sahagun, C. (2008). El impuesto sobre la renta de las personas físicas en Castilla y León desde la perspectiva de género: una propuesta a favor de las mujeres asalariadas (Premio de Estudios 2008). Valladolid: Consejo Económico y Social de Castilla y León. [Online] Available from: www.cescyl.es/es/publicaciones/premios/irpf-castilla-leon-perspectiva-genero-propuesta-favor-mujer (accessed 22 July 2015).

List of legislation

Ley 26/2014, 27 November 2014. Madrid. BOE-A-2014-12327.

Ley 39/2010, 22 December 2010. Madrid. BOE-A-2010-19703.

Ley 35/2006, 28 November 2006. Madrid: BOE-A-2006-20764.

Ley 30/2003, 13 October 2003. Madrid: BOE-A-2003-18920.

Real Decreto Ley 20/2011, 30 December 2011. Madrid. BOE-A-2011-20638.

PART III
Women, work and childcare

9

CHILDCARE AS AN INVESTMENT IN INFRASTRUCTURE

Sue Himmelweit

Introduction

The last time that I saw Ailsa was on International Women's Day in 2013. The evening before she had met with Nicola Sturgeon, the then deputy First Minister of Scotland. Ailsa was thrilled because at that meeting it was confirmed that hence-forth the SNP Scottish Government would be referring to childcare as a form of investment in infrastructure. And Nicola Sturgeon was as good as her word, saying at the SNP conference in November 2014, days before becoming Scotland's First Minister:

> An extension of childcare on the scale we plan will require, not just revenue investment, but major capital investment in our education estate. Our flag-ship infrastructure project in this parliament has been the new Forth Bridge – the Queensferry Crossing ... But friends, I want to make one of our biggest infrastructure projects for the next parliament a different kind of bridge. I want it to be comprehensive childcare, giving our young people the best start in life and a bridge to a better future.
>
> (Sturgeon, 2014)

Insisting on talking about childcare in this way is a longstanding practice of both the UK and Scottish Women's Budget Groups[1] and of feminist economists more generally. This insistence is a response to the relative neglect in policy discourse of attention to 'social infrastructure' compared to the more widely recognised physical infrastructure. Feminist economists have stressed that economic develop-ment requires a well-functioning social infrastructure that includes accessible care services, not only to enable people to be employed and to contribute to output and growth, but also because the fundamental aim of economic development should be to improve the wellbeing of the population as a whole. Moreover, given the current gender division of labour, the relative neglect of social infrastructure, including the provision of care, has adverse effects on gender equality. This is because investment in social infrastructure tends both to alleviate unpaid care work, which usually falls to women, and to generate more jobs for women, while in physical infrastructure investment the jobs generated tend to go to men.

Using the terminology of 'investment in infrastructure' captures two characteristics of high quality childcare. The first is that it has benefits that result in an increase in the wealth of society as a whole, in terms of better educated, happier people. The second is that it has benefits that accrue over time: better educated children grow into more productive, happier adults. Being for the future, not just the present, not only makes investment spending more politically acceptable, it *should* also mean that it is accounted for differently in the National Accounts, as a form of capital rather than current spending.

As governments increasingly make rules for themselves about budget deficits and the circumstances in which they will allow themselves to borrow, such accounting distinctions matter. The social infrastructure consists of what can be termed 'human and social capital', that is, wealth that resides in individuals and the institutions of society. However, the National Accounts do not count expenditure on the services that directly create such capital as coming from the capital account (although perversely, spending on the buildings in which such services are provided, schools, hospitals and care homes, is counted as coming from the capital account, such buildings are a form of physical infrastructure). So, in practice, money used to employ builders counts as 'capital' spending, while money used to employ childcare workers and teachers is counted as 'current' expenditure.

This is not a Scottish, or even a UK, problem but is laid down in the international System of National Accounts (SNA) (United Nations, 2008). As the Institute of Fiscal Studies points out, the SNA's distinction between capital and current spending is inadequate because some of what is counted as current spending, such as on education, benefits future generations. Basing fiscal rules on that 'crude' distinction risks discouraging such spending (Bloom et al., 2001: 2).

Feminist economists recognise that the use of this inadequate accounting system has important gender implications, not only in the type of employment that is favoured, but also because it fails to recognise the long-run significance of spending on the areas of public policy with most effect on women's lives, including on care services. One reason therefore to keep referring to childcare as 'investment in infrastructure' is to get this inadequate accounting system, with the gender bias in its implications for employment and policy change, reformed.

One of the last papers that Ailsa wrote was *The Economic Case for Investing in High-Quality Childcare and Early Years Education*, co-authored with Jim Campbell and Diane Elson, and published by Women in Scotland's Economy Research Centre (WiSE) in November 2013. In this chapter I will first outline the economic ideas that are being harnessed in the general notion of investment in (social) infrastructure, and then present Ailsa and her co-authors' arguments for seeing childcare specifically as such an investment. I will then raise some issues about why, as campaigners for gender equality, we might want to be a bit cautious about not overusing this terminology. This is both because it can be misused, distracting attention from the case for spending on childcare as a public service, and because it can render more difficult the case for spending on some areas which are of just as much significance to women's lives but cannot so easily be seen as providing benefits over a period of time. I will conclude with some reflections on when and where the use of investment type arguments is helpful in arguing for policies that promote gender equality and their possible impact on Scottish politics in particular.

The meaning of investment in infrastructure

The notion of 'investment' captures the idea of spending now in order to receive returns in the future. So spending on high quality childcare is an investment because resources are allocated to it now (to pay childcare workers' wages etc.) in the expectation of future gains (happier, better educated children, who experience more wellbeing throughout their lives and as adults will work with higher productivity). Investing entails creating 'capital', a stock of something that lasts and over its lifetime continues to generate gains. When a machine is bought, it functions as a form of 'capital' because it provides a flow of benefits throughout its lifetime, by enabling workers to produce goods (or more goods than they would be able to without that piece of machinery). By analogy, high quality childcare is an investment in the personal qualities of children, providing a flow of benefits for the children themselves (better educated so able to command higher wages throughout their careers, and also better adjusted so living happier lives) and the economy more generally (better educated, more productive population, fewer social problems, etc.) over many years. Those personal qualities are a form of 'human capital', a term well-recognised by economists as applying to education to explain the increased earnings of educated workers, but less frequently used to talk about the long-term benefits of high quality care services.

There is no universally accepted definition of infrastructure. One writer, Hirschman (1958), provides a useful definition of it as 'capital that provides public services'. Talking about infrastructure as a form of capital means that it is built up through investment. But for capital to count as infrastructure a further condition must also hold: that the eventual flow of benefits must be in the form of public services. What Hirschman, as an economist, meant by 'public services' are those services that for their full benefits to be realised need to be at least partially funded by the state rather than solely by individual users purchasing them for themselves on the market. This is because if left to pay for such a service themselves, direct users will purchase only as much as needed for the benefit they themselves receive. But if there are wider benefits to society these will not be taken into account by these purchasers, and society as a whole would benefit from more being provided and used than the direct users would choose to purchase. Leaving such a service's provision to the market, with everyone just paying for their own use, will therefore not be efficient, and the state will need to pay towards its provision to ensure that it is not underused. For example, if parents have to pay fees for childcare, only those parents who consider it worthwhile and affordable for themselves and their children will use childcare, but the state may subsidise fees or provide childcare on the grounds that society as a whole benefits from the children of parents who cannot afford childcare, or would not choose to pay its fees, receiving childcare too.

The notion of investing in infrastructure brings together two ideas: that of spending now for a future stream of benefits and that this future stream takes the form of public services whose provision, if left to individual purchasers on the market, would not be efficient. Spending on childcare exemplifies both those ideas perfectly.

In practice, the term 'infrastructure' is typically used to talk about large physical construction projects such as the building of bridges or high-speed railway lines. And again these generally satisfy both characteristics of investing in infrastructure: that resources are spent now to provide a stream of benefits in the future, and that these benefits would not then be efficiently provided or used if funding was just left to individuals being charged for what they chose to use. In the example of a bridge that provides the service of enabling people to cross a river in a remote area, the cost of any extra person or vehicle using it is effectively zero.[2] As a result, any charge for its use will mean that some people do not use it who would benefit from doing so, and this is inefficient since it costs nothing for them to use it. To avoid inefficiencies these infrastructure projects have to be publicly financed.

Economists recognise that there are different forms of infrastructure, but they do not always agree on how to distinguish them. One account distinguishes between 'economic infrastructure' that directly contributes to the economy and 'social infrastructure' that comprises 'those basic activities and services which, in addition to achieving certain social objectives, indirectly help various economic activities'. Examples cited of social infrastructure include 'education, health service, sanitation and water supply' and of economic infrastructure 'irrigation, power, transport and communication'. However childcare, as so often happens, is not mentioned at all. By these definitions high-quality childcare should count as infrastructure, and be classified as social infrastructure, since it achieves the social objective of enabling children to be well looked after and indirectly helps the economy by enabling their parents to take employment.

That distinction between direct and indirect benefits to economic activities can be challenged: for example, the benefits of a better cared-for, more educated workforce in helping economic activities can be argued to be quite direct. Instead feminist economists tend to make a different distinction, and distinguish 'social' from 'physical' infrastructure by the type of capital being created, with the former being the economy's stock of human and social capital, residing in the people and the institutions of society, as opposed to its stock of physical capital. By this distinction, focusing on the type of capital created, spending on a high quality childcare system would again be classified as investment in social infrastructure since, as argued above, it adds to the human capital of children (and indirectly to those of parents who it enables to enter education or gain workplace experience) and because having a well-functioning childcare system adds to a society's stock of social capital.

Ailsa's arguments

Ailsa and her co-authors do not mention infrastructure in their paper, although they include investment in its title. Nevertheless, they start in immediately with childcare's public benefits. These they claim include greater economic growth, reduced gender inequality and more sustainable welfare provision. All these are seen as consequences of the increased labour market participation of parents, and of mothers in particular, that high quality childcare and early years education would enable. They also point to positive effects on local economic regeneration through both improving the quality of provision for children in deprived areas and giving parents access to wider labour market opportunities. The educational and social development of children is also mentioned as a public as well as private benefit, and so is a possible increase in fertility. Thus the public benefits cited are wide-ranging and go well beyond the benefits of the childcare system to its direct users alone (whether these are seen as the children or their parents).

The paper explicitly makes the case that money spent on high quality childcare and early years education should be seen as an investment because it generates a stream of benefits in the future. And it argues that the pay of childcare workers is as much of an investment in human capital as that of the construction workers who build the nursery is in physical capital. Thus it effectively makes the case for spending on high quality childcare and early years education being investment in 'social infrastructure', though without using the latter term.

Ailsa and her co-authors divide the stream of benefits from investing in high-quality childcare into different time-scales: short, medium and long term. In the short term if there is unemployment, any government spending provides a stimulus to employment. However, each pound of spending on childcare provides a particularly effective stimulus because it is nearly all spent on wages, unlike spending on physical infrastructure, much of which needs to be spent on materials. Further, because childcare workers are not highly paid, spending on employing them will in practice generate far more jobs than spending that employs higher paid workers. Relatedly, because childcare workers do not have high incomes, they are likely to spend most of their wages, and particularly so because most are likely to be women, some of whom will need to buy local services to replace their own caring labour at home. So childcare spending is likely to have particularly high and local multiplier effects and thus be a particularly good stimulus to local and national employment (better, in this respect, than spending on physical infrastructure). These are clearly public benefits rather than ones accruing to the direct users of childcare alone.

The medium-term arguments are the ones mentioned above. First, that women will be able to take jobs more easily if they can find high quality, affordable childcare. Public provision at an affordable price will benefit low-earning/low-skilled women particularly, who cannot afford the high market price of good quality childcare and may leave the labour market as a result, or change to less desirable jobs that fit around the childcare they can afford. High quality, affordable childcare will thus promote greater equality in employment opportunities between those with and those without responsibilities for young children (mostly women), and across classes, since the benefits will be felt by the low paid particularly. And this will result in greater gender equality between men and women both in the labour market and society more generally, and within households. Another effect is likely to be a reduction in poverty rates, since women's earnings are often crucial to keeping families out of poverty, and are particularly important for those who are or become lone parent families, an important consideration since one-third of children in the UK live in a lone parent family at some point in their childhood (Rowlingson and McKay, 2014: 31). And finally, Ailsa and her co-authors point to greater fertility, through lowering the cost of childbearing in terms of labour market and career opportunities, as a potential gain. However, while lowering the personal costs of childbearing to women is undoubtedly beneficial and promotes equality, whether women choosing to have more children as a result should be used as an argument for providing childcare is far more controversial. Some would argue that national boundaries impose a distorted way of looking at population planning, that an aging population does not need to be seen as a problem and that if Scotland's low population replacement rate needs tackling, immigration would be a greener and more feminist approach than targeting fertility (MacInnes and Pérez Díaz, 2006).

Finally, the paper talks about a positive long-term impact on children's futures, in terms of their educational attainment, which has been shown to be greatest for spending on early years education, and on their health, behaviour and future earnings. This would have a positive impact on society through greater productivity and labour market participation, increased healthy life expectancy, reduced poverty rates and greater social cohesion. And this, Ailsa and her co-authors argue, would reduce the need for state expenditure in the future, and generate additional revenues.

The points made in the paper about spending on high quality childcare being an investment and as having wider benefits on society are persuasive, and we saw earlier how effective they have been in influencing policy on childcare and early years provision in Scotland. We should, however, stress that Ailsa and her co-authors' arguments are for the benefits of spending on *high quality* childcare. One could assess the provision of low quality childcare in similar ways, but would get a very different answer.

Some points of caution

In this section I want to sound a small note of caution. The arguments presented so far have some limitations in their scope and therefore some caution needs to be taken in how they are deployed. Ailsa and her co-authors make the argument for high quality childcare being an investment in two ways, both of which are commonly deployed in arguments about public investment more generally. The first is in terms of the wellbeing of members of society in the future: spending resources now will result in increased flows of wellbeing in the future. Whether such investment is justified will depend on one's assessment of those future gains relative to the costs today. And since the gains are in terms of wellbeing, it is matter of political debate how those benefits are assessed (which may of course be influenced by to whom they are seen as going) and whether they are seen as justifying the initial costs.

But there is another, apparently more technical, argument that is frequently used to justify public expenditure in terms of investment: that expenditure now will (more than) pay for itself in the long run, by in the future either reducing the need for flows of state spending and/or generating additional flows of revenue. Put like this, it appears to be a purely technical issue; provided the sums work out the expenditure should be made if future net gains to the exchequer (at an appropriate rate of discount) outweigh current costs. If that is the case, making such an investment appears to be a no-brainer. Such arguments are frequently used for rehabilitative or preventative health care, that spending now avoids greater spending on health or social care in the future. Free childcare for disadvantaged two-year-olds has also been justified in terms of preventing problems that would lead to future spending.

There are a number of problems with such arguments. The first is they tend to overshadow the benefit of the service provision in itself. Thus the above argument for providing childcare for disadvantaged two-year-olds appears to have nothing to do with the benefits to the two-year-olds themselves (or to their parents). This is just one aspect of a broader problem with this approach, that it appears to turn social and political debate into a technical matter. What the state pays for or how it receives its revenue is not a given; social norms, history and politics shape what the state decides to pay for and how it raises its revenue. Preventative care is only cost saving for the government if the problems that it prevents would result in costs for it. And that depends not only on what policy is now but what it is likely to be in the future. If policy shifts so that whatever would be prevented is no longer seen as a public responsibility, future suffering may be prevented by early intervention, but not future expenditure.

To make an investment argument, the full benefits and costs to direct recipients, to their families and to society more generally have to be accounted for; whether they would be paid for by the state or anyone else is irrelevant to whether the benefits justify the costs. Taking net gains to the exchequer as shorthand for benefit to society as a whole will not do, because systemic biases are introduced that way. In particular unpaid care provided free by family members will rarely be accounted for (though the cost of benefits paid by the state to carers would be, but these notoriously undervalue the costs of the time and effort such carers contribute). Similarly, the wage rates used to value both costs of preventative care and savings of subsequent costs reflect the current low valuation put on care work, which may not persist if the gender pay gap continues to fall.

Looking at investment in terms of savings to the state is therefore a dangerous procedure, because it appears to turn a political and social issue into a technocratic one. A proper evaluation of investment involves making explicit the assumptions built into the process and is therefore open to question. An interesting example of this was the debate engendered by the costing of a drug that delays the onset of dementia by the UK's National Institute for Health and Care Excellence (NICE), the body that evaluates drugs and other treatments and decides on cost effectiveness grounds whether the National Health Service should adopt them (NICE, 2012). The Alzheimer's Society argued that the benefits of the drug had been undervalued because no account was taken of the benefits to carers, in terms of their quality of life, that any delay in the onset of dementia would bring and therefore that NICE's 'model is based on costs that are too low' (Alzheimer's Society, 2004).

But NICE argued that its mandate meant that it should be concerned only with costs to the National Health Service (NHS) and to Personal Social Services (PPS), the two branches of the state that incur costs when care is provided or financed by the state; costs borne by carers that are not reimbursed by the NHS or PPS were therefore not taken into account.

So care time that is paid for by the state is accounted for. But whether such care time is paid or unpaid does not change the benefits of the drug in saving care time, nor does it impinge on the fundamental issue of the benefits of the drug to its potential users. Ironically, the Citizens Council convened by NICE to discuss the values that should underlie its standards and guidance advocated that unpaid and informal carers' costs and benefits *should* be taken into account in such calculations (NICE Citizens' Council, 2013). So NICE recognised that its evaluations inherently depend on political and social values, but then failed to follow the recommendations of the Citizens Council that it set up to advise on such values.

Finally, we need to remember that the investment argument is not specific to or even the main reason for public expenditure. Investment arguments can be used to justify expenditure at all levels: for individuals, households, firms and the state. The argument for *public* expenditure is about public services, that they would be underprovided if left to individual choice through the market that typically does not take into account wider benefits to society. This argument applies to the present benefits of public services in the here and now, just as much as to any future benefits.

The danger of overusing the investment argument when other arguments would do is that for many public services, and in particular for some other forms of care, it is harder to make an investment argument. For example, it is hard to claim such long-lasting benefits for long-term care of the elderly or use the prevention argument for those whose condition is unlikely to improve. It may also be somewhat harder to make the more medium-term argument in terms of the benefits of increased labour market participation of those currently caring unpaid for such people, since the amount of time spent caregiving for adults increases with age, with the highest amounts of time devoted to caregiving continuing to rise after retirement age (ONS, 2011).

However, the care of all these people can still be perfectly well justified as a public service. There are benefits to all of us in living in a society which cares well for the old and long-term disabled, and in knowing that we ourselves and our relatives can hope to be well cared for if we ever need to be. These benefits alone are sufficient to justify public expenditure on it. An investment argument adds to it by stressing the long-term benefits of having such a care system, but is not essentially needed.

So the danger of over-emphasising the investment side of providing high quality childcare is that it may detract from what really matters. First, just like elder care, high quality childcare is a public good in itself, of benefit to children and society in general in the here and now and, if it is not publicly funded, too little will be provided. Second, using an investment argument for childcare may undermine the case for public support of other forms of care where the investment argument is not as salient. It is important that such arguments are not used to set the needs of different types of care recipients against each other.

Conclusion

The argument for investing in childcare was powerfully made by Ailsa and her co-authors, and has played an important part in feminist arguments for a different form of national accounting in which investment in social infrastructure is recognised on a par with investment in physical infrastructure. Indeed both the UK and the Scottish Women's Budget Groups have given support to Plan F, a long-term feminist economic plan to invest in creating a caring and sustainable economy. This plan is built on investing in social infrastructure – care, health, education and training services, and social security, as well as in well-insulated housing, renewable energy and environmentally friendly public transport, on the grounds that this 'would improve both wellbeing and productivity, both in the short run but also in ways that persist over time, benefiting people not only today but in years to come' (SWBG and WBG, 2015: 1).

In this chapter I have outlined some of the economic arguments behind the case Ailsa and her co-authors made and also sounded a note of caution about not overusing investment arguments, or rather using them in the right place to augment, rather than replace, a public good argument.

Is Scotland's childcare infrastructure there? No. Like provision in the rest of the UK, it has some way to go still. But as Ailsa's obituary in *The Scotsman* noted, Ailsa provided: 'the economic case ... underpinning the Scottish Government's proposals for free, universal childcare' (The Scotsman, 2014).

With the Labour Party now also talking about childcare in terms of investment, we can but wait to see what happens in the next Scottish parliament. If Scotland gets its childcare infrastructure, it will be fitting recognition of the arguments Ailsa made so well with her co-authors, and worked so hard to put on the political agenda.

Notes

1 The UK Women's Budget Group (www.wbg.org.uk) and the Scottish Women's Budget Group (www.swbg.org.uk) produce analyses of their respective governments' spending plans, budgets and policies to promote a better understanding of the impact of government decision making on women and to improve the quality of that decision making so that public resources are allocated for the benefit of all. They are both independent of government and all political parties.
2 This argument relies on an extra person's use incurring no extra cost. If there is congestion the cost of an extra person's use is not zero, in which case well-designed charges may be required for efficient use.

References

Alzheimer's Society (2004). *Drugs for the Treatment of Alzheimer's Disease*. [Online] Available from: www.alzheimers.org.uk/site/scripts/download_info.php?fileID=525 (accessed 12 July 2015).

Bloom, N., Emmerson, C. and Frayne, C. (2001). *The Main Parties' Tax and Spending Proposals*. IFS Election Briefing Note No. 10. [Online] Available from: www.ifs.org.uk/uploads/publications/election/ebn10.pdf (accessed 27 July 2015).

Campbell, J., Elson, D. and McKay, A. (2013). *The Economic Case for Investing in High-Quality Childcare and Early Years Education*. WiSE Briefing Sheet, November. Glasgow: Glasgow Caledonian University. [Online] Available from: www.gcu.ac.uk/media/WiSEBriefingPaperNov13.pdf (accessed 6 July 2015).

Hirschman, A. O. (1958). *The Strategy of Economic Development*. New Haven, Connecticut: Yale University Press.

MacInnes, J. and Pérez Díaz, J. (2006). '"Low" fertility and population replacement in Scotland'. *Populations, Spaces & Places*, 13(1): 3–21.

NICE (2012). *The guidelines manual: appendices B–I*. [Online] Available from: http://www.nice.org.uk/article/pmg6b/chapter/Appendix-G-Methodology-checklist-economic-evaluations (accessed 12 July 2015).

NICE Citizens' Council (2013). *What Aspects of Benefit, Cost and Need Should NICE Take Into Account When Developing Social Care Guidance?* [Online] Available from: www.nice.org.uk/Media/Default/Get-involved/Citizens-Council/Reports/CCReport16SocialCareValues.pdf (accessed 12 July 2015).

ONS (2011). *Unpaid Care Provision: By Age and Sex in England and in Wales, 2011*. [Online] Available from: www.ons.gov.uk/ons/guide-method/census/2011/carers-week/index.html (accessed 27 July 2015).

Rowlingson, K. and McKay, S. (2014). *Lone Parent Families: Gender, Class and State*. Abingdon: Routledge.

The Scotsman (2014). *Obituary: Professor Ailsa McKay, Professor of Economics, Tuesday 11 March 2014*. [Online] Available from: www.scotsman.com/news/obituaries/obituary-professor-ailsa-mckay-professor-of-economics-1-3335185 (accessed 27 July 2015).

Sturgeon, N. (2014). *Nicola Sturgeon Address to SNP Conference*. [Online] Available from: www.snp.org/media-centre/news/2014/nov/nicola-sturgeon-address-snp-conference (accessed 22 June 2015).

SWBG and WBG (2015). *Plan F: A Feminist Economic Strategy for a Caring and Sustainable Economy*. [Online] Available from: www.swbg.org.uk/content/publications/PLAN-F-2015.pdf (accessed 27 July 2015).

United Nations (2008). *System of National Accounts*. [Online] Available from: http://unstats.un.org/unsd/nationalaccount/sna.asp (accessed 15 July 2015).

10

INTEGRATING ECONOMIC AND SOCIAL POLICY

Childcare – a transformational policy?

Gary Gillespie and Uzma Khan

Introduction

Professor Ailsa McKay took the view that all economic policy is social, and all social policy is also economic. She challenged us to think differently; she questioned the scope and relevance of economic models as they are currently constructed with a view to looking beyond the obvious. Childcare is an example of a policy that has many dimensions. Ailsa helped to develop and shape the direction of childcare provision in Scotland today. In advising Parliament and the Scottish Government, she used this opportunity for engagement to go further than childcare alone, and set the policy in the wider context of gender equality more broadly as well as in the context of women's labour market participation, with implications for occupational segregation and the gender pay gap. Ailsa saw childcare policy as one lever for improving outcomes for women more generally and as part of a well-defined package of support and provision.

Ailsa's legacy and influence are reflected in the recognition of the close interaction between the social and wellbeing aspects of economic policy that are central to Scotland's Economic Strategy (SES). This chapter reflects on her interactions with the Scottish Government and the Council of Economic Advisers. It provides a personal reflection of her contribution to the wider debate around childcare, economic opportunities and women's labour market outcomes and her influence on the Scottish Government's updated economic strategy reflecting the importance of an integrated inclusive framework. The latter is reflected in the wider international literature with growing recognition of the importance of inequality, equality and inclusive growth through the work of the Organisation for Economic Co-operation and Development (OECD), International Monetary Fund (IMF), World Bank and other key academics (Stiglitz, 2012; Piketty, 2013).

The chapter begins by setting out the economic framework under which the Scottish Government is developing its policies for sustainable economic *and* inclusive growth. It goes on to describe the context for the development of childcare policy in view of women's labour market participation and outcomes, the role and importance of funded childcare provision and an overview of Ailsa's specific contribution to the development of the Scottish Economic Strategy.

In this context, childcare is an example of a policy which has impacts on more than one outcome or objective and in that sense is a policy which has to be considered in a wider socio-economic context. Therefore while we discuss childcare specifically in this chapter, Ailsa's key contribution to Scotland's economic strategy is the recognition of the important interaction of social and economic policies and the need to focus on economic outcomes beyond the standard metrics of Gross Domestic Product (GDP) or employment.

Scotland's economic strategy

The Scottish Government published its updated economic strategy in March 2015 setting out its vision for Scotland's economy and society. At the heart of the strategy are the two mutually supportive goals of increasing competitiveness and tackling inequality to achieve sustainable economic growth. These ambitions are underpinned by priorities for policy action in four key areas – the '4Is': Investment, Innovation, Internationalisation and Inclusive Growth (Figure 10.1). The emerging framework was presented at 'A Commemorative Conference for Professor Ailsa McKay' held on 22 January 2015, and benefitted from contributions at the conference.

The essence of the framework is to recognise the wider linkages between the economy and societal outcomes – it puts the interaction of economic and social

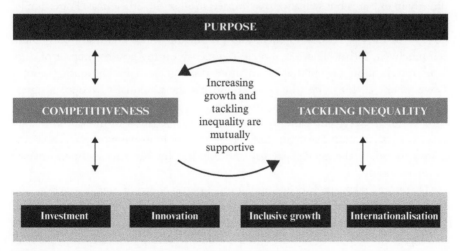

FIGURE 10.1 Scottish economic strategy: framework
Source: Scottish Government (2015a)

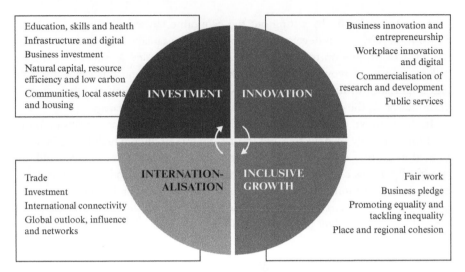

FIGURE 10.2 The four priorities
Source: Scottish Government (2015a)

policy at the heart of the government's purpose to create growth that is 'inclusive' and benefits all the people of Scotland. Professor McKay was a strong proponent of developing a socio-economic framework that captured the importance of creating equality of opportunity and tackling inequality at source in order to improve outcomes particularly for women and children.

As Figure 10.2 depicts, each of the '4Is' within the SES framework impact on each other and are mutually dependent. Within each sphere, policy decisions, investment choices, market, regulatory or technological change may impact directly in one area but will also have impacts in all of the other areas. For example, publicly funded childcare provision is primarily viewed as an investment in the context of early years development and part of the wider education curriculum (Himmelweit, 2016). There is also clear evidence on the positive impact of early years intervention on children from more disadvantaged backgrounds (Scottish Government, 2015b). This investment also has the potential to reduce a significant barrier to continued labour market participation among women which, in turn, can help overcome patterns of entrenched segregation in the labour market relating to occupational structure and retention of skills in the workplace, and ultimately to reduce the gender pay gap and improve the diversity and performance of the economy.

Therefore, taking a broader and more holistic view of the interaction and impacts of policies across the '4Is' can create a more inclusive growth model. In this respect, childcare is a key policy lever in enabling equality of opportunity to participate fully in economic life – it has a direct bearing on improving women's economic participation and, consequently, better economic and social outcomes for women and children.

Rationale for greater childcare provision in Scotland

In Scotland, the provision of childcare is a mixed economy – with different systems in place for children aged under 3, and for those aged over 3 years old. For children under 3, formal childcare is primarily offered by the private sector, although there is also some workplace and local authority provision. Formal childcare for the under 3s is paid for directly by parents, offset to some extent through workplace salary sacrifice voucher schemes, or through the childcare element of Working Tax Credit. Currently around 5 per cent of employers offer childcare vouchers that can be used for childcare for children of any age (HM Treasury, 2014). Around 32,000 families with children in Scotland were in receipt of the childcare element of Working Tax Credit in 2013–2014 (HMRC, 2015: 12).

Formal childcare for over 3s is similarly part-funded through these channels. In addition, a funded part-time pre-school entitlement is available for all 3- and 4-year-olds. In settings where full-day provision is offered, the pre-school entitlement can be combined with the purchase of wraparound childcare hours (usually on a full-day or half-day basis).

There has been a significant expansion in childcare provision in recent years, following a marked change in the recognition of the importance of childcare provision as a key policy for the Scottish Government. The onset and impact of the financial recession which led to a fall in women's employment rates in Scotland triggered a strong desire for action in this area. The Scottish Government in partnership with the Scottish Trades Union Congress (STUC) established a Women's Employment Summit in 2012 as a response to falling employment, of which Professor McKay was a key contributor. Ailsa McKay also influenced policy making at the heart of the Scottish Government through her interactions with the Council of Economic Advisers (CEA) – the work of the Council in 2013 included a scoping study of key childcare issues in Scotland to form the introduction to a programme of work to examine the issue more thoroughly. In this role, Ailsa presented the issue more broadly, highlighting childcare in the context of both its social and economic importance (Council of Economic Advisers, 2013).

Subsequently, the expansion in childcare provision has been supported by the rationale to improve women's outcomes in the labour market following the recession. In 2013, all 3- and 4-year-olds were entitled to 475 hours (12.5 hours per week) of funded early learning and childcare entitlement. The Scottish Government increased the entitlement for 3- and 4-year-olds to 600 hours a year (15 hours per week) in August 2014, and extended this provision to disadvantaged 2-year-olds (constituting around 15 per cent of 2-year-olds). In August 2015 this provision was expanded to 27 per cent of 2-year-olds, with further future expansion for all 3- and 4-year-olds and eligible 2-year-olds towards an entitlement of 1140 hours a year (30 hours a week) by 2021, which is equivalent to school term time.

Childcare policy in context of women's participation and outcomes

Trends in women's employment

The global financial crisis of 2008 impacted in Scotland with output contracting by 5 per cent over five quarterly periods, which was broadly in line with the OECD average and slightly lower than the aggregate for the UK and EU. The labour market response was similar to the UK with more people staying in employment, but working typically less hours and on more flexible and less secure conditions. Within the labour market, there were differential impacts on workers relating to age, gender, skills and sector. These impacts have changed over time, initially concentrated on the contraction in the production and construction sectors and then the services sector more generally, which has had impacts on participation by gender.

Women's participation in the labour market is influenced by a range of factors, but childcare is seen as a key factor in determining economic participation, particularly for those with younger children. There has been a significant change in labour market outcomes for women in Scotland over the last few decades and more recent trends indicate their employment continues to rise. In both the UK and in Scotland, the period following the 2008/2009 recession did not lead to a substantial fall in labour force participation compared to previous recessions. Employment rates fell for both men and women as unemployment increased in Scotland during 2009 and we can see from Figure 10.3 there was a difference in the timing of the impact by gender, which related to the sectoral falls in output at that time (large falls in output in construction and production as these sectors contracted).

From 2013, increases in overall economic activity in Scotland have been driven by increases in female participation rates as more women are re-entering the labour market. Scotland now has the highest female employment rate in the UK at 72.2 per cent (March to May 2015).

Between January to March 2015, latest data also show that Scotland has the second highest female employment rate in Europe, only slightly lower than Sweden. Furthermore, the gender employment gap has narrowed in the last three years having decreased from 9.1 to 4.2 percentage points (March–May 2012 compared to March–May 2015). Figure 10.3 shows the trend in employment split by men and women since the early 1990s.

Nevertheless, despite the recent improvements in female labour market statistics, there are still notable differences between men's and women's outcomes. The rate of male employment is still markedly higher than the female employment rate in every age bracket over 24, but with a particularly sizeable difference between the 25–34 age bracket as shown in Figure 10.4.

There are also significant gender differences in reasons for economic inactivity. For instance, around 38 per cent men in this category were inactive on health

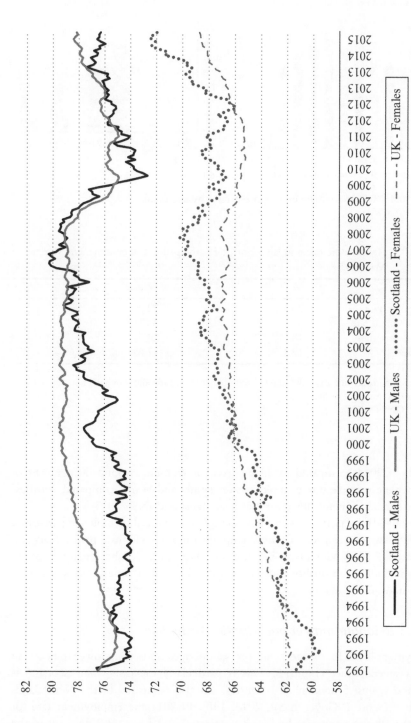

FIGURE 10.3 Trends in employment rate; men and women: Scotland and UK

Source: ONS (2015b)

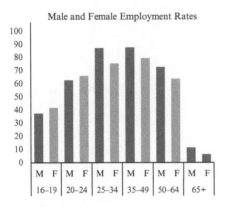
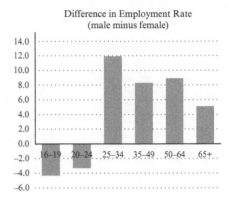

FIGURE 10.4 Male and female employment rates by age band
Source: ONS (2015a)

TABLE 10.1 Gender differences in labour market participation and employment March–
May 2015

	Male	Female
Employment rate	76.4%	72.2%
Unemployment rate	6.3%	4.6%
Economic inactivity	18.3%	24.2%
Part-time★	12.1%	41.6%

★ Part-time figures are not seasonally adjusted and exclude those individuals who did not state whether
they worked part-time or full-time.
Source: ONS (2015b)

grounds in 2014, compared to 25 per cent of women. Around 30 per cent of
women were inactive due to looking after family and home, compared with less
than 8 per cent of men (Office for National Statistics (ONS), 2013).

A notably larger portion of women in employment are also employed part-time.
Similarly, women are predominantly employed in low-skill, low-paid sectors and
occupations – all of which have implications for progressive labour market opportunities including job quality and job security. Table 10.1 summarises key labour
market statistics by gender.

Barriers to labour market participation – childcare

Employment levels for women with pre-school-age children are lower in Scotland
than in several other countries. This is particularly the case when Scotland is
compared against Scandinavian countries, but also compared to the Netherlands
or France (Scottish Government, 2013: 148). In 2011 the employment rate for
mothers with the youngest child aged between 3 and 5 was 61.2 per cent in the

UK compared to 83.6 per cent in Iceland, 81.3 per cent in Sweden, 77.8 per cent in Denmark, 76.0 per cent in Finland and 75.6 per cent in Netherlands (OECD, 2014). Furthermore, a cross sectional study of EU-15 countries found that of all the drivers of employment rate gaps between mothers and non-mothers, the presence of public childcare provision had the strongest effect (De Henau et al., 2010: 43–77).

There are likely to be a variety of reasons for different employment rates and labour market participation rates of women with young children across countries. Nevertheless, the costs and availability of childcare in Scotland are perceived to be key barriers to women's participation in the labour market (see Scottish Government, 2012). European Commission research on gender equality suggests that access to affordable childcare is a significant issue – its research showed that 73 per cent of mothers in the UK who did not work or worked part-time because of inadequate childcare services cited childcare as being too expensive (European Commission, 2013).

The overall picture in Scotland and UK is that childcare costs are high and rising. Results from the 2014 Scottish Childcare Report highlight that the average yearly cost for sending a child under the age of 2 to nursery part-time (25 hours) is £5,514 (Rutter and Stocker, 2014), which is broadly similar to the annual cost in the UK (£5,710). Childcare costs have continued to rise over the last five years and are now 27 per cent higher than in 2009 (up £1,214). For families who require full-time pre-school nursery care spending between 20–30 per cent of their income on childcare is the norm.

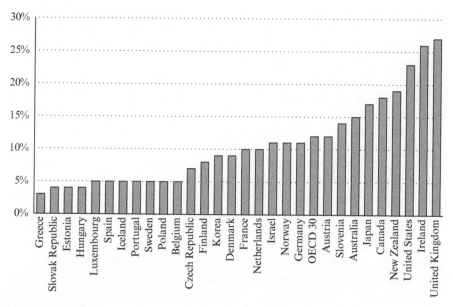

FIGURE 10.5 Childcare costs as a percentage of net family income
Source: OECD (2011)

Figure 10.5 uses OECD data to set out the cost of childcare as a percentage of wages in families where both partners earn 100 per cent of the average wage. The data suggest that in the UK childcare costs account for more than twice as much of average net family income – 27 per cent, compared to an average of 12 per cent in the OECD 30. This is driven by the magnitude of upfront childcare costs in the UK, which the OECD estimated to be equivalent to 46 per cent of the average wage in 2008, compared to 27 per cent of the average wage in the OECD 30. Associated benefits and tax reductions reduced the 'net cost' of childcare to around 18 per cent of the average wage in the OECD 30, but only to 41 per cent of the average wage in the UK. The OECD also noted that formal childcare costs significantly reduced returns to paid employment in the UK, with high childcare costs substantially increasing average effective tax rates for parents of young children (OECD, 2011).

Impacts of expanding childcare provision

Government support for childcare provision can be motivated by a number of factors including improving women's access to labour markets, children's outcomes, economic efficiency, social justice and gender equality. Increasing the availability and provision of state-funded childcare is expected to generate financial savings to families from spending less on purchasing childcare, particularly on those households where childcare costs form a significant proportion of household expenditure.

Reducing barriers to labour market participation through improving childcare provision can have a number of positive economic effects, including wider impacts than those directly measured by GDP. By increasing the labour supply of women, this could help close the gender gap in employment rates, but also the quality and type of jobs undertaken by women.

The indicative analysis in Figure 10.6 shows the potential impact on female labour supply by assessing the labour market status and aspirations of women with dependent children of pre-school age. This analysis was used to inform the discussion at the CEA meeting in Aberdeen in August 2013, which Professor McKay attended (Council of Economic Advisers, 2013).

Figure 10.6 is based on the labour market status of those women with a dependent child who are the head of the household, spouse, partner, civil partner or cohabitee. All other female family members are excluded. On this basis, it shows that in 2012 there were estimated to be around 200,000 women in Scotland with dependent children, of whom the youngest dependent child was aged between 1 and 5. Of those employed, around 70 per cent were in part-time employment. Of those inactive, almost 85 per cent were inactive for reasons of looking after the family or home, while 10,400 (19 per cent) of those inactive for family reasons would like to work but were unable to because of family commitments. Furthermore, an estimated 3,000 women felt that the lack of sufficient childcare provision prevented them from being economically active.

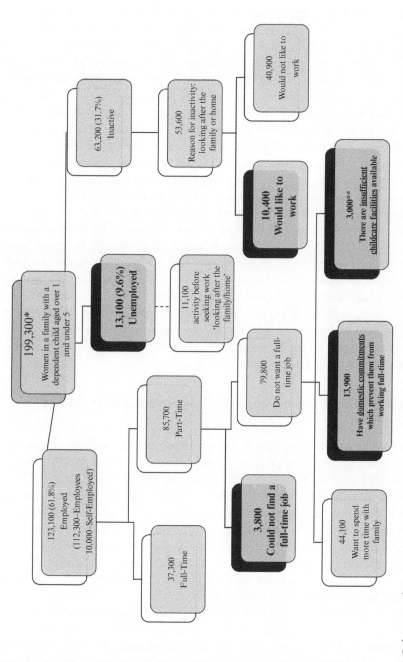

FIGURE 10.6 Labour market status and aspirations of women with dependent children – youngest dependent aged 1–5, Scotland, 2012
Source: ONS (2013)

The analysis in Figure 10.6 merely presents a snapshot of the economic circumstances of women with children under 5 in Scotland in 2012. Improving both provision and access to childcare will reduce one of the key barriers faced by some parents with young families when seeking employment. Whilst the positive benefits will initially accrue to families with young children, the impact of the policy will build as new cohorts of families benefit year-on-year with subsequent impacts on participation rates for women as they continue in employment throughout their lifetime. Taking into account the dynamic effects of childcare policy over time, it has the potential to influence multiple outcomes and Professor McKay argued that it should be viewed in the wider context of a socio-economic framework.

For example, boosting participation can have numerous spill-over benefits in key areas such as skills, employability, education attainment and, at an aggregate level, productivity in the Scottish economy. In turn, this will benefit business and help make Scotland an even more attractive location for investment. Increasing international evidence supports this notion. Recent research by the International Monetary Fund (IMF) (2013) emphasises the role that women's increased labour force participation can play in delivering economic growth. The report also highlights the importance of paternal leave, access to childcare and flexible working in encouraging participation and the role of leadership from those in public and private sector organisations in creating opportunities and role models for women. Christine Lagarde, Head of the IMF, stated: 'Increasing women's economic participation can, in turn, lead to higher growth... It makes economic sense to increase women's labor participation' (Lagarde, 2015).

Modelling the economic impact of improved labour market participation

In standard economic models, it is difficult to measure the impact of enhanced childcare directly but it is possible to simulate the impact indirectly, through improved labour force participation on key economic variables such as GDP and employment. Analysis undertaken by the Scottish Government (2014) shows the potential impacts on the Scottish economy relating to different levels of women's participation in the labour market. The modelled scenarios estimate the potential impacts that could arise when the female participation rate in Scotland increased by 2, 4 and 6 percentage points respectively. This analysis was motivated at that time by the observed differences in rates of participation in 2012 between Scotland with Finland, Netherlands, Norway and Sweden.

The potential impacts of the increases in female participation rates set out in the scenarios below on output and tax revenues in the Scottish economy have been estimated using a Computable General Equilibrium model of the Scottish economy. The results of this modelling include the first round effects of changes in labour market participation, but also indirect effects that would occur over the longer term. Figure 10.7 sets out the results of this estimation.

The analysis suggests that increases in women's labour market participation would

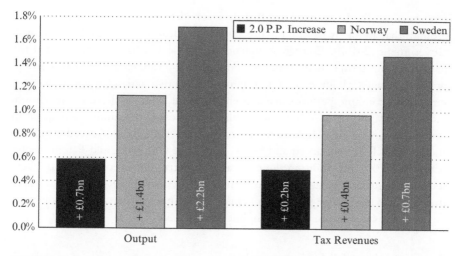

FIGURE 10.7 Impact on the Scottish economy of increased women's labour market
participation
Source: Scottish Government (2014a)

have positive impacts on output and on tax revenues. However, the model has
its limitations, only quantifying potential economy level impacts associated with
increases in women's participation, rather than increases generated by a specific
policy. In this respect, and with regards to childcare, it is widely recognised that
such a model would not capture the broader range of impacts and spill-over benefits that are likely to be associated with a change in childcare policy. Such spill-over
benefits could include:

- increased output arising from a productivity boost from more optimal allocation of skilled workers to jobs;
- increased social inclusion and gender equality arising from reduced barriers to
  women's participation in the labour market;
- greater choice and flexibility for women in employment, leading to improvements in job quality;
- improvements in child outcomes (cognitive and non-cognitive) arising from
  greater participation in formal early learning and childcare, particularly among
  disadvantaged children;
- reducing rates of child poverty and safeguarding families at risk of experiencing
  poverty;
- an improvement in the birth rate through greater provision of childcare.

Improved childcare provision can, therefore, have significant positive impacts on
equality, child and educational outcomes more generally, because more children
will be involved in formal early learning and childcare. These benefits include
cognitive, language and social development and improved confidence and peer

relationships. Evidence suggests that it is children from disadvantaged backgrounds that are likely to gain the most from early learning and childcare (Scottish Government, 2015b). Emerging evidence from the US has also highlighted the particular long-term benefit from early education and care interventions for groups of disadvantaged children such as improved cognitive and schooling outcomes, improved economic performance and employment, improved crime prevention, more stable family relationships and health in the lives of programme participants to age 40. Studies include High/Scope Perry (Barnett et al., 2005), Abecedarian Early Intervention Project (Barnett and Masse, 2007) and Chicago Child-Parent Center (Ou et al., 2011). In addition there are also potential impacts on cohesion where increases in guaranteed state provision can improve equality of access in areas where there may be less private provision of childcare. In this respect, childcare policy is a key policy lever, not just for growth, but *inclusive growth*.

Transforming childcare provision

The economic case for investing in high quality childcare and early years education and the issues around current provision and costs of childcare in Scotland was set out in a paper published by Women in Scotland's Economy (WiSE) research centre (Campbell et al., 2013).

An important difference between Scotland and other countries arises from the proportion of national income spent on family benefits, and on the type of benefits purchased. The UK spent over 4 per cent of GDP on family benefits in kind, services, cash benefits and tax breaks to families in 2009, substantially above the OECD average of 2.6 per cent. Around 58 per cent of this expenditure was directed via cash transfers.[1] This approach differs from that adopted in several other countries, including the Nordic countries, France and Belgium, where the majority of expenditure is on services (Figures 10.8 and 10.9).

In addition to differences in resource allocation mechanisms, there is also considerable diversity in how pre-school childcare is delivered across different countries (Scottish Government, 2013). Countries like Sweden, Norway and Denmark offer universal entitlements to childcare places, with a mixed economy of public sector, private sector and voluntary sector provision. Scandinavian countries, along with France, also operate mixed systems of payment, with funding contributions made by the state and by parents (subject to parental income levels). Countries vary as to whether their childcare systems integrate care and pre-school education, while uptake rates also vary across countries, with Scandinavian countries experiencing high uptake rates. In particular, parental leave and childcare are highly integrated in Scandinavian countries, and are geared to support employment.

There is evidence to suggest that the mechanism used to support early learning and childcare and the degree of public support for childcare is a significant determinant of maternal employment rates through its effects on childcare uptake and labour force participation (Scottish Government, 2015b). In Scotland levels of uptake of formal pre-school childcare vary across age groups. Available research and

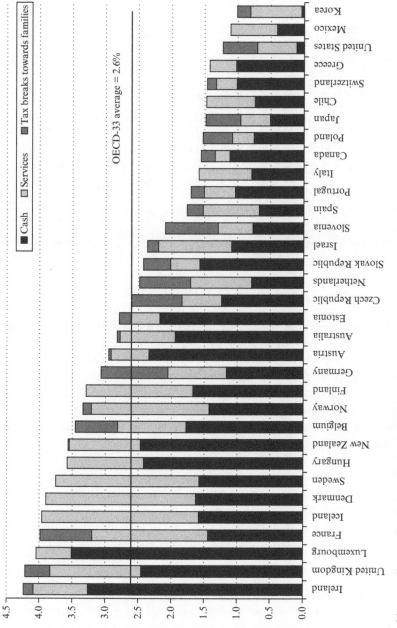

FIGURE 10.8 Public spending on family benefits in kind (services), in cash and tax measures, % GDP, OECD countries, 2009

Source: OECD (2014)

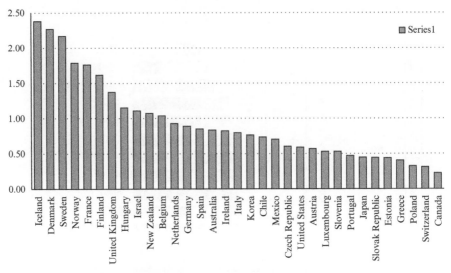

FIGURE 10.9 Public spending on family benefits in kind (services) as a percentage of GDP, 2009
Source: OECD (2014)

data indicate that around 30 per cent of children aged between 1 and 2 were registered with a formal childcare provider in 2012 (Care Inspectorate, 2013). Around 68 per cent of parents of children aged between 2 and 3 made use of formal childcare and 99 per cent of children aged 3 and 4 used some form of formal provision (Bradshaw et al., 2008: 166).

Research also shows that countries with a greater degree of publicly funded childcare also have higher maternal employment rates (IPPR, 2014; European Commission, 2009). The OECD's *Doing Better for Families* report makes clear that:

> Financial support for (public and private) childcare providers and parents reduces a key barrier to employment participation for many parents with young children … [Participation] rates tend to vary across countries according to the degree of public childcare supports, especially for children under 3.
>
> (OECD, 2011: 131)

It follows that improvements in female participation rates are likely to improve women's pay by improving labour market attachment and resulting in greater accumulation of skills and experience. By improving provision and access to childcare, therefore, there is a strong link to better socio-economic outcomes. Research by the European Commission shows how the enrolment rate of children in formal childcare appears to be inversely correlated with the gender pay gap (European Commission, 2013: 24).

Professor McKay advocated a transformational change in childcare provision, around an opportunity to re-think the funding mechanism and the extent of public funding, entitlement and delivery implications for expanding childcare considerably. Her view was that this could create a virtuous cycle of economic growth and social benefits by creating the potential situation where higher tax revenues generated by increased labour market participation could offset the costs of expansion. Her arguments were based on the impact of changing Scotland's childcare offer – with a focus on generating improved outcomes and opportunities, which would have a wider transformational impact on equality and the outcomes within the economy.

Final reflections

This chapter has provided a personal reflection on the input of Professor Ailsa McKay to the development of childcare policy in Scotland. Her legacy though is much greater. Her influence on economic policy in Scotland is reflected in the wider debate relating to the outcomes of public policy and the importance of understanding the interaction of social and economic policy and the importance of equality of opportunity.

Her input to the work on equality in Scotland both as part of the Equality Budget Advisory Group (EBAG) and also in advising the Scottish Parliament Equalities Committee helped bring these issues into the mainstream of Scottish public life. The legacy from this work is evident throughout public policy in Scotland today.

Finally, her personal energy, vision and resilience in building research capability and evidence in an area which was outwith much of the traditional mainstream of economics is testament to her personal conviction. It is also a great loss to this area of public policy, given the increasing recognition of this wider agenda internationally and, as First Minister Nicola Sturgeon said in a recent speech in New York on ethics and sustainability: 'It shone through in the work of the late Professor Ailsa McKay – who made such a major contribution, not just to Glasgow Caledonian University, but to public policy in Scotland – and who is very much missed' (Sturgeon, 2015).

Note

1 This figure will have changed since 2009, given changes to the UK welfare system since that period. A summary of key changes relating to welfare expenditure in Scotland has been published by the Scottish Government (Scottish Government, 2014b).

References

Barnett, W.S. and Masse, L.N. (2007). 'Comparative benefit-cost analysis of the Abecedarian program and its policy implications'. *Economics of Education Review*, (26): 113–125.
Barnettt, S., Belfield, C.R., Nores, M., Schweinhart, L.J., Montie, J. and Xiang, Z. (2005).

Lifetime Effects: The High/Scope Perry Preschool Study Through Age 40. Ypsilanti. Michigan: High/Scope Press.

Bradshaw, P., Cunningham-Burley, S., Dobbie, F., MacGregor, A., Marryat, L., Ormston, R. and Wasoff, F. (2008). *Growing Up In Scotland: Year 2: Results From the Second Year of a Study Following the Lives of Scotland's Children.* Edinburgh: Scottish Government.

Campbell, J., Elson, D. and McKay, A. (2013). *The Economic Case for Investing in High-Quality Childcare and Early Years Education.* WiSE Briefing Sheet, November. Glasgow: Glasgow Caledonian University. [Online] Available from: www.gcu.ac.uk/media/WiSEBriefingPaperNov13.pdf (accessed 6 July 2015).

Care Inspectorate (2013). *Childcare Statistics 2012: Table 8.* [Online] Available from: www.careinspectorate.com/index.php?option=com_content&view=article&id=8146&Itemid=756 (accessed 30 July 2015).

Council of Economic Advisers (2013). *Minutes of the Fourth Meeting of the Council.* [Online] Available from: www.gov.scot/Topics/Economy/Council-Economic-Advisers/Meetings/30-08-2013 (accessed 30 July 2015).

De Henau, J., Meulders, D. and O'Dorchai, S. (2010). 'Maybe baby: comparing partnered women's employment and child policies in the EU-15'. *Feminist Economics,* 16(1): 43–77.

European Commission (2009). *The Provision of Childcare Services: A Comparative Review of 30 European Countries.* Luxembourg: Publications Office of the European Union.

European Commission (2013). *Barcelona Objectives: The Development of Childcare Facilities For Young Children in Europe With a View to Sustainable and Inclusive Growth.* Luxembourg: Publications Office of the European Union. [Online] Available from: http://ec.europa.eu/justice/gender-equality/files/documents/130531_barcelona_en.pdf (accessed 30 July 2015).

Himmelweit, S. (2016). 'Childcare as an investment in infrastructure'. In Campbell, J. and Gillespie, M. (eds) *Feminist Economics and Public Policy: Reflections on the Work and Impact of Ailsa McKay.* Abingdon: Routledge, pp. 83–93.

HMRC (2015). *Child and Working Tax Credit Statistics, Geographical Analysis.* [Online] Available from: www.gov.uk/government/statistics/personal-tax-credits-finalised-award-statistics-geographical-statistics-2013-to-2014 (accessed 01/08/2015).

HM Treasury (2014). 'New scheme to bring tax-free childcare for 25 million working families'. [Online] Available from: www.gov.uk/government/news/new-scheme-to-bring-tax-free-childcare-for-25-million-working-families (accessed 28 July 2015).

IMF (2013). *Women, Work and the Economy.* Washington D.C.: International Monetary Fund.

IPPR (2014). *Childmind the Gap: Reforming Childcare to Support Mothers Into Work.* [Online] Available from: www.ippr.org/publications/childmind-the-gap-reforming-childcare-to-support-mothers-into-work (accessed 1 August 2015).

Lagarde C. (2015). *Fair Play – Equal Laws for Equal Working Opportunity for Women.* Blog [Online] Available from: http://blog-imfdirect.imf.org/2015/02/23/fair-play-equal-laws-for-equal-working-opportunity-for-women/ (accessed 3 August 2015).

OECD (2011). *Doing Better for Families.* Paris: OECD. [Online] Available from: www.oecd.org/els/soc/doingbetterforfamilies.htm (accessed 5 August 2015).

OECD (2014). OECD *Family Database.* [Online] Available from: www.oecd.org/social/family/database (accessed 5 August 2015).

ONS (2015a). *Annual Population Survey April 2014 – March 2015.* Newport: ONS.

ONS (2015b). *Labour Force Survey March – May 2015.* Newport: ONS.

ONS (2013). *Annual Population Survey 2012.* Newport: ONS.

Ou, S.R., Reynolds, A.J., Robertson, D.L., Temple, J.A. and White, B.A. (2011). 'Age 26 cost-benefit analysis of the child-parent center early education program'. *Child Development*, 82(1): 379–404.

Piketty, T. (2013). *Capital in the 21st Century*. Cambridge, Massachusetts: Harvard University Press.

Rutter, J. and Stocker, J. (2014). *The 2014 Scottish Childcare Report*. London: Family and Childcare Trust.

Scottish Government (2012). *Findings of the Scottish Government Childcare Commission and Scottish Trades Union Congress 2012 Women's Employment Summit*. [Online] Available from: www.employabilityinscotland.com/media/218392/early_learning_and_childcare_-_women_s_employment_summit_-_report_of_key_points.pdf (accessed 30 July 2015).

Scottish Government (2013). *Early Childhood Education and Care Provision: International Review of Policy Delivery and Funding*. [Online] Available from: www.scotland.gov.uk/Resource/0041/00416230.pdf (accessed 5 August 2015).

Scottish Government (2014a). *Childcare and Labour Market Participation – Economic Analysis*. [Online] Available from: www.gov.scot/Resource/0044/00441783.pdf (accessed 3 August 2015).

Scottish Government (2014b). *UK Government Cuts to Welfare Expenditure in Scotland – Budget 2014*. [Online] Available from: www.gov.scot/Resource/0045/00455865.pdf (accessed 21 August 2015).

Scottish Government (2015a). *Scotland's Economic Strategy*. Edinburgh: Scottish Government.

Scottish Government (2015b). *Maximising Economic Opportunities for Women in Scotland*. [Online] Available from: www.gov.scot/Resource/0047/00473060.pdf (accessed 4 August 2015).

Stiglitz, J. (2012). *The Price of Inequality*. New York: W.W. Norton & Co.

Sturgeon, N. (2015). *Caledonian Lecture 2015*. 8 June, Glasgow Caledonian University, New York.

11

SCOTLAND AND THE GREAT RECESSION

An analysis of the gender impact

Jim Campbell, Ailsa McKay and Susanne Ross

Introduction

The causes of the financial crisis, which precipitated the deepest economic recession since the great depression of the early 1930s, have been well documented and debated (Crotty, 2009; Krugman, 2009; Stiglitz, 2009; Claessens et al., 2014). What has not been explored to the same extent is the gender impact of the recession and the subsequent economic recovery (Karamessini and Rubery, 2013; Rubery and Rafferty, 2013; McKay et al., 2013; Pearson and Elson, 2015). This chapter provides an analysis of how the recession and the recovery process in Scotland have impacted on men and women, as well as considering the longer term implications of this impact.

The great recession in Scotland

Scotland entered into recession in the third quarter of 2008 and remained there for five quarters until quarter three of 2009. The Scottish economy experienced a peak to trough decline in output of 5.6 per cent, compared to 6.3 per cent for the UK as a whole (Gillespie, 2013: 14). The recovery in Scotland proceeded at a much slower pace than the UK as a whole during 2010, with GDP in Scotland expanding by 1.2 per cent compared to 2.1 per cent in the UK. However recovery stalled in 2010 resulting in only 0.5 per cent growth in Scotland in 2011 compared to 0.8 per cent in the UK (Scottish Government, 2012). By the end of 2012, Scottish GDP was still 2.4 per cent below its pre-recession peak (Fraser of Allander Institute, 2013: 4). Nonetheless during 2013 and 2014 economic recovery took hold and by the third quarter of 2014, Scotland was 2 per cent above its pre-recession peak (Fraser of Allander Institute, 2015: 8).

Table 11.1 indicates that, as expected, the great recession resulted in a fall in

TABLE 11.1 Employment in Scotland (16–64) 2008–2015 (thousands)

Period	Total (%)	Men (%)	Women (%)
Dec 07 – Feb 08	2509 (74.4)	1303 (79.1)	1206 (69.9)
Dec 09 – Feb 10	2399 (70.5)	1233 (74.1)	1166 (66.9)
Dec 14 – Feb 15	2532 (74.2)	1274 (76.3)	1258 (72.1)

Source: Office for National Statistics (2015a)

TABLE 11.2 Unemployment in Scotland (16–64) 2008–2015 (thousands)

Period	Total (%)	Men (%)	Women (%)
Dec 07 – Feb 08	130 (4.9)	74 (5.4)	56 (4.4)
Dec 09 – Feb 10	209 (8.0)	131 (9.6)	78 (6.3)
Dec 14 – Feb 15	165 (6.1)	98 (7.1)	67 (5.1)

Source: Office for National Statistics (2015a)

the number of people in employment (the great recession is defined as the period between December–February 2008 and December–February 2010). Despite the recovery being long and somewhat erratic, total employment had more or less returned to pre-recession levels by early 2015. The most noticeable change is that the gap between male and female employment rates has narrowed significantly from 9.2 percentage points in 2008 to 4.2 percentage points in 2015. This has been driven largely by increases in female employment, which now stands at its highest level since comparable records began, as well as male employment rates deteriorating at a faster pace than the female rate over the great recession (Scottish Government, 2015a).

During the great recession, total employment in Scotland fell by 110,000, a fall in the employment rate of 3.9 percentage points. Two-thirds of the decrease was accounted for by the decline in male employment. Therefore, in terms of the employment effects of the recession, men appear to have suffered more than women. This is not unique to Scotland and indeed the tendency for this recession to have a disproportionate impact on the employment of men led some commentators to describe it as a 'mancession', a phrase coined in the USA to describe the trends in unemployment in the recession's early stages (Perry, 2009; Wall, 2009).

Male employment declined by 70,000, a reduction of 5.4 per cent during the recent economic downturn and continued to fall during the recovery phase. It was not until late 2011 to early 2012 that male employment levels started to recover. Despite this, over the whole period from 2008 to 2015, total male employment decreased by 2.2 per cent. By comparison, female employment fell by 40,000, a decline of 3.3 per cent compared to pre-recession levels. However, female employment levels made a stronger recovery than male employment and by 2015 were 4.3 per cent higher than their 2008 levels.

As Table 11.2 shows, during the recessionary period, unemployment in Scotland

TABLE 11.3 Economic inactivity in Scotland (16–64) 2008–2015 (thousands)

Period	Total (%)	Men (%)	Women (%)
Dec 07 – Feb 08	733 (21.7)	270(16.4)	463 (26.9)
Dec 09 – Feb 10	797 (23.4)	299 (18.0)	498 (28.6)
Dec 14 – Feb 15	717 (21.0)	297 (17.8)	420 (24.1)

Source: Office for National Statistics (2015a)

rose by 57,000 for men and 22,000 for women, with men accounting for 72 per cent of the increase in total unemployment. Since the onset of the expansionary phase in 2010, male unemployment levels have recovered at a much faster rate, falling by 33,000, a 25 per cent decline compared to a reduction of 11,000 or 14 per cent for women. Over the whole period from 2008 to 2015, male unemployment has risen by 24,000, an increase of 32 per cent, while female unemployment rose by 11,000, an increase of 20 per cent. Men therefore accounted for 68 per cent of the increase in total unemployment over this period.

The overall picture therefore suggests that although men suffered the most from rising unemployment during the great recession, since the initial recovery phase women's unemployment has recovered at a much slower pace. Although both men's and women's unemployment remain higher than pre-recession levels, the unemployment gap between men and women has widened from 1 percentage point in 2008 to 2 percentage points in 2015.

Given the acute fall in output experienced during the recent downturn, it is perhaps surprising that the levels of unemployment experienced by both men and women have not risen more sharply. Indeed previous recessions in the early 1980s and early 1990s were characterised by much higher rates of unemployment, despite the loss in output being lower than the great recession (Hogarth et al., 2009; Vaitilingam, 2010; UK Commission for Employment and Skills, 2014a).

During the great recession, the number of people classified as economically inactive, that is neither in work or actively seeking work, rose by 64,000, an increase of 8.7 per cent (Table 11.3). This compares to an increase in unemployment over the same period of 79,000. As Table 11.3 indicates, both men and women experienced an increase in economic inactivity during the great recession, with a subsequent fall as the economy recovered. However, the fall in economic inactivity for women during the economic recovery was much more significant than that experienced by men. As a result, over the whole period 2008 to 2015, economic inactivity rose by 10 per cent for men but fell by 9.3 per cent for women. Therefore during the recovery women have experienced an increase in employment and a fall in unemployment. Economic inactivity has fallen to record lows for women and the gap between male and female economic inactivity rates has subsequently narrowed from 10.5 per cent in 2008 to 6.3 per cent in 2015.

Another labour market consequence of the financial crisis and subsequent recession in both the UK and Scotland has been an increase in the level of part–time employment for both men and women. Part-time employment is normally defined

TABLE 11.4 Full-time and part-time employment in Scotland (thousands)

Period	Total FT (%)[1]	Total PT (%)[1]	Male FT (%)[2]	Male PT (%)[2]	Female FT (%)[3]	Female PT (%)[3]
2008	1903 (75.2)	628 (24.8)	1196 (89.9)	135 (10.1)	706 (58.9)	494 (41.1)
2010	1799 (72.7)	677 (27.3)	1120 (87.7)	157 (12.3)	678 (56.7)	520 (43.3)
2014	1850 (72.5)	703 (27.5)	1148 (87.2)	170 (12.8)	702 (56.9)	533 (43.1)

1 As % of the total number in employment
2 As % of the total number of males in employment
3 As % of the total number of females in employment
Source: Office for National Statistics (2015a)

as working less than 30 hours per week (Organisation for Economic Co-operation and Development, 2015).

Although traditionally women have a much greater propensity to work part-time, the number of men employed on part-time contracts increased by 16.7 per cent during the recession, compared to 5.3 per cent for women, as Table 11.4 shows. This contrasts with a fall in the number of men employed on full-time contracts which declined by 6.4 per cent compared to 4.0 per cent for women over the same period. Interestingly, in the recovery period male part-time employment has continued to rise. Over the whole period 2008 to 2015, total part-time employment has risen by 75,000, around 45 per cent of which is accounted for by men. Male part-time employment grew by 25.9 per cent during this period, whilst full-time male employment fell by 4.0 per cent. In contrast, female part-time employment grew by 7.9 per cent, while full-time employment declined by 0.6 per cent. However part-time employment amongst men is still relatively low, accounting for around 1 in 8 men in employment compared to more than 3 in 8 women in employment.

Whilst the majority of people working part-time do so through choice, a growing number do so because they could not find a full-time job. In 2008, 10.4 per cent of people in part-time employment fell into this category rising to 16.2 per cent in 2014 (Office for National Statistics (ONS), 2015a). These figures are not disaggregated by gender at a Scottish level but it would seem reasonable to assume that a significant proportion of both men and women on part-time contracts would have preferred a full-time contract.

A more flexible and precarious labour market

In addition to increasing use of part-time employment, evidence also suggests that the labour market is becoming increasingly precarious with the growing use by employers of more flexible forms of employment such as zero hours and short hours contracts and the growth of self-employment. Table 11.5 reveals that over

TABLE 11.5 Self-employment in Scotland (16+) (thousands)

Period	Total (%)[1]	Male (%)[2]	Female (%)[3]
2008	269 (10.6)	188 (14.1)	81 (6.7)
2010	271 (10.9)	187 (14.6)	84 (7.0)
2014	302 (11.8)	200 (15.1)	102 (8.2)

1 As a % of total number in employment
2 As a % of the total number of males in employment
3 As a % of the total number of females in employment
Source: Office for National Statistics (2015a)

the whole period 2008 to 2014, self-employment has risen by 33,000, an increase of 12 per cent. Although the majority of self-employed individuals are men, since the onset of the recession female self-employment has increased at a much faster rate than their male counterparts, rising by 26 per cent compared to 6 per cent over the period. Self-employed women are also twice as likely to work part-time compared with their male counterparts, with the levels of female part-time self-employment driving the overall increases in total self-employment since 2008 (Scottish Government, 2015a).

Whilst the rise in the level of self-employment can be seen as evidence of a more dynamic and entrepreneurial economy, it should also be recognised that people may enter self-employment not through choice but rather necessity. The increase in self-employment in the UK since the great recession has attracted a different type of person in terms of gender, hours of work, occupation and sector of employment (Philpott, 2012). In the UK as a whole women account for around 60 per cent of the net increase in self-employment since the start of the recent downturn and nearly 90 per cent of the additional self-employed who work less than 30 hours per week. Sectors not traditionally associated with self-employment such as education, information and communications, financial services and social security show the biggest increases (Philpott, 2012). The evidence therefore would seem to suggest that the increase in self-employment, which may be seen as an indicator of economic recovery, has occurred more as a result of the lack of demand for labour than entrepreneurialism spurred by growth.

The number of individuals working on zero hours contracts in the UK, with no guarantee of minimum working hours per week, increased to 700,000 in 2014. This equates to 2.3 per cent of those in employment, the majority of whom (55 per cent) are women. Two-thirds of people on zero hours contracts reported that they work part-time. Whilst statistics are not available over the whole period from 2008 to 2015, evidence suggests that the number of individuals working on zero hours contracts increased by 19 per cent between 2013 and 2014 (ONS, 2015b).

In addition to zero hours contracts, there were 820,000 workers in 2014 in the UK who were employed on short hours contracts, 72 per cent of whom were women. These contracts refer to individuals who are employed for between 0 to 19 hours per week. These types of contracts are popular amongst employers, as they only need to start paying national insurance contributions for individuals who work more than 18 hours per week. The main sectors using these contracts were retail, education, accommodation and food services, with health and social care between them accounting for 71 per cent of all those on short hours contracts (Trade Union Congress, 2015).

Despite economic recovery taking hold, the increasing incidence of precarious forms of employment, such as zero hours and short hours contracts, is becoming an embedded feature of the post-recession UK labour market, reinforcing low paid and insecure forms of employment. This change, combined with the increasing use of part-time employment during the recession, may help to explain why unemployment did not reach the same levels experienced in previous recessions. The great recession resulted in an increase in both unemployment and underemployment.

Underemployment in Scotland

The ONS (2014: 25) defines underemployment as: 'those people in employment who are willing to work more hours, either by working in an additional job, by working more hours in their current job, or by switching to a replacement job'.

Underemployment provides a useful indicator of the underutilisation of labour and skills present in the labour market. According to this hours-constrained definition, underemployment in Scotland has risen from 7.0 per cent in 2008, marginally below the UK rate of 7.1 per cent, to 8.6 per cent in 2014, lower than UK rate of 9.9 per cent (ONS, 2014, 2015a). In 2014 there were 216,500 individuals in Scotland who would have liked to work longer hours; of these, 43 per cent were female part-time workers compared to 21 per cent of male part-time workers (Scottish Government 2015a). This change is so dramatic that it now makes the unemployment rate:

> a poorer indicator of the degree of slack in the labour market than it has been in the recent past. Further, estimates of the 'output gap' that rely on the unemployment rate may be giving a seriously misleading estimate of the degree of excess capacity in the UK labour market.
>
> (Bell and Blanchflower, 2013: 8)

Table 11.6 indicates that underemployment levels are generally much higher for women, reflecting the fact that the majority of part-time workers are women. Over the period of the great recession, underemployment in Scotland increased by 57,000, a rise in the underemployment rate of 2.4 percentage points, 44 per cent of which was accounted for by increases in female part-time underemployment. Over the whole period 2008 to 2014, underemployment increased by 42,000, predominantly driven by rising levels of underemployment among female part-time workers. Given the disproportionate experience of men and women in terms of underemployment, the question therefore remains whether rising female

TABLE 11.6 Underemployment in Scotland (16+) 2008–2014 by gender and work patterns (thousands/rate)

Period	Male All (%)	Male FT (%)	Male PT (%)	Female All (%)	Female FT (%)	Female PT (%)
2008	80 (6.1)	48 (4.1)	32 (24.7)	95 (8.0)	27 (3.8)	68 (14.0)
2010	111 (8.7)	64 (5.7)	47 (31.1)	121 (10.2)	28 (4.1)	93 (18.2)
2014	95 (7.3)	49 (4.3)	46 (28.2)	122 (9.9)	28 (3.9)	94 (18.0)

Source: Scottish Government (2015a)

underemployment will remain as a long-term consequence of the great recession and recovery.

At a UK level, underemployment by major occupational grouping has risen across all categories since 2008. The highest increase in underemployment was experienced by individuals working in elementary occupations which include cleaning, personal services such as bar work and basic security functions. Underemployment in these occupations rose from 14.1 per cent of the total employed in 2008 to 21.1 per cent in 2014. Underemployment in sales and customer service occupations increased by 5.7 per cent to 18.7 per cent of the total employed in that category, making this the occupation group with the second highest percentage of underemployed workers (ONS, 2014).

Underemployment also varies by age, with young workers aged between 16 and 24 most likely to be underemployed. In 2008 in Scotland 13.7 per cent of 16–24-year-olds in work were underemployed rising to 19.4 per cent in 2014 (Scottish Government, 2015a).

In addition to younger workers, the self-employed are more likely than the employed to classify themselves as underemployed (ONS, 2014). Pre-recession the percentage of underemployed self-employed workers was lower than that of employees. However since 2008 self-employed people experienced a sharper rise in underemployment, from 6.3 per cent in 2008 to 9.7 per cent in 2014 compared to an increase of 2.7 percentage points for employees over the same period. In 2014 the rates for both self-employed and employees were fairly similar at 9.7 per cent and 9.9 per cent respectively (ONS, 2014).

The International Labour Organisation (ILO) uses a broader definition of underemployment than the ONS and defines it as: 'all those who worked or had a job during the reference week but were willing and able to work more adequately' (ILO, 2015).

The ILO definition measures underemployment not just in terms of hours worked but also in terms of under-utilisation of skills, for example, graduates working in low-skilled employment. There is limited data available on skills-related underemployment partly because it is difficult to measure. However the UK Commission for Employment and Skills (2014b) found that, in a survey undertaken by UK employers, the percentage of staff reported as over-qualified or over-skilled for the job they were doing was 17 per cent in Scotland. There is some research to support the contention that women work below their current skills levels in an attempt to manage the balance between paid and unpaid work (Equal Opportunities Commission, 2005; Perrons, 2009). In other words, mothers returning to the formal labour market take part-time employment below their qualifications and skill levels. This choice is made under conditions of constraint such as inability to find suitable, affordable childcare. This is reinforced by the lack of part-time and/or flexible jobs available at senior management level which may, at least partly, explain female under-representation at the top of organisational hierarchies.

Impact on different sectors of the economy

As Table 11.1 shows over the period of the great recession, employment in Scotland fell by 111,000, representing a 4 per cent fall in total employment. Over a third of the job losses were in male-dominated manufacturing and construction sectors. In September 2008 these two sectors accounted for 15 per cent of workforce jobs in Scotland but 40 per cent of the decline in workforce jobs between 2008 and 2010. The more female-dominated wholesale and retail sectors (14 per cent of the Scottish workforce in 2008) shed 21,000 jobs during this period, 12 per cent of the total loss, while the more gender neutral financial and insurance services sector accounted for 10 per cent of the employment loss, mostly in the first year of the downturn. These four sectors, manufacturing, construction, financial services, and wholesale and retail, accounted for around one-third of Scottish employment in 2008 but experienced the majority (61 per cent) of the job losses between 2008 and 2010. Other sectors, particularly in the public sector, such as health and education where women tend to dominate the workforce, were sheltered from the great recession to some extent, with education experiencing a rise in employment of 0.5 per cent over the period of the great recession (ONS, 2015a).

Since 2010, 91.5 per cent of the jobs lost during the great recession have been recovered. The largest increases in employment were seen in administration and support service activities, human health and social work, manufacturing, education and public administration, and defence and compulsory social security. These five sectors accounted for 51.7 per cent of the increased employment during this period (ONS, 2015a). At least three of these sectors are heavily dominated by the public sector. Indeed there is a perception that the Scottish economy, in comparison to the rest of the UK, is over reliant on public sector employment. In the fourth quarter of 2014 there were 531,000 people employed in the public sector in Scotland, which represents 20.5 per cent of total employment in Scotland. In the UK as a whole in the fourth quarter of 2014 public sector employment accounted for 17.1 per cent of those employed (ONS, 2015c; Scottish Government, 2015b). These figures exclude employment in various financial institutions which were taken into public ownership as a result of the financial crisis in 2007/2008, including the Royal Bank of Scotland, Halifax Bank of Scotland and Lloyds TSB. Scotland accounts for around 10 per cent of total public sector employment in the UK.

As expected, the great recession affected the level of private sector employment more than the public sector. Between the fourth quarter of 2007 and the fourth quarter of 2009 the level of private sector employment in Scotland fell by 4 per cent compared to a slight rise in public sector employment (excluding the financial institutions) of 0.02 per cent. In contrast, between the fourth quarter 2009 and fourth quarter 2014 public sector employment (excluding the nationalised financial institutions) declined by 8.9 per cent whilst private sector employment increased by 9.1 per cent (Scottish Government, 2015b). As a result of financial pressures faced by public bodies in the UK to meet efficiency savings targets, many public bodies are increasingly using arm's length external organisations to outsource the delivery of public services to private sector organisations. This has resulted in approximately 1,000 local government staff in Scotland being transferred into the private sector over the four-year period to 2013, further reducing the size and structure of the public sector workforce in Scotland (Audit Scotland, 2013). The public sector in Scotland, as elsewhere, is dominated by women, with over two-thirds (69 per cent) of employees being female in 2013 (Audit Scotland 2013). So, as the size of the public sector declines, the impact will be disproportionately felt by women.

Impact of government policies

The main driver of the decline in public sector employment has been the austerity policies pursued by governments in the aftermath of the financial crisis. What differentiates the great recession from previous ones is not just its level and intensity but also the reaction of governments. Initially, as the scale of the global financial meltdown became apparent, governments throughout the world intervened to prevent the collapse of the banking sector. In October 2008 the UK government rescued two of the UK's leading banks, Halifax Bank of Scotland (HBOS) and the Royal Bank of Scotland (RBS). At the time of the rescue they had a combined balance sheet worth around £3 trillion, more than twice the GDP of the UK (National Audit Office, 2009: 5). According to the National Audit Office report the purchase of shares by the public sector together with the offer of guarantees, insurance and loans reached £850bn. To put that into context, total public spending in the UK in 2010/2011 was in the region of £700bn.

However once some stability had been restored to the financial system, governments, partly as a result of pressure from financial markets, became more concerned about the growing levels of public sector debt and their attention switched from saving the banking system to curbing public expenditure and raising taxation in order to reduce the level of government debt. Cuts in state support in care services, alongside restrictions in welfare benefits, pension reform and reduced public spending have therefore dominated the UK policy arena since the great recession.

Conclusions

The cumulative effects of increased deregulation of the labour market alongside welfare reforms have been to expose women to greater risks of job losses, particularly in the public sector, and real reductions in income over the longer term. With the election of a Conservative majority government in May 2015, pressure on public spending and particularly welfare spending is likely to intensify given the Government's commitment to achieve a budget surplus by 2019/20 (HM Treasury, 2015). However, reductions in spending on state supported care services do not imply a reduction in demand for those services, but rather a transfer of responsibility from the public to the private sphere. Thus women will find that their opportunities for formal labour market participation are further restricted due to the demands placed on their time performing necessary work at home without pay. Patterns of participation in the formal labour market therefore are different for men and women (Thomson, 2016) and women's 'choices' in the reconciliation of paid employment are often dependent upon other factors with respect to their roles and responsibilities in the household (Himmelweit, 2016).

The great recession did not result in the massive increases in headline unemployment levels experienced in other less severe recessions in the 1980s and 1990s. In part this can be explained by the increase in economic inactivity and part-time working, as well as a significant increase in underemployment which tends to affect women more than men. In addition, despite the austerity agenda driven by the UK government, male employment opportunities since the downturn have been more beneficial compared to female employment opportunities.

It remains to be seen whether the increases in underemployment that have occurred in the wake of the recent recession and recovery will become a permanent feature of Scotland's labour market. If changes in working patterns, such as the increase in part-time employment, rising underemployment, self-employment and the upsurge in zero-hours and short hours contracts, remain the norm, the financial and economic independence of many of Scotland's female workers could be under threat, placing women at even greater risk of in-work poverty.

References

Audit Scotland (2013). *Scotland's Public Sector Workforce*. Edinburgh: Audit Scotland.

Bell, D.N.F. and Blanchflower, D.G. (2013). 'Underemployment in the UK revisited'. *National Institute Economic Review*, May, No 224, F1–F15.

Claessens, S., Ayhan Kose, M., Laeven, L. and Valencia, F. (2014). *Financial Crisis: Causes, Consequences and Policy Response*. New York: IMF.

Crotty, J. (2009). 'Structural causes of the global financial crisis: a critical assessment of the "new financial architecture"'. *Cambridge Journal of Economics*, 33: 563–580.

Equal Opportunities Commission (2005). *Britain's Hidden Brain Drain: The EOC's Investigation Into Flexible and Part-Time Working*. Manchester: Equal Opportunities Commission.

Fraser of Allander Institute (2013). *Economic Commentary*. Vol. 37, No. 1. Glasgow: University of Strathclyde, pp. 3–20.

Fraser of Allander Institute (2015). *Economic Commentary*. Vol. 38, No. 3. Glasgow: University of Strathclyde, pp. 3–29.

Gillespie, G. (2013). *State of the Economy*. March 2013. Edinburgh: Scottish Government.

HM Treasury (2015). *Summer Budget 2015 Key Announcements*. [Online] Available www.

gov.uk/government/news/summer-budget-2015-key-announcements (accessed 16 September 2015).

Himmelweit, S. (2016). 'Childcare as an investment in infrastructure'. In Campbell. J. and Gillespie, M. (eds.) *Feminist Economics and Public Policy: Reflections on the Work and Impact of Ailsa McKay*. Abington: Routledge, pp. 83–93.

Hogarth, T., Owen, D., Gambin, L., Hasluck, C., Lyonette, C. and Casey, B. (2009). *The Equality Impacts of the Current Recession*. Equality and Human Rights Commission Research Report No. 47. Manchester: Equality and Human Right Commission.

ILO (2015). *Unemployment Statistics*. [Online] Available from: www.ilo.org/global/statis tics-and-databases/statistics-overview-and-topics/underemployment/lang--en/index. htm (accessed 31 July 2015).

Karamessini, M. and Rubery, J. (eds) (2013). *Women and Austerity: The Economic Crisis and the Future for Gender Equality*. Abingdon: Routledge.

Krugman, P. (2009). *The Return of Depression Economics and the Crisis of 2008*. London: Penguin Books.

McKay, A., Campbell, J., Thomson, E. and Ross. S. (2013). 'Economic recession and recovery in the UK: what's gender got to do with it?' *Feminist Economics*, 19(3): 108–123.

National Audit Office (2009). *Maintaining Financial Stability Across the United Kingdom's Banking System*. National Audit Office Report by the Comptroller and Auditor General HC 91 Session 2009–2010, 4 December. London: The Stationary Office. [Online] Available from: www.nao.org.uk/wp-content/uploads/2009/12/091091.pdf (accessed 31 July 2015).

ONS (2014). *Underemployment and Overemployment in the UK, 2014*. Newport: ONS. [Online] Available from: www.ons.gov.uk/ons/dcp171776_387087.pdf (accessed 31 July 2015).

ONS (2015a). *Regional Labour Market, May 2015*. Newport: Office for National Statistics. [Online] Available from: www.ons.gov.uk/ons/rel/subnational-labour/regional-la bour-market-statistics/may-2015/index.html [Accessed 31/7/2015].

ONS (2015b). *Analysis of Employee Contracts That Do Not Guarantee a Minimum Number of Hours*. Newport: Office for National Statistics. [Online] Available from: www.ons.gov. uk/ons/dcp171776_396885.pdf (accessed 31 July 2015).

ONS (2015c). *Public Sector Employment, Q4, 2014*. Newport: Office for National Statistics. [Online] Available from: www.ons.gov.uk/ons/dcp171778_391987.pdf (accessed 31 July 2015).

Organisation for Economic Co-operation and Development (2015). *OECD Labour Force Statistics 2014*. Paris: OECD Publishing.

Pearson, R. and Elson, D. (2015). 'Transcending the impact of the financial crisis in the United Kingdom: towards Plan F – a feminist economic strategy'. *Feminist Review*, 109: 8–30.

Perrons, D. (2009). *Women and Gender Equity in Employment: Patterns, Progress and Challenges*. Institute for Employment Studies Working Paper: WP23. Brighton: Institute for Employment Studies. [Online] Available from: www.employment-studies.co.uk/ system/files/resources/files/wp23.pdf (accessed 31 July 2015).

Perry, M. (2009). 'It's a "Man-Cession" in the lipstick industry', weblog, *Carpe Diem*, 9 December. [Online] Available from: http://mjperry.blogspot.co.uk/2008/12/its-man-cession-in-lipstick-economy.html (accessed 31 July 2015).

Philpott, J. (2012). *The Rise in Self-Employment*. London: Chartered Institute of Personnel and Development.

Rubery, J. and Rafferty, A. (2013). 'Women and recession revisited'. *Work, Employment and Society*, 27(3): 414–432.

Scottish Government (2012). *Economic Pocket Databank March 2012*. Edinburgh: Scottish Government.

Scottish Government (2015a). *Local Area Labour Markets: Statistics from the Annual Population Survey 2014*. Edinburgh: Scottish Government.

Scottish Government (2015b). *Public Sector Employment in Scotland: Statistics for 4th Quarter 2014*. Edinburgh: Scottish Government.

Stiglitz, J. (2009). 'The anatomy of murder: Who killed America's economy?' *Critical Review*, 21(23): 329–339.

Thomson, E. (2016). 'Occupational segregation and Modern Apprenticeships in Scotland'. In Campbell, J. and Gillespie, M. (eds.) *Feminist Economics and Public Policy: Reflections on the Work and Impact of Ailsa McKay*. Abington: Routledge, pp. 124–136.

Trade Union Congress (2015). 'Zero-hours contracts just the tip of the iceberg for low-paid and insecure jobs, says TUC'. [Online]. Available from: www.tuc.org.uk/econom ic-issues/zero-hours-contracts-just-tip-iceberg-low-paid-and-insecure-jobs-says-tuc (accessed 31 July 2015).

UK Commission for Employment and Skills (2014a). *The Labour Market Story: The UK Following Recession: Briefing Paper July 2014*. Wath-upon-Dearne: UK Commission for Employment and Skills.

UK Commission for Employment and Skills (2014b). *UK Commission's Employer Skills Survey 2013: UK Results Evidence Report 81*. Wath-upon-Dearne: UK Commission for Employment and Skills.

Vaitilingam, R. (2010). *Recession Britain: Findings from Economic and Social Research*. Swindon: Economic and Social Research Council.

Wall, H. J. (2009). 'The "Man-Cession" of 2008–09: it's big, but it's not great'. *The Regional Economist*, 18(4): 4–9.

12

OCCUPATIONAL SEGREGATION AND MODERN APPRENTICESHIPS IN SCOTLAND

Emily Thomson

Introduction

Occupational segregation by gender is an enduring feature of modern labour markets. The clustering of men and women into occupations based on gendered stereotypes also forms part of the explanation for the gender pay gap. Government funded vocational training programmes such as the Scottish Modern Apprenticeship programme are recognised to be reinforcing wider patterns of occupational segregation and gendered gaps in earnings (see for example Thomson et al., 2005; Campbell et al., 2005, 2006, 2011; the Equality and Human Rights Commission (EHRC) Scotland, 2014). Evidence shows that the labour market outcomes in female-dominated occupations do not compare favourably with male-dominated areas, particularly in terms of pay (McIntosh, 2007; Jones and Dickerson, 2007; Fong and Phelps, 2008; Learning and Skills Council, 2009; Winterbotham et al., 2014). Similarly, due to differences in the rate of government funding across different occupational areas there can be a considerable bias towards public investment in male trainees' skills over females (Campbell et al., 2009).

For over a decade between 2004 and 2014, researchers from Glasgow Caledonian University, led by Professor Ailsa McKay, conducted research and analysis on gender issues in the Scottish Modern Apprenticeship programme, providing a key evidence base for debates around occupational segregation and training in Scotland. In 2015, occupational segregation in the MA programme continues to be a significant cost to the Scottish economy, as well as being an example of where a lack of gendered analysis leaves occupational segregation unchallenged. This chapter summarises this research and explores its impact on Scotland's flagship vocational training programme. The research demonstrates that the MA programme perpetuates gender segregation in the labour market but that, as a key national training programme and first point of entry into the labour market for young people, it has the potential to challenge occupational segregation. The comprehensive body of research led by Ailsa has contributed to the development of positive policy changes. For example, the Scottish Government has made a commitment to tackle occupational segregation in the MA programme and also in the economy as a whole, has increased the level of publicly available data broken down by gender and, perhaps most importantly, has recognised the important contribution which a feminist economics perspective and a gendered analysis of the problem of occupational segregation and the inequalities it engenders can make.

Occupational segregation: causes and consequences

Gender segregation in labour markets is one of the most pervasive articulations of women's inequality compared to men. In all modern labour markets men's and women's paid employment is clustered to some extent into occupations that are dominated by their gender (Chang, 2003; Blau et al., 2013). Occupational segregation by gender can be horizontal or vertical. Horizontal segregation occurs where stereotyped assumptions about male and female capabilities and preferences concentrate women into predominantly 'female' occupations (and men into 'male' occupations). The jobs that are female dominated are associated with lower pay and lower status, therefore occupational segregation contributes significantly to the gender pay gap (see for example Olsen and Walby, 2004; Perales Perez, 2010; Couppié et al., 2014). Vertical segregation occurs where women are over-represented towards the bottom of organisational hierarchies and men tend to dominate the senior managerial positions.

Within the discipline of economics, attempts to explain the pervasiveness of occupational segregation and resultant gender pay differentials can be considered under two main headings: mainstream human capital and discrimination theories and feminist/gender theories (see for example Anker, 1997). Focussing on the supply side of the labour market, the human capital school (Becker, 1964) starts from the assumption that all workers and employees are 'rational' and that the market for labour can be viewed as any other product market. Income inequality is explained as the consequence of the differences between individual workers in terms of education, training and experience. The theory asserts a causal relationship between education and work skills, between skills and productivity and between productivity and earnings. According to the human capital perspective, women earn less than men in the labour market because of their inferior endowments of human capital due to lower initial investments in education as well as broken patterns of experiences within the labour market as a result of child rearing. Hence, women are paid less because they are less 'productive'. From this theoretical standpoint it is assumed that women are willing to trade earnings for expediency in terms of the flexibility and overall compatibility of low paid work with domestic responsibilities (Hakim, 2000; Hansen and Wahlberg, 2008). Hence, women's concentration in occupations at the lower end of the earnings distribution is an expression of their preferences. As such, occupational segregation is largely unproblematic because it is an expression of women's choices as free, rational, economic agents.

Within the mainstream economic perspective, theories of labour market discrimination focus on the demand side of the labour market in explaining occupational segregation (Becker, 1964, 1971). According to this theory, employers make decisions based on 'imperfect information' about the likely productivity of certain workers. Employer preferences are formed by considering the transaction costs associated with hiring and training workers and employers will only invest in these workers if they can be guaranteed a return in the form of increased productivity on their investment. Women are seen to be a riskier investment because employers assume they are less committed to paid work due to their endogenous preferences for unpaid work and their reproductive role, so they are more likely to leave paid work, resulting in higher transaction costs. Therefore, employers who have a 'taste' for discrimination will hire fewer women, hence female/male-dominated occupations emerge.

Human capital and discrimination theories embed many gender-stereotypical assumptions that make their explanations unacceptable to those seeking to address gender inequalities in the labour market and in earnings. Feminist economic theory, on the other hand, would argue that labour markets, like other 'economic' activities, cannot be viewed in isolation from the rest of society and social processes that shape participation in the paid labour market. Human capital and discrimination theories do not take into account the broader societal influences that determine what occupational choices are most 'suitable' for women and men (Hartmann, 1987; Folbre and Hartmann, 1988; Bergman, 1989). A feminist economics approach challenges the very definition of 'rational choice' that the mainstream presents as axiomatic. Gendered stereotypes and social expectations about the different roles and responsibilities of women and men can be understood as 'structures of constraint' (Folbre, 1994) which heavily influence the notions of preference and free choice. Under these conditions the market fails to allocate workers to jobs and/or training places efficiently, creating major labour market rigidities and restricting individual career choices and aspirations. From a feminist economics perspective, understanding the causes and consequences of occupational segregation is crucial to the formulation of labour market policies if gender inequality in labour markets is to be addressed. The Scottish Modern Apprenticeship (MA) programme provides an example of where a lack of gendered analysis in education and training policy has passively reinforced gendered inequalities, rather than actively challenging them.

The Scottish Modern Apprenticeships programme: where are the women?

The MA is a training programme giving individuals the opportunity to combine employment and training by following an industry-designed training framework. In Scotland, the government makes a contribution to funding the programme, the amount of which varies according to the occupation and level of training. Introduced in 1994 to address a perceived lack of intermediate vocational skills in the UK economy, it targeted 16–19-year-olds (school leavers) initially, but has been opened to all ages from 2002. The public sector contribution to funding for apprentices over the age of 19, however, is not guaranteed. Successful completion of an apprenticeship results in the award of an accredited work-based qualification, known as a Scottish Vocational Qualification (SVQ) at levels 2, 3, 4 and 5 and a set of 'core skills' (communication, numeracy, information technology, working with others and problem solving). Level 2 SVQ is an entry level qualification, a stage below that of the European Qualification Framework (EQF) level 1, while level 5 SVQs are equivalent to EQF level 3 or a UK honours degree (European Commission, 2015).

MA frameworks include occupations in the 'traditional' sectors where the notion of apprenticeship training is well established, such as in construction and engineering; and in 'non-traditional' sectors where the concept of apprenticeship training is relatively new, mainly in service sector and caring occupations. All apprentices have employed status meaning that, if not in employment already, potential candidates must find a suitable vacancy with an apprenticeship attached. In Scotland, education and training are devolved to the Scottish Parliament and a range of agencies are involved in the design and delivery of MAs (Campbell et al., 2013). The Scottish Government develops policy on MAs and provides the funding for Skills Development Scotland (SDS), the national non-departmental skills body, established in 2008. SDS delivers the programme, sets funding levels, administers funds and has a key role in marketing the MA to potential candidates and increasing awareness of the MA amongst employers.

The latest data published by SDS indicates that there were 34,472 MAs in training in Scotland at the end of June 2015. Of those, 10,383 were women, a female participation rate of 30 per cent. If broken down by age category (see Table 12.1), women are most prevalent in the 20–24-year-old category (40 per cent participation) with lower rates of female participation evident in the 'target' 16–19-year-old category (28 per cent) and in the 25+ age group (23 per cent). The majority of MAs (62 per cent) are in the target school leaver age group. This is largely explained by the fact that government funding is only guaranteed for individuals in this age group as the MA is a cornerstone of Scotland's Youth Employment Strategy (Scottish Government, 2014a).

Women are also under-represented in the higher level MA frameworks (see Table 12.2). Women account for around a quarter of MAs at level 3 or 4 SVQ and the figure drops to only 6 per cent at level 5. MAs at level 5 form a very small cohort, with only 123 apprentices in training at this level. In 2014, the average

TABLE 12.1 Female participation rates by age

Age group	All	16–19	20–24	25+
Female	10,383 (30%)	5,955 (28%)	3,201 (40%)	1,227 (23%)
Male	24,089 (70%)	15,329 (72%)	4,749 (60%)	4,011 (77%)
TOTAL	**34,472**	**21,284**	**7,950**	**5,238**

Source: SDS (2015a)

TABLE 12.2 Female participation rate by SVQ level of attainment

SVQ level	Level 2	Level 3	Level 4	Level 5
Female	3,875 (48%)	6,289 (25%)	212 (30%)	7 (6%)
Male	4,268 (52%)	19,024 (75%)	501 (70%)	116 (94%)
TOTAL	**8,143**	**25,313**	**713**	**123**

Source: SDS (2015a)

TABLE 12.3 Female participation in the 'top ten' occupational frameworks 2015 and change from 2009

Occupational framework	In training 2009	% female 2009	In training 2015	% female 2015	change in % points
Engineering	3627	1.8%	4282	3.8%	+2
Automotive★	2269	1.0%	2851	1.8%	+0.8
Social Services: Children and Young People + Social Services and Healthcare★★	322	85.7%	2519	91.9%	+6.2
Hospitality	626	46.0%	2417	52.5%	+6.5
Business Administration	989	83.7%	2099	72.0%	−11.7
Construction: Building	7644	1.3%	2168	1.9%	+0.6
Electrical Installation	3236	1.1%	1560	1.3%	+0.2
Hairdressing and Barbering	371	94.8%	1477	91.9%	−2.9
Retail	262	67.5%	1473	55.0%	−12.5
Freight Logistics	N/A	N/A	1209	6.0%	N/A

★ In 2009 this framework was known as Vehicle Maintenance and Repair.
★★ In 2009 this framework was known as Health and Social Care. By 2015 this occupational area has been split into two frameworks, underlining the massive expansion of MA training in this area.
Source: SDS (2015a)

hourly pay for a level 2 and 3 MA in Scotland was £6.61 compared to an average of £14.45 per hour for level 4/5, which is a substantial difference in mean hourly pay (Winterbotham et al., 2014).

The severe under-representation of women in level 5 MAs is driven not only by the fact that the overall cohort is so small, but also that most 'professional level' MAs are in construction. This highlights the nature of gendered segregation on the MA programme – it is both vertical in that women are concentrated in the lower levels of attainment, and horizontal as women are concentrated in the non-traditional service sector and caring occupations. Table 12.3 outlines the female participation rates in the ten most popular (current) occupational frameworks (by numbers 'in training'). These ten frameworks account for 64 per cent of the whole MA programme. Of these frameworks only two, hospitality and retail, are close to gender balance, while five are heavily male dominated (including the largest, engineering) and three are heavily female dominated. Included in this table are female participation rates in 2009, the earliest year for which gender disaggregated data is publicly available on the SDS website.

Although the frameworks are not directly comparable in some cases, the figures overall indicate that, while gender based occupational segregation in most of the largest occupational areas is reducing, the pace of change is very slow. Progress towards desegregation in male-dominated fields has been less successful than in female-dominated occupational areas, with the exception of social services/health care in which the proportion of female apprentices in this area has increased by 6 percentage points as the framework has increased in numbers.

It is evident that the MA programme displays quite severe gender-based occupational segregation and this segregation underpins inequality of outcomes between male and female apprentices, particularly in terms of the wage premium associated with this type of training and level of qualification. A cost-benefit analysis of apprenticeships and other vocational qualifications indicates that there are significant variations in the estimated wage returns to apprenticeships in different occupational sectors (McIntosh, 2007). The analysis found that an apprenticeship qualification increases the average wage of an individual working in the construction sector by 32 per cent, whereas in retail there is no observed effect on apprenticeship in wages. Similarly, a study undertaken by Walker and Zhu (2007) indicates that men in Scotland can expect a wage increase of over 20 per cent on average with a MA qualification but women in Scotland can expect less than half that at just under 10 per cent. Other research indicated a gender pay gap in English apprenticeships of 21 per cent (Fong and Phelps, 2008). A review of the benefits of completing an apprenticeship, carried out by the Learning and Skills Council National Office in England, indicated that the average annual wage after completion of an apprenticeship was £16,900 for men and £13,100 for women – a difference of 22.5 per cent in favour of men (Learning and Skills Council, 2009). This conclusion is supported by research investigating job outcomes by job level and qualification that found the impact was most apparent for those with trade apprenticeship qualifications: around 12 per cent of men with trade apprenticeships were in higher level jobs compared to 3 per cent of women (Jones and Dickerson, 2007). The latest apprenticeship pay survey, published by the Department of Business Innovation and Skills in December 2014, indicates that male MAs in Scotland are paid on average £1.16 per hour more than female MAs (a mean of £6.98 versus £5.82) (Winterbotham et al., 2014). This represents an apprenticeship pay gap of 17 per cent compared to the overall gender pay gap of 11.5 per cent in Scotland (Office for National Statistics, 2014) strengthening concerns that MAs may be reinforcing women's disadvantage in the labour market in Scotland.

What's gender got to do with it? Assessing the impact of Professor Ailsa McKay's research on occupational segregation in Scottish MAs

Women have always been under-represented among MAs in Scotland, with female participation rates averaging at around a third of all MAs since gender disaggregated data has been publicly available. A Scottish feminist activist group, the Scottish Women's Budget Group (SWBG), of which Ailsa McKay was a founding member, highlighted the fact that MAs were heavily male dominated as early as 2002, when only a fifth of MAs were female according to unpublished data obtained by SWBG. These comments followed a review of the MAs programme in Scotland (SQW Ltd, 2001) that indicated female apprentices were concentrated in a small number of non-traditional frameworks and that these frameworks were associated with low participation and high drop-out rates (SWBG, 2002). SWBG was concerned that the review had failed to undertake any gendered analysis of these issues or the high levels of gender-based occupational segregation in MAs, particularly given the commitment to equality that had been enshrined in the Scottish Devolution Settlement in 1999 (O'Cinneide, 2009).

The issue of gender-based occupational segregation was taken up again in September 2003 when the (then) Equal Opportunities Commission (EOC) launched a General Formal Investigation (GFI) into the segregation of women and men in training and work. The GFI chose to focus on the MA programme to explore issues of gender segregation and concentrated on five of the most gender-segregated employment sectors – childcare, construction, plumbing, engineering, and information and communications technology. In view of specific concerns about MAs in Scotland, Ailsa McKay made the case to the EOC for a separate study to be undertaken in Scotland when the GFI was launched in England and Wales (see Thomson et al., 2004). She subsequently led a separate research project, carried out in Scotland under the terms of the GFI in England and Wales. The starting point for this research was that occupational segregation has significant economic, as well as social, costs to the Scottish economy. Challenging the levels of occupational segregation within the MA programme, as a key entry level training programme, was therefore crucial to delivering on the (then) Scottish Executive's[1] strategy for economic development. Furthermore, the research was undertaken from an explicitly feminist economics perspective, which recognised gender as a social construct that heavily influences labour market 'choices' and had the overall goal of ending women's economic and social inequality.

In February 2005, the final report of the Scottish component of the EOC's GFI was published (Thomson et al., 2005). This report confirmed that patterns of participation were significantly differentiated by gender: men dominated the 'traditional' frameworks such as construction and women were concentrated in 'non-traditional' frameworks, where there was no established tradition of the apprenticeship mode of training, such as childcare. The 'traditional' frameworks were found to be of longer average duration than those in non-traditional areas, more resource intensive and associated with enhanced rates of pay for apprentices in training and in the wider labour market. The key recommendation of the Scottish component of the GFI was for the development of a national strategy for Scotland to tackle occupational segregation that should be government led. The report also recommended that relevant data (including information on apprenticeship pay) be made available in the public domain in a readily accessible format and that positive action on promoting industries to atypical candidates should become a priority for relevant stakeholders (Thomson et al., 2005).

Gender-disaggregated data were subsequently published on a regular basis and eventually became easily accessible via the SDS website after its establishment in 2008. However, the (then) Scottish Executive did not agree with the development of a national strategy for action on occupational segregation, but rather established the cross-departmental Occupational Segregation Working Group (OSWG) to 'take forward action on occupational segregation' in 2006 (Macpherson, 2008: 4). This group became the main focus of activity on occupational gender segregation but unfortunately it did not make any recommendations concerning the MA programme.

The Scottish Executive formally consulted on the future of the MA programme in 2006 and in 2009 the Scottish Government held an 'Apprenticeship Summit' to consider the impact of the global recession on the programme's operation. Neither exercise reported any analysis of gender-based occupational segregation in the programme, or the low participation rates of women (see Scottish Executive, 2006, and Scottish Government, 2009). The EOC requested that Alisa and colleagues undertake research on the progress of occupational segregation in the MA programme. The updated research recognised that little progress had been made (Campbell et al., 2009). The Gender Equality Duty[2] required government ministers to set out priority areas for action to address gender equality across the work of the Scottish public sector: occupational segregation became one of two Ministerial priorities in 2009, the other was violence against women (Scottish Government, 2010). A review of evidence and national policies for tackling occupational segregation (Reid Howie Associates and Equality Plus, 2010) highlighted the need for action, underpinned directly by the GFI research and analysis. In September 2012, Ailsa made the keynote speech at the first ever Women's Employment Summit, a joint initiative by the Scottish Government and the Scottish Trades Union Congress. The event included extensive discussions about occupational segregation in education and training and led to the re-establishment of the OSWG in April 2013 which had disbanded in 2008 (Close the Gap, 2014a).

Discussion

In 2014, the EHRC in Scotland published a series of three research reports, one of which focused on diversity data for Modern Apprenticeships (and their equivalents) across Scotland, England, Wales, Northern Ireland (EHRC, 2014; Sosenko and Netto, 2013). This research acknowledged the body of work by Ailsa McKay and colleagues and it highlighted the fact that Scotland's investment in apprenticeships, compared to that of the other UK countries, was consistently skewed towards men due to high levels of occupational segregation, particularly male domination of the most populous MA frameworks (Sosenko and Netto, 2013).

Ailsa gave evidence to the Wood Commission in November 2013 (Scottish Government, 2014b). The commission was set up in January 2013 to consider the quality of intermediate vocational education and training and the 'connectivity' between young people and employers in the context of high youth unemployment in Scotland. The final report made a specific recommendation to SDS to develop an action plan on gendered inequalities in the MA programme, as well as more general recommendations around gender-based occupational segregation within schools and colleges. The recommendation to SDS was underpinned by a call for 'realistic but stretching improvement targets' on which SDS would be required to report annually (Scottish Government, 2014b: 38). Targets are an important step towards reducing occupational segregation, but on their own they are not enough to guarantee better outcomes for female apprentices, particularly in terms of pay or drop-out rates and:

> perhaps there needs to be more radical changes to the funding, delivery and design of the MA programme to enable stakeholders to improve the outcomes for young women. For example, strategies to support young women into training and employment must be flexible to accommodate women's caring responsibilities, and might include direct support for childcare.
>
> (Close the Gap, 2014b)

In response to the Wood Commission's final report, Angela Constance, Cabinet Secretary for Training, Youth and Women's Employment, in a speech to the Scottish Parliament, outlined a commitment to tackling occupational segregation in the MA programme including encouraging 'non-traditional' career choices for men and women through the work of SDS (Constance, 2015). She also announced a total investment of £4.5 million in activities which included addressing segregation, although the precise allocation for work to tackle occupational segregation was unclear. The Scottish Government announced additional funding in order to increase the number of MAs in training from 25,000 to 30,000 by 2020 and the First Minister of Scotland, Nicola Sturgeon, outlined her aims for the programme to be accessible to more young women (SDS, 2015b). However, increasing overall female participation rates in MAs without addressing underlying occupational divisions will do little to address the gender inequalities that the current operation of the programme reinforces – the persistent problem of occupational segregation and the negative impact it has on women's pay and progression.

Conclusion

There is ample evidence that the research Ailsa led and developed, starting from the observations of SWBG in 2002, has impacted on policy approaches to education and training in two major ways. Firstly, her feminist economics approach contributed to the understanding of gender-based occupational segregation in the Scottish MA as a policy *problem* that should be addressed rather than an unproblematic expression of free choice and individual agency. Secondly, the data gathered during the GFI and in subsequent updates have provided robust evidence on which to build positive action strategies and from which to measure progress towards gender equality in Scottish MAs. While still very much a 'wicked problem', occupational segregation in this training programme has at least begun to be addressed by relevant stakeholders, thanks in large part to the work of Ailsa McKay and colleagues. This is reflected in recent reports such as EHRC Scotland (2014) and Sosenko and Netto (2013) and in the recommendations of the Commission for Developing Scotland's Young Workforce – the 'Wood' Commission (Scottish Government, 2014b).

The evidence suggests some reduction in levels of segregation in the last decade, particularly in the male-dominated areas, but progress is very slow. Men are still concentrated in sectors where the concept of apprenticeship training is embedded and women in the 'non-traditional' sectors. This results in significant inequalities in male and female apprenticeship wage rates and expected earnings on completion of training. As a publicly funded training programme, the Scottish government must ensure that the MA programme is not only equally accessible to women and men, but that their participation in the programme challenges gendered stereotypes, rather than reflecting and reinforcing them. Addressing gender inequalities within the MA programme is a long-term objective and will require engagement and commitment from all stakeholders, including employers. The work of Ailsa McKay and colleagues has, at the very least, succeeded in putting the issue of occupational segregation firmly on the policy agenda, providing an evidence base on which positive change can begin to develop and bringing some feminist economics analysis into policy discourse. It is a real source of sadness that Ailsa McKay did not live to see the impact that her work is beginning to have on the training opportunities for Scotland's women.

Notes

1 The 'Scottish Executive' was the name used initially by the administration in Scotland, changing to the 'Scottish Government' when the minority SNP administration took office in 2007.
2 The gender equality duty came into force in 2007. The Equality Act 2006 created a 'duty' on public authorities to eliminate unlawful sex discrimination and promote equality of opportunity between men and women. It was a significant step towards a pro-active approach to ensuring equality of outcomes, as opposed to the reactive 'equal opportunities' approach that had hitherto dominated public policy discourse on equalities in the UK (Webb, 1997).

References

Anker, R. (1997). 'Theories of occupational segregation by sex: an overview'. *International Labour Review*, 136 (3): 315–339.
Becker, G.S. (1964). *Human Capital: A Theoretical and Empirical Analysis*. New York: National Bureau of Economic Analysis.
Becker, G.S. (1971). *The Economics of Discrimination, Second Edition*. Chicago: Chicago University Press.

Bergman, B. (1989). 'Does the market for women's labor need fixing?' *Journal of Economic Perspectives*, 3: 43–60.

Blau, F., Brummond, P. and Yung-Hsu Liu, A. (2013). 'Trends in occupational segregation by gender 1970–2009: adjusting for the impact of changes in the occupational coding system'. *Demography*, 50: 471–492.

Campbell, J., Gillespie, M., McKay, A. and Meikle, A. (2009). 'Jobs for the girls and for the boys: promoting a smart, successful Scotland three years on'. *Scottish Affairs*, 66 (1): 65–83.

Campbell, J., McKay, A. and Thomson, E. (2005). 'How modern is the modern apprenticeship?' *Local Economy*, 20 (3): 294–304.

Campbell, J., McKay, A. and Thomson, E. (2006). 'From gender blind to gender focused: re-evaluating the Scottish Modern Apprenticeship Programme'. *Scottish Affairs*, 57(1): 70–89.

Campbell, J., McKay, A., Ross, S. and Thomson, E. (2013). *How Modern is the Modern Apprenticeship in Scotland*. Glasgow: Women in Scotland's Economy Research Centre, Glasgow Caledonian University.

Campbell, J., Thomson, E. and Pautz, H. (2011). 'Apprenticeship training in England: Closing the Gap'. *Journal of Contemporary European Studies*, 19(3): 365–378.

Chang, T. (2003). 'A social psychological model of women's gender-typed occupational mobility'. *Career Development International*, 8(1): 27–39.

Close the Gap (2014a). *Women and Work: What Comes Next in a Post-Referendum Scotland?* [Online] Available from www.closethegap.org.uk/content/resources/CTG-Working-Paper-13---Women-and-work-what-comes-next-in-a-post-referendum-Scotland.pdf (accessed 2 September 2015).

Close the Gap (2014b). *The Wood Commission Publishes Final Report on Developing Scotland's Young Workforce*. Blog post. [Online] Available from: www.closethegap.org.uk/news/blog/the-wood-commission-published-report-on-developing-scotlands-young-work-force/ (accessed 7 August 2015).

Constance, A. (2015). *Response to the Wood Commission on the Young Workforce*. Speech delivered to the Scottish Parliament, 25 June 2014. [Online] http://news.scotland.gov.uk/Speeches-Briefings/Response-to-the-Wood-Commission-on-the-Young-Work force-e36.aspx (accessed 6 August 2015).

Couppié, T. Dupray, A. and Moullet, S. (2014). 'Education-based occupational segregation and the gender wage gap: evidence from France'. *International Journal of Manpower*, 35(3): 368–391.

European Commission (2015). *Descriptors Defining Levels in European Qualifications Framework*. [Online] Available from: https://ec.europa.eu/ploteus/content/descriptors-page (accessed 19 August 2015).

EHRC Scotland (2014). *Modern Apprenticeships: Equality and the Economy, Spreading the Benefits*. Glasgow: Equality and Human Rights Commission.

Folbre, N. (1994). *Who Pays for the Kids? Gender and the Structures of Constraint*. London: Routledge.

Folbre, N. and Hartmann, H. (1988). 'The rhetoric of self-interest and the ideology of gender'. In Klamer, A., McCloskey D.N. and Solow R.M. (eds) *The Consequences of Economic Rhetoric*. New York: Cambridge University Press, pp. 184–206.

Fong, B. and Phelps, A. (2008). *Apprenticeship Pay: 2007 Survey of Earnings by Sector*. Research Report 08 05. London: Department for Innovation, Universities and Skills.

Hakim, C. (2000). *Work-Lifestyle Choices in the 21st Century Preference Theory*. Oxford: Oxford University Press.

Hansen, J. and Wahlberg, R. (2008). 'Occupational gender composition and the gender wage gap in Sweden'. *Research in Labor Economics*, 28: 353–369.

Hartmann, H. (1987). 'Changes in women's economic and family roles in post-World War II United States'. In Beneria, L. and Stimpson, C.R. (eds) *Women, Households and the Economy*. New Brunswick: Rutgers University Press, pp. 33–64.

Jones, P. and Dickerson, A. (2007). *Poor Returns: Winners and Losers in the Job Market*. Equal Opportunities Commission Working Paper Series No. 52, Manchester: Equal Opportunities Commission.

Learning and Skills Council (2009). *The Benefits of Completing an Apprenticeship*. Coventry: Learning and Skills Council National Office.

Macpherson, S. (2008). *Tackling Occupational Segregation in Scotland: A Report of Activities from the Scottish Government Cross-Directorate Occupational Segregation Working Group*. Edinburgh: Employment Research Institute.

McIntosh S. (2007). *A Cost Benefit Analysis of Apprenticeship and Other Vocational Qualifications*. Department for Education and Skills Research Report RR834. London: Department for Education and Skills.

O'Cinneide, C. (2009). *The Place of Equal Opportunities in the Devolution Settlement: A Legal Analysis*. Glasgow: Equality and Human Rights Commission Scotland.

Office for National Statistics (2014). *Annual Survey of Hours and Earnings: Provisional Results*. [Online] Available from: www.ons.gov.uk/ons/rel/ashe/annual-survey-of-hours-and-earnings/2014-provisional-results/stb-ashe-statistical-bulletin-2014.html#tab-Gender-pay-differences (accessed 25 June 2015).

Olsen, W. and Walby, S. (2004). *Modelling Gender Pay Gaps*. Manchester: Equal Opportunities Commission.

Perales Perez, F. (2010). 'The impact of occupational sex-segregation on wages: evidence from Britain'. *Essex Graduate Journal of Sociology*, 10: 35–53.

Reid Howie Associates and Equality Plus (2010). *Reporting on Progress Towards Equality of Opportunity for Women and Men Made by Public Authorities in Scotland: Ministerial Priorities for Gender Equality. Tackling Occupational Segregation*. Edinburgh: Scottish Government.

Scottish Executive (2006). *Building on Our Success – Improving Modern Apprenticeships: Consultation Analysis Report*. [Online] Available from: www.scotland.gov.uk/Publications/2006/12/12103147/20 (accessed 6 August 2015).

Scottish Government (2009). *Making Training Work Better: Modern Apprenticeships*. [Online] Available from: www.gov.scot/Topics/Education/skills-strategy/making-skills-work/ntp/mtwbkq (accessed 6 August 2015).

Scottish Government (2010). *Gender Equality Ministerial Priorities Reports*. [Online] Available from: www.gov.scot/Topics/People/Equality/violence-women/MinisPrioGenEquReport2010 (accessed 6 August 2015).

Scottish Government (2014a). *Developing the Young Workforce, Scotland's Youth Employment Strategy, Implementing the Recommendations of the Commission for Developing Scotland's Young Workforce*. Edinburgh: Scottish Government.

Scottish Government (2014b). *Education Working for All! Commission for Developing Scotland's Young Workforce Final Report*. [Online] Available from: www.gov.scot/Publications/2014/06/4089 (accessed 6 August 2015).

SDS (2015a). *Modern Apprenticeship Performance Report June 2015*. [Online] Available at www.skillsdevelopmentscotland.co.uk/media/1367942/ma_breakdown_by_level_q1_2015-16.pdf (accessed 7 August 2015).

SDS (2015b). *New Apprenticeships Announced*. [Online] Available from www.

skillsdevelopmentscotland.co.uk/news-and-events/news/new-apprenticeships-announced/ (accessed 25 June 2015).

Sosenko, F. and Netto, G. (2013). *Scotland-Focused Analysis of Statistical Data on Participation in Apprenticeships in Four UK Countries*. Edinburgh: Heriot Watt University.

SQW Ltd (2001). *Review of Modern Apprenticeships in Scotland*. Edinburgh: Scottish Executive Central Research Unit.

SWBG (2002). *Accounting for Gender: A Response to the Annual Expenditure Report Of the Scottish Executive: The Scottish Budget 2003*. Edinburgh: Scottish Women's Budget Group.

Thomson, E., McKay, A., Campbell, J. and Gillespie, M. (2004). *Modern Apprenticeships and Gender Based Occupational Segregation in Scotland: A Position Paper*. Glasgow: Equal Opportunities Commission Scotland.

Thomson, E., McKay, A., Campbell, J. and Gillespie, M. (2005). *Jobs for the Boys and the Girls: Promoting a Smart, Successful and Equal Scotland*. Glasgow: Equal Opportunities Commission Scotland.

Walker, I. and Zhu, Y. (2007). *The Labour Market Effects of Qualifications*. Glasgow: Futureskills Scotland.

Webb, J. (1997). 'The politics of equal opportunity'. *Gender, Work and Organisation*, 4(3): 159–169.

Winterbotham, M., Davies, B., Murphy, L., Huntley Hewitt, J. and Tweddle, M. (2014). *Apprenticeship Pay Survey 2014*. London: Department for Business Innovation and Skills.

13

WOMEN WORKING TOGETHER

Ann Henderson

Introduction

With the establishment of the Scottish Parliament in 1999, Ailsa McKay was always ready to take all opportunities to advance a challenge to the traditional way of approaching budgets and public expenditure, speaking up for women and for a different, more equal, way of organising our society. This chapter examines some of the alliances that were built in that period, with a particular focus on women's experiences of the labour market, their campaigns to improve their rights and working conditions and the effectiveness or otherwise of policy interventions and public spending decisions.

It also reflects on historical evidence of women's unequal treatment in the world of work and the importance of women's activism, including in trade unions. This shows how some policy issues have concerned women for many decades, but also that progress has been made and governments and workplaces can be responsive where they can see the benefits of change. This can apply to benefits for women themselves, in the interests of economic necessity or where these coincide, for example in the provision of high quality childcare that can contribute to improved economic growth as well as benefiting women and children.

Building alliances from 1999

I was working in the Scottish Parliament in 1999, as a researcher with Mike Watson MSP (at that time Convenor of the Scottish Parliament Finance Committee and a member of the Social Inclusion, Housing and Voluntary Sector Committee). In November 1999 I attended a meeting in Edinburgh with speakers from the UK Women's Budget Group and women from Scotland, including Ailsa, who were advocating the establishment of a Scottish Women's Budget Group.

Subsequently the Scottish Parliament Finance Committee recommended that the Equal Opportunities Committee was to have a role in the budget scrutiny process. Women worked together from inside and outside the Parliament to build on the opportunity this presented to try to ensure that the scrutiny would challenge orthodox approaches on budget priorities and policy decisions (McKay et al., 2002). For me, this was to be the start of a long, supportive and enjoyable relationship with Ailsa, feminist economics and family. That initial approach, of sharing knowledge and taking our arguments through various different routes simultaneously, was to be replicated throughout the time that Ailsa and I knew each other.

I took up a post at Scottish Trades Union Congress (STUC) in 2007. The STUC is the autonomous trade union centre in Scotland, representing over 590,000 workers and their families. Since 2002, the formal working arrangements between the STUC and Scottish Government have included twice-yearly meetings between the STUC and the First Minister, in the context of an agreed Memorandum of Understanding (Scottish Government and STUC, 2015).

Ailsa McKay was a welcome visitor and speaker at the STUC annual Women's Conferences. A key common interest was the impact of the great recession on women in Scotland and work on this issue with Ailsa and the Women in Scotland's Economy (WiSE) Research Centre was a two-way exchange. We explored and questioned how well the data matched up with women's experiences.

Political changes in Scotland brought new opportunities for debate as well, following the election in 2011 which resulted in a Scottish National Party majority and a Scottish Government that was committed, amongst other things, to holding a referendum on independence. It transpired that the pre-Referendum period provided a distinct space for debate and reflection on improving the position of women in Scotland's economy and society.

Women, work and the recession

Following the economic recession of 2008 and the decline of manufacturing industries in Scotland over a longer period, the labour market is very different from that of 100 years ago. But the challenges for women of equal pay, the rate for the job, the value attached to paid and unpaid work, remain.

Whilst a direct comparison is not possible as not all women's work was accurately recorded, the figures from the 1901 census show that 24 per cent of the female workforce were employed in domestic labour (servants), falling to 6 per cent by 1971. By 1981 only 1 per cent of women in work were recorded as employed in domestic service. This is likely to actually be a little higher, with unrecorded work and casual labour, but the shift is significant. In 1901 21 per cent of women in work were employed in textiles compared to only 3 per cent by 1981. On the other hand, women's employment in the professional and scientific category, which includes teachers and nurses, rose from 5 per cent in 1901 to 24 per cent in 1981 (McIvor, 2004).

The female employment participation rate in Scotland, as a percentage of women of employable age, was calculated as 33 per cent in 1901, 39.7 per cent in 1971, then rising very quickly to 68.1 per cent by 1981. The Scottish Government reported in 2015 the highest ever female participation rate in Scotland of 72.4%. The gap between male and female employment is narrowing, with male employment participation rates now at 76.1%. The report also observes that, as a general trend, between 2008 and 2014 in both Scotland and the UK, the number of people employed part-time increased. However women's part-time work increased more than men's, by 18.1 per cent compared with 12.7 per cent (Scottish Government, 2015).

The changes in women's labour market participation raise questions about the quality of women's work that are discussed further below. However, a more immediate and shared concern arose following the recession in 2008 that, despite wide assumptions of the recession being about the loss of men's jobs, particularly in the early stages, the data indicated that women's employment also appeared to be suffering.

Women's Employment Summit

One of the formal meetings between the STUC and the Scottish Government in February 2012 picked up on this issue when a discussion about labour market figures showed a fall in women's employment in Scotland. In response to this an STUC/ Scottish Government Women's Employment Summit was planned to bring policy makers, employers, economists and trade union women together. This took place in September 2012 (Employability in Scotland, 2015a).

In planning the Summit, the STUC and Scottish Government worked closely with Ailsa and we shared a commitment to make sure that it delivered some change for women's lives in Scotland, placing women's experiences at its heart. Over 150 participants attended the event that was chaired by STUC president Agnes Tolmie, a leading member of UNITE the Union. Speakers included prominent figures from business, education, social services organisations and trade union representatives from both local and national levels. Importantly, the Scottish Government's commitment was reflected in keynote addresses from the then First Minister, Alex Salmond MSP; the Minister for Youth Employment Angela Constance MSP; and the Deputy First Minister, and Cabinet Secretary for Investment, Infrastructure and Cities, Nicola Sturgeon MSP.

One contribution that made welcome headlines that day came from the Deputy First Minister, Nicola Sturgeon MSP, when she outlined a commitment to investing in childcare 'as infrastructure' in Scotland's economy, a commitment that she reinforced following her appointment as First Minister in November 2014 (Sturgeon, 2014).

The Women's Employment Summit led to work being taken forward across government departments in collaboration with representatives from the STUC and the establishment of the Ministerial Advisory Group on Women and Work. Responsibility for women's employment was added to the remit of Angela

Constance MSP, Minister for Youth Employment. She convened the Group on Women and Work that included Ailsa McKay and members from the STUC, organisations interested in childcare policy, business and academia (Employability in Scotland, 2015b).

In 2012 and 2013, a series of seminars organised through the Scottish Universities Insight Institute 'Constitutional Futures – Gender Matters in a New Scotland' contributed to developing this agenda further, involving representatives from academia, Scottish Government, the STUC and organisations from across Scottish civic society. Taking advantage of the space created during the run up to the referendum on independence and the enthusiasm for taking every opportunity presented, a key issue they examined was the value of women's work, paid and unpaid, to the Scottish economy. Ailsa McKay worked with other key seminar participants to argue for a different way of responding to the challenges facing the Scottish economy, placing childcare policy high on the agenda (Scottish Universities Insight Institute, 2013).

Reflecting the growing interest in women's employment, Ailsa McKay also had a significant engagement with the Council of the Economic Advisers in 2013 on childcare and the economy. She argued that childcare was a key lever with the potential to have a transformative effect on the economy and wider and longer-term economic and social impacts (Scottish Government, 2013; Campbell et al., 2013).

The interest in the transformational potential of childcare is reflected in work by Siraj and Kingston (2015) and the Commission for Childcare Reform (2015). Most significant, however, is the impact of this and other work on government policy and the Scottish Government now has plans for a large expansion of childcare provision for pre-school children (Gillespie and Khan, 2016). The rise in female employment and indications from the Scottish Government of increasing childcare support are welcome messages that should benefit women entering the labour market, the economy and the welfare of the child. However, this will need to include development of the childcare infrastructure in Scotland and recent trends indicate that there has been a reduction in childcare facilities: 'The number of early learning and childcare (ELC) centres in Scotland peaked in 2005 (to 2,836) and has been steadily decreasing since. In September 2014 there were 2,449 local authority or partnership ELC providers in Scotland' (Scottish Government, 2014).

The Care Inspectorate's annual publication of childcare statistics for 2013 shows this decline is not limited to one service type:

> The total number of registered services decreased by 1.3 per cent from 10,099 at 31 December 2012 to 9,968 at 31 December 2013; 6,185 childminding and 3,783 daycare of children services. This was the result of a 1.4 per cent decrease in childminders, the first since 2008, and a 1.1 per cent decrease in daycare of children services, a continuing trend.

(Care Inspectorate, 2014: 5)

A very small increase is noted in out-of-school services. In policy terms, if we are expecting to see significant investment in 'childcare infrastructure', close attention needs to be paid to an apparent mismatch between ambition and evidence of current capacity.

Valuing women and the world of work

While an expansion of high quality childcare has the potential to support women's greater participation in the labour market, childcare itself is one of the sectors that is dominated by female workers. This raises a further concern – the value attached to women in the workforce, their terms and conditions and their place in the labour market.

This is a long-standing debate. The childcare sector is part of what is sometimes described as the 'five Cs' – caring, cleaning, cooking, clerical and checkout – all areas in which women dominate. In the 1990s 50 per cent of women in work were concentrated in these lower paid jobs (Boston, 2015: 417). In September 2013, the Office for National Statistics identified that women make up 87 per cent of those employed in the caring and leisure professions; 77 per cent of those in administrative and clerical jobs; and 63 per cent of those in retail and customer service (Office for National Statistics, 2013: 11).

This concentration of women employees in certain sectors is not new, nor are feminist concerns about women's over-representation in low paid and often unrewarding work. Over 100 years ago, Cicely Hamilton, an actress, writer and suffragist wrote: 'One wonders why it should be 'natural' in women to do so many disagreeable things. Does the average man really believe that she has an instinctive and unquenchable craving for all the unpleasant and unremunerative jobs?' (Hamilton, 1981 [1909]: 68).

Such work is also carried out, primarily by women, in the home. Whilst it is generally undervalued in terms of effort, skills and contribution to the economy, there are important historical examples of where government policy has demonstrated an awareness of the importance of caring, nutrition and cleanliness.

During World War I, as more and more women in the UK were required to work in the war industries, concern grew over the working conditions and the health of the workforce. Long hours and poor health were not good for productivity. In 1915 the Minister of Munitions set up a committee to look at the hours and health of women workers. In September 1916 it recommended a maximum 60 hour working week and the appointment of welfare supervisors to assist with accommodation, health, diet, travelling and cleanliness. These welfare supervisors were resented by many of the working women, and in 1917 the Joint Committee of Industrial Women's Organisations called for representation in the factories from amongst the women themselves, as best understanding their workplace concerns, and called for the recognition of a trade union in every workshop and factory (Boston, 2015: 125). This is one early but powerful example of women taking the lead in speaking up and promoting the role of collective bargaining and workplace representation.

The Department of Munitions also oversaw a range of improvements to working conditions including: the development of appropriate protective clothing for the women; provision of toilets, restrooms and first aid facilities; and pregnant women were to be taken off nightshifts and heavy work. Day nurseries were provided for women with children and those who did have to work nightshift were given an allowance to help with the costs of childcare at night (Boston, 2015: 126).

It is interesting to note how the government could put provisions in place quickly to keep women in work and in better health when the economy required it, yet how quickly the benefits can be forgotten or removed from workplace practice. As recently as 2012, an examination of the higher attrition rates amongst women graduates in Science, Technology, Engineering and Mathematics subjects suggests there could be some lessons to learn from the past. The study found that contributory factors included concerns about a culture in construction and engineering that did not invest in decent toilet and rest room provision, did not respect family when women became pregnant, nor respond with flexibility. Arguably, different kinds of responses, implemented in the past, could support better retention rates in a skilled workforce (Royal Society of Edinburgh, 2012).

The pay gap and work of equal value

Another crucial issue that employers, policy makers and the trade union movement have still to resolve is the question of equal pay. Historically, women were often employed on lower rates of pay, causing divisions amongst the workforce. Women were generally blamed for dragging pay down, as if in some way it was their responsibility rather than that of the employer or government. As far back as 1888 the Trade Union Congress (TUC) adopted a policy, proposed by delegate Clementina Black, that: 'it is desirable, in the interests of both men and women, that in trades where women do the same work as men, they shall receive equal treatment' (Women's Trade Union Provident League, 1889).

Similarly, when Margaret Irwin, Secretary to the first Scottish Trades Union Congress, held in Glasgow in 1897, spoke of the importance of universal suffrage, in connection with working conditions, it was agreed that:

> in view of the important legislative measures relating to the social and industrial conditions of women which are at present before the country, it is desirable as a matter of right to allow women a direct voice in the making of the laws which so seriously affect them, by extending the parliamentary franchise on the same footing as to men.
>
> (STUC, 1897)

In the early twentieth century, pay in many sectors remained at different rates for men, women and children and the trade unions often concentrated more on

making sure the women left the factories, workshops and yards for the men returning from the war, rather than on bargaining for the rate for the job in the men's
absence. Writing before the end of the World War I, Mark Starr, a miner in Wales,
made this enlightened observation in an education pamphlet on the economy:

> While women's entrance into industry may – especially if the male workers
> do not tackle the problem intelligently – at first have disastrous results, still,
> if she finally gains economic independence and becomes the true equal and
> comrade of man, undreamt of beneficial results will accrue.
>
> (Starr, 1919: vi)

The Second World War brought the same challenges: wage differentials were not
addressed, although a number of other policy interventions were made to better
support women coming into work. The government, once again, wanted women
with children to enter into the workforce. When Minister for Labour Ernie Bevin
MP announced this, he included a commitment for government to provide childcare facilities for working mothers (Boston, 2015: 96). Facilities were opened and a
wider interest was taken in women's lives. This included recognition that productivity would be higher if the workforce was healthier and a recognition that women
had more 'external' worries and responsibilities with shopping, cleaning and
cooking at home. This led to government taking an interest in travelling to work,
shopping hours, canteens and communal laundries, as well as nurseries. Debates
at contemporary TUC and STUC conferences showed a similar wide range of
concerns from women workers about health and safety, long hours, sanitation and
child welfare, as well as continuing the fight for equal pay.

After the Second World War, the expansion of the welfare state, the public
sector and the nationalisation of key industries, such as rail and energy, ensured the
maintenance of some of those workplace improvements in terms and conditions.
The 1927 Trade Union Act (which placed restrictions on the ability of trade unions
to strike and picket) was repealed in 1946.

However, despite the introduction of equal pay legislation in the 1970s, the
gender pay gap endures. Close the Gap (2014) identifies the pay gap as 11.5 per cent
(comparing men's full-time hourly earnings with women's full-time hourly earnings,
using the mean) or 32.4 per cent if the comparison is between men's full-time hourly
earnings and women's part-time hourly earnings.

In the public sector in Scotland there remain thousands of equal pay cases that
are still working through the employment tribunal system. Despite the strong cases
presented on behalf of women, their claims are being contested at large and arguably
unjustifiable cost to the public purse. The Scottish Government Cabinet Secretary
for Communities, Social Justice and Pensioners, Alex Neil MSP commented:

> In my own area, the Labour-controlled North Lanarkshire Council has
> spent thousands of pounds fighting the workers who are fighting for equal
> pay. That is outrageous ... I certainly think that maximum political pressure

should be applied to all the recalcitrant local authorities that are not playing fair with their own employees.

(Scottish Parliament, 2015)

The impact of the economic recession and the austerity policies being pursued by government will have a particular effect on women and their experience of the world of work. Jobs are being lost with the continuing decline in sectors dominated by male employees. But the total number of public sector jobs in Scotland continues to fall, affecting women more since they outnumber men in the public sector by a ratio of almost two to one (McKay et al., 2013). The trade union with the largest representation in local government, UNISON Scotland, highlights that Scotland's budget is being slashed by more than £6 billion in real terms, estimating 50,000 jobs have already been lost in Scotland and thousands more are predicted to go as the 2015–2016 local authority budget decisions are made (UNISON, 2014).

As local authority services are reduced, the effect is also felt in local communities and families. This has an impact on many women, faced with picking up the service gaps whilst also trying to remain in the labour market (TUC, 2015). This can limit the time available for paid work, but working part-time often gives the employer the choice over flexibility and cutting costs, rather than providing the worker with job security and good terms and conditions. The lack of choice about this for women at various stages in their working lives will only be compounded if public services are further reduced. Any debate on women and the labour market cannot take place in a vacuum, as public funding is cut from services such as transport, community centres, libraries, parks, lunch clubs, art galleries, sporting facilities and health and social care.

Women and the trade union movement

Trade unions have an important role in gaining and protecting rights of workers. The returns for the STUC annual Congress in 2015 show that women now make up over 50 per cent of the membership of affiliated trade unions. However, the majority of people in employment, both men and women, are not members of trade unions. In 2014, the percentage of the workforce holding trade union membership across the UK was 25.6 per cent (Department of Business Industry and Skills, 2015). In Scotland the proportion is slightly higher at 30.4 per cent. Across the UK, 55 per cent of union members were female in 2014, up from 45 per cent in 1995. For the thirteenth consecutive year, women were more likely than men to be a trade union member. The proportion of female employees who were in a trade union was around 28 per cent in 2014, compared with 22 per cent for male employees (Department of Business Industry and Skills, 2015: 5).

The progress that has been made on working conditions requires regular review as we look to the future. The protection provided by legislation such as the Health and Safety at Work Act (1974), the Equality Act (2010) and other regulations governing maternity and paternity leave may need greater public resources to ensure enforcement and improvement. However, following the election of the Conservative Government at Westminster in the UK General Election of May 2015, this looks unlikely. The proposals for the Trade Union Bill, working its way through the parliamentary process at the time of writing, will place further constraints on the rights to organise at work, and restrictions on facility time and other union matters, will reduce capacity for equality representatives and health and safety representatives to give voice to those who need it in the workplace, as Grahame Smith, General Secretary STUC, highlighted:

> It [the Bill] is about shifting the balance in industrial relations even more in favour of employers and will result in more insecurity at work, higher levels of inequality, and more workplace deaths and injuries. It will not be good for workers and it will not be good for employers or the economy.
>
> (STUC, 2015a)

The reduction of the working week was fought for long and hard, the eight-hour day campaign providing the key focus for the early days of organising into trade unions. Reducing paid work from 60 or 70 hours a week, to 35 or 40 hours a week, was widely understood to be of benefit to all working people and to society more generally. Employment is about much more than the hourly rate, with a wide range of terms and conditions to be taken into account including holidays, sick pay, maternity pay and parental leave, pensions and job security. Trade unions and employers have devised policies for better support of women experiencing domestic abuse, and bullying and sexual harassment are regarded more widely as unacceptable in the workplace.

Women's voices and representation

Such developments reflect women's greater influence in the workplace today. However, although often unreported, women have long been at the forefront of fighting for their own dignity and that of those they represent. Speaking of her time in the cotton mills of Lancashire, in the early 1890s, Selina Cooper described how women did not wear any sanitary protection, bleeding onto their petticoats and the factory floor and monthly menstruation was seen as an attractive time for the male manager to force himself onto the factory girls. Selina was nearly sacked for showing one of the girls how to make sanitary towels from rags (Liddington, 1984: 53).

The records of STUC Women's Conferences show the struggles for decency, health protection and representation in public and political life continued through-out the twentieth century. Conference debates over the years include inadequate maternity provision in hospitals, equal pay, housing, health and safety, women as Justices of the Peace, discrimination against part-time workers and pensions.

Working together on feminist economics

Reflecting women's involvement in the broad range of trade union concerns, education has been a consistent priority for trade unions. Interestingly, the STUC Women's Committee annual reports include its training schools for women representatives and the topics reflect a broad range of concerns from trade union structures and legislation (STUC, 1966, 1973) to Equal Opportunities and the impact of local government reorganisation on trade union organisation, representation and negotiation (STUC, 1974).

That tradition of combining education with organisation through the STUC Women's structures continues today and is the context in which joint work was developed with Ailsa McKay and WiSE. There was a common interest in encouraging women to engage with economics and public finance by making them more accessible. This included an interest in sharing knowledge and understanding about the operation, language and influences of economics that led to two successful joint STUC/WiSE training Schools held in Glasgow which Ailsa led and another in May 2015.

The STUC, in working with Ailsa McKay, sought to bring together our workplace experiences with the analysis and critique that feminist economics encourages. There are questions to be asked and questions to be answered, if we are to make further progress on the real value of women's contribution to society to social and economic analysis. Far more radical solutions are needed, alongside honesty in addressing what has, and has not, worked in the past.

Ailsa gave our work together high priority. Her enthusiasm and open approach was infectious, and the STUC Schools in September 2012 and March 2014 reflected a growing confidence amongst the trade union women who participated. Sadly the 2014 STUC Women's Weekend School turned out to be the last weekend of Ailsa's life. Her powerful and passionate contribution to that school is remembered by all who were present, as these quotes from participants at the 2014 Weekend School show (STUC, 2014).

> I have always known there was gender inequality but I didn't fully realise just how bad it was or how far back it went. This weekend has spurred me on to help change things.
>
> I've learned the importance of speaking up, and giving other women a hand up the ladder.
>
> The course has given me confidence to say: I count and so do my values.

In May 2015, Professor Diane Elson, University of Essex and UK Women's Budget Group, along with Angela O'Hagan and Morag Gillespie of WiSE and Glasgow Caledonian University, and Val Wright from Glasgow University, worked with the STUC Women's Committee to deliver the third weekend School on 'Women Understanding the Economy'.

Women from a wide range of trade unions, workplaces and different parts of Scotland came together to learn from the tutors and each other, and share their experiences. We took strength from the women who led the rent strikes during World War I, the struggles then and now for political representation and for investment in child and women's health, considered 'Plan F' as an alternative comment on and strategy for budget decisions of governments today (Women's Budget Group, 2015) and learned from Marilyn Waring's experiences in New Zealand. Suggestions from the women participants for the way ahead included: increased provision of public sector housing, a Citizen's Basic Income, a significant increase in wages in the care sectors, setting the 'rate for the job' through national collective bargaining, and a 'whole life cycle' approach to employment. Evaluations (STUC, 2015b) reinforced why women must engage more closely with economics:

> Informative, educational, thought provoking, action provoking. The subjects were ones that I have not had debates about before in any union forum, but ones that I can now take back.
>
> This school was a real eye opener for me.
>
> Has completely transformed my understanding of economics. It's so encouraging to see that it can be what it should be – about people and for communities.

Conclusions

Recognising the contribution that women make to the economy and to society through paid and unpaid work will bring benefits for all. Policies that perpetuate inequality and discrimination will not. The women and men who spoke up in the past for a fairer world had their eyes on the future. Ailsa McKay was doing the same, working across disciplines and communities, with all who shared that confidence in our collective ability to make a real difference.

Ailsa's legacy is far reaching, and I know that all the members of the STUC Women's Committee are proud to be able to continue to ground her work in the lived experiences of women in Scotland today, strengthening women's voices for change.

References

Boston, S. (2015). *Women Workers and the Trade Unions*. Revised edition. London: Lawrence and Wishart Limited.

Campbell, J., Elson, D. and McKay, A. (2013). *The Economic Case for Investing in High-Quality Childcare and Early Years Education*. WiSE Briefing Sheet, November. Glasgow: Glasgow Caledonian University. [Online] Available from: www.gcu.ac.uk/media/WiSEBriefingPaperNov13.pdf (accessed 6 July 2015).

Care Inspectorate (2014). *Childcare Statistics 2013*. [Online] Available from: www.careinspectorate.com/images/documents/1423/Childcare_Statistics_2013.pdf (accessed 1 September 2015).

Close the Gap (2014). *Statistics – the Pay Gap*. [Online] Available from: www.closethegap. org.uk/content/gap-statistics/ (accessed 6 July 2015).

Commission for Childcare Reform (2015). *Meeting Scotland's Childcare Challenge: The Report of the Commission for Childcare Reform*. Edinburgh: Children in Scotland. [Online] Available from: www.childreninscotland.org.uk/sites/default/files/FinalChildcareCommission ReportJune2015.pdf (accessed 25 August 2015).

Department of Business Industry and Skills (2015). *Trade Union Membership 2014: Statistical Bulletin*. [Online] Available from: www.gov.uk/government/statistics/trade-union-sta-tistics-2014 (accessed 25 August 2015).

Employability in Scotland (2015a). *Women's Employment Summit – 12 September 2012*. [Online] Available from: www.employabilityinscotland.com/key-clients/women-and-work/womens-employment-summit-12-september-2012 (accessed 23 July 2015).

Employability in Scotland (2015b). *Strategic Group on Women and Work*. [Online] Available from: www.employabilityinscotland.com/key-clients/women-and-work/strategic-group-on-women-and-work/ (accessed 23 July 2015).

Gillespie, G. and Khan, U. (2016). 'Integrating economic and social policy: childcare – a transformational policy?' In Campbell, J. and Gillespie, M. (eds) *Feminist Economics and Public Policy: Reflections on the Work and Impact of Ailsa McKay*. Abingdon: Routledge, pp. 94–111.

Hamilton, C. (1981 [1909]). *Marriage as a Trade*. London: The Women's Press.

Liddington, J. (1984). *The Life and Times of a Respectable Rebel: Selina Cooper (1864–1946)*. London: Virago.

McKay, A., Fitzgerald, R., O'Hagan, A. and Gillespie, M. (2002). 'Scotland: using political change to advance gender issues'. In Budlender, D. and Hewitt G. (eds) *Gender Budgets Make More Cents*. London: Commonwealth Secretariat, pp. 133–151.

McKay, A., Thomson, E. and Ross, S. (2013). *Where Are Women in Scotland's labour Market?* WiSE Briefing Sheet, January. Glasgow: Glasgow Caledonian University. [Online] Available from: www.gcu.ac.uk/media/gcalwebv2/theuniversity/centresprojects/wise/A4%20WiSE%20Briefing%20Paper_Jan%2013.pdf (accessed 26 August 2015).

McIvor, A., (2004). 'Women and work in twentieth century Scotland'. In Dickson, A. and Treble, J.H. (eds) *People and Society in Scotland Vol III*. Edinburgh: John Donald, imprint of Birlinn Limited.

Office for National Statistics (2013). *Full Report – Women in the Labour Market*. London: ONS.

Royal Society of Edinburgh (2012). *Tapping All Our Talents. Women in Science, Technology, Engineering, and Mathematics: A Strategy for Scotland*. Edinburgh: RSE.

Scottish Government (2013). *Council of Economic Advisers – Fourth Meeting – 30 August 2013*. [Online] Available from: www.gov.scot/Topics/Economy/Council-Economic-Advisers/Meetings/30-08-2013 (accessed 23 July 2015).

Scottish Government (2014). *Early Learning and Childcare Key Trends*. Web page, updated December 2014. [Online] Available from: www.gov.scot/Topics/Statistics/Browse/Children/TrendNursery (accessed 28 June 2015).

Scottish Government (2015). *Maximising Economic Opportunities for Women in Scotland*. [Online] Available from: www.gov.scot/Publications/2015/03/2036 (accessed 23 August 2015).

Scottish Government and STUC (2015). *SG/ STUC Memorandum of Understanding*. Edinburgh: Scottish Government. [Online] Available from: www.gov.scot/Publications/2015/05/7975 (accessed 23 July 2015).

Scottish Parliament (2015). *Official Report 4 February 2015 Portfolio Question Time*. [Online]

Available from: www.scottish.parliament.uk/parliamentarybusiness/report.aspx?r=97
64&i=89427 (accessed 23 August 2015).

STUC (1897). *Report of the Inaugural Conference.* Glasgow: STUC archives, Glasgow
Caledonian University.

STUC (1966). *Report of the STUC Women's Conference 1966.* STUC Archive. Glasgow:
Glasgow Caledonian University.

STUC (1973). *Report of the STUC Women's Conference 1973.* STUC Archive. Glasgow:
Glasgow Caledonian University.

STUC (1974). *Report of the STUC Women's Conference 1974.* STUC Archive. Glasgow:
Glasgow Caledonian University.

STUC (2014). Evaluation forms returned by delegates at the STUC/WiSE Women's
Weekend School, March 2014, unpublished. Glasgow: STUC.

STUC (2015a). *STUC on the Trade Union Bill.* News release. 15 July [Online] Available
from: www.stuc.org.uk/news/1177/stuc-on-the-trade-union-bill (accessed 12/09/15).

STUC (2015b). Evaluation forms returned by delegates at the STUC/ WiSE Women's
Weekend School Cumbernauld, May 2015, unpublished. Glasgow: STUC.

Scottish Universities Insight Institute (2013). *Constitutional Futures: Gender Equality Matters
in a New Scotland.* [Online] Available from: www.scottishinsight.ac.uk/Programmes/
Programmes20122013/Constitutionalfutures.aspx (accessed 23 July 2015).

Siraj, I. and Kingston D. (2015). *An Independent Review of the Scottish Early Learning and
Childcare (ELC) Workforce and Out of School Care (OSC) Workforce.* Edinburgh: Scottish
Government.

Starr, M. (1919). *A Worker Looks at History.* Third edition. London: The Plebs League.

Sturgeon, N. (2014). *Nicola Sturgeon Address to SNP Conference.* [Online] Available from:
www.snp.org/media-centre/news/2014/nov/nicola-sturgeon-address-snp-conference
(accessed 22 June 2015).

TUC (2015). *The Impact on Women of Recession and Austerity.* [Online] Available from: www.
tuc.org.uk/economic-issues/equality-issues/gender-equality/equal-pay/impact-wom-
en-recession-and-austerity (accessed 12 September 2015).

UNISON (2014). *The Cuts Don't Work – The Impact of 'Austerity' on Scotland's Public Services.*
Glasgow: UNISON Scotland's Bargaining and Campaigns Team.

Women's Budget Group (2015). *Plan F: A Feminist Economic Strategy for a Caring and sustainable Economy.* [Online] Available from: http://wbg.org.uk/wp-content/uploads/2015/02/
PLAN-F-2015.pdf (accessed 12 September 2015).

Women's Trade Union Provident League (1889). *Annual Report.* Cited in Boston, S. (2015).
Women Workers and the Trade Unions. Revised edition. London: Lawrence and Wishart
Limited.

PART IV
Citizen's Basic Income

14

ON JUSTIFYING A CITIZEN'S BASIC INCOME

Chris Pierson

Ailsa McKay's *Future of Social Security Policy* (McKay, 2005) is an impassioned call to promote the idea of a Citizen's Basic Income (CBI), grounded in a feminist political economy. In Chapters 5 and 6, she reviews some of the most important historical examples of the case made for a guaranteed basic income or social dividend (or some close equivalent). She traces these arguments back through the ideas of the Guild Socialists and the Social Credit movement, and the unconventional economics of Henry George, to a foundational moment in Tom Paine's Agrarian Justice (1899 [1797]), first published in the feverishly radical 1790s. In this she follows the most celebrated, and sophisticated contemporary advocate of a Basic Income, Philippe van Parijs, whose 1995 book, *Real Freedom for All*, established at length the philosophical case for the maximum feasible basic income (van Parijs, 1995). Recognising in van Parijs, 'the most prominent of theorists within the contemporary CBI literature', she goes on to review his position, at some length, in Chapter Seven (McKay, 2005: 196). Ailsa's core insight here is that a universal CBI may secure the interests of women in a way that more traditional welfare state policies have consistently failed to do. A CBI is oriented around lives which are not so narrowly 'economic' as the mainstream economics, of which Ailsa was such a determined critic, supposes. In particular, a CBI may be better suited to the multi-dimensional, lived experiences of women that a feminist political economy like Ailsa's helps to disclose. In practice, feminist writers have taken a range of views of the consequences of a CBI for women, arguing that it may have a downside as well as an upside; (see, for example, the contributions of Ann Withorn, Ann Orloff, Ingrid Robeyns, Tony Fitzpatrick, Carole Pateman, Anne Alstott, as well as Ailsa McKay in Widerquist et al., 2009). Ailsa was clearly persuaded that it had a real potential to improve the lives of women.

As we have seen, in the *Future of Social Security Policy*, Ailsa traces the idea of some sort of social dividend back to Tom Paine writing in the 1790s. But there is in fact a much older, critical tradition of thinking about our claims to an income (and to private property) which may yield a still stronger claim to a basic income and, to this extent, give still more force to Ailsa's case. Often this much older discourse, steeped in patriarchal values and a Christian ontology, systematically excluded women. But it is still a resource which is worth exploring, and perhaps selectively appropriating, not least for what it tells us about the (quite provisional) relationship between labour and property, a provisionality that both the modern world and most of its economists have forgotten. I will suggest that it has some very real consequences for our thinking about labour, property and income in the here and now – not least in justifying an extensive Citizen's Basic Income. In fact, there are two arguments to present here. One is very old, is deeply inscribed in Christian-Catholic social theory and is perhaps best represented in the work of Thomas Aquinas. The other is modern and secular and has its best (if unknowing and probably unwilling) representative in David Hume. The core of both sets of ideas is disarmingly simple.

The right to live

Although Aquinas is often seen as a foundational figure for later Christian social and political theory, he also stands at the end of a millennium-long tradition of theorising about Christianity's engagement with what we might call the secular world (though that's not a good term for the mundane part of an order saturated with religious values). As is well known, Jesus's own reported teaching on property and wealth was deeply ambiguous, as was the early experience of the church (living in community at Jerusalem). And this is reflected in one enduring tradition of Christian theorising about private and collective property: Many of the earliest Christian sources are explicitly hostile to wealth and private property. Here's the Preaching of Peter (an early second century source):

> God has given all things to all of his creation. Understand then, you rich, that you ought to minister, for you have received more than you yourselves need. Learn that others lack the things you have in superfluity. Be ashamed to keep things that belong to others. Imitate the fairness of God, and no man will be poor.
>
> (Peter, 2005 [100–150CE]: 22–24)

And this sensibility can be found across the late ancient and the medieval worlds: from St Ambrose, Bishop of Milan at the time of Augustine's arrival in the city in the fourth century, to the followers of St Francis in the fourteenth. Here's Ambrose:

> How far, O ye rich, do you push your mad desires? Shall ye alone dwell upon the earth? Why do you cast out your consort in nature and claim for yourselves the possession of nature? The earth was made in common for all, both rich and poor.
>
> (Ambrose, 1927 [c.387], 47).

And St Francis:

> The Rule and life of the friars is to live in obedience, in chastity and without property. We should have no more use or regard for money in any of its forms than for dust. The friars should be delighted to follow the lowliness and poverty of our Lord Jesus Christ, remembering that of the whole world we must own nothing.
>
> (The Rule of St Francis cited in Habig, 1973)

But at least from the dissemination of Clement of Alexandria's late second-century tract, '*Who is the rich man that shall be saved?*' (1994 [c180–210CE]), answering Jesus's seemingly rhetorical question in the case of the rich young man encountered in the gospels, the orthodox position of the church was to make its peace with private property. Here the definitive authority was Augustine. In the beginning, the world was granted to humankind in common. (This is a commonplace in the literature of property that persists right through to John Locke and beyond.) But in the fallen world of the City of Men, where the righteous must co-exist with the damned, we need private property (just as we need the state, the law and the executioner) to keep the peace. There is nothing especially good or righteous about the possession of property – in fact, it is morally neutral. Those who have it should use it to do good works but it is avarice not the possession of wealth that is a sin. Alongside this went an insistence that the possession of private property was an aspect of the civil (rather than divine) law. It was kings and emperors, rather than God himself directly, who allocated title to land and goods. Private property was not strongly associated with *desert* and title was contingent, even if recognising its integrity was essential to the really good end, which, in this world, was keeping the peace. Certainly, no one had a *natural* right to what they possessed – whether through labour or any other title (on Augustine on property, see Pierson, 2013: 71–74).

The right of necessity

If we leap forward to the work of Thomas Aquinas (in the middle of the twelfth century), we again find reservations about the standing of private property. As is well known, Aquinas's teaching can be understood as an attempt to reconcile the philosophy of Aristotle (always referred to as the philosopher by Aquinas) with the theology of the Christian church, all within the rubric of the recently rediscovered Roman Law. Aquinas rehearses Aristotle's largely practical reasons for favouring private ownership (principally arguments about maximising productivity and minimising violent conflict) but also the ancient Greek's insistence that generally property should be 'common in use'. According to Aquinas, private property is not itself a part of the natural law – and the world had originally been granted in common to all humanity – but it is not against the natural law. It is rather 'an addition to natural right devised by human reason':

The human will can make anything just by common agreement provided that the thing in question has nothing about it which is repugnant in itself to natural justice; and it is in matters of this kind that positive right has its place.
(Aquinas, 2006 [1265–1274], *Summa Theologiae*, II–II q57 a2 ad2)

Aquinas describes external things in two different ways. 'With regard to their nature', they belong to God and the divine will; 'with regard to the use of them', God has ceded to man 'a natural dominion over external things' (Summa Theologiae, II–II q66 a1 responsio). The question that follows immediately is 'whether it is lawful for anyone to possess something as his own'. Here again, Aquinas offers a two-fold distinction:

Two things pertain to man with regard to external things. One is the power to procure and dispose of them; and, in this regard, it is lawful for man to possess property ... The other thing which pertains to man with regard to external things is their use. In this respect, man ought to hold external things not as his own, but as common: that is, in such a way that he is ready to share them with others *in the event of need*.
(*Summa Theologiae*, II–II q66 a2 *responsio*; emphasis added)

The claims of private property are pragmatic and provisional. They derive much more from the overall social good that they generate than from the authenticity of any individual's claim:

For there is no reason why a piece of land considered simply as such should belong to one man rather than another; but considered with respect to how best to cultivate the land and make peaceable use of it, it has a certain commensuration to be the property of one man rather than another, as the Philosopher shows at *Politics II*.
(*Summa Theologiae*, II–II Q57 a3 *responsio*)

When the Church Fathers had insisted upon common ownership (and here Aquinas cites Basil and Ambrose) they were referring to the requirement for community of use and this remains. Thus, 'a rich man does not act unlawfully if he anticipates someone in taking possession of something which was originally common property but then shares it with others; but he sins if he excludes others indiscriminately from use of it'. In response to Ambrose's injunction 'let no man call his own that which is common', Aquinas insists that the Bishop of Milan is referring (only) to 'ownership with regard to use'. That is why Ambrose can add an insistence that 'he who spends too much is a robber' (*Summa Theologiae*, II–II q66 a2 ad.2 and ad.3).

Private property is then lawful and good (in so far as it contributes to the common good and human flourishing). It is avarice, not the possession of riches, which is a sin. Nonetheless this yields to the owner a title which is strictly limited. In the end, real *dominium* lies with God and possessions must be used in ways that are consistent with his will. Use remains common (however obscure and constrained this claim may be). The (unlimited) accumulation of riches is not, in itself, a legitimate end. There may be differences of wealth (given that Aquinas believes that different stations in life require different resources for their proper and normal support) but the function of wealth is principally to serve the common good (after all, this is why God placed the rest of his creation at the service of humankind in general). Liberality – generosity with one's goods – is a requirement. It does not (normally) place a justiciable right in the hands of the poor but it is nonetheless a requirement rather than a recommendation that those who have superfluous goods should share them with the less fortunate. *In extremis*, as Aquinas most famously argued, all is common and taking the property of another under these circumstances is not theft. More than this, 'whatever anyone has in superabundance is due under the natural law to the poor for succour'. In cases of dire necessity, 'someone can also take another's property secretly in order to succour his neighbour in need' and this without committing the sin of theft (*Summa Theologiae*, II–II q66 a7 ad.3). The essence of the late medieval position that Aquinas articulated was this: private ownership was a legitimate 'addition' to the natural law – because it made for social peace and better enabled men to meet God's command to 'be fruitful and multiply'. But this was always qualified by the insistence that, in times of dire need, the prior requirement of commonality (and to preserve life) re-asserted itself. God did not will that any should perish because of the exclusivity of private ownership. Private property was a derivative or secondary component of the natural law. It was welcomed or tolerated in so far as it enabled the prior (in time and importance) requirement that mankind should 'be fruitful, and multiply'. Where the private property regime did not serve this purpose – of allowing all to flourish – its legitimacy could be challenged – to the point where *taking from the rich to give to the poor was not theft*.

The radical contingency of private property

The second and more unlikely source for thinking differently about the sources of a basic income I take from the work of David Hume. Hume's own politics are generally regarded as more or less conservative but Hume was, at least epistemologically, a radical and it is possible to give a left-Humean reading of his work on justice and property (which turn out to be more or less the same thing).

Hume argues that justice is an artificial virtue and that property is the product of convention. Given that the typical qualities of the human mind are '*selfishness* and *limited generosity*', neither self-interest nor benevolence (public or private) can provide the requisite 'natural' motive to justice. More than this, if we imagine (as sometimes the poets have done) circumstances of comparative abundance or, indeed, of extreme scarcity, justice would no longer have any meaning. Similarly, if we imagine human nature so transformed that every individual treated the interests of every other as equal to his own, justice would again have no work to do. It follows 'that 'tis only from the selfishness and confin'd generosity of man, along with the scanty provision nature has made for his wants, that justice derives its origins' (Hume 2000 [1739–1740]: 317–318, 3.2.2).

So, it is from the contingent (but, as it happens, more or less universal) circumstances of the human condition that the need for justice (and property) arises. Men and women are naturally sociable; indeed, in the first instance human society arises from the instinctual attraction of the sexes and their procreation. Given our natures and our needs, we are driven towards society. But, at the same time, our natures (and our passions) do not naturally make us fit for a social life beyond the immediate confines of our family (and its affections) and 'rude and savage men' would have no conception of justice or respect for property. But, in time, men come to recognise both the 'infinite advantages' to be derived from living in an extended society and that the 'principal disturbance' in society arises from external goods, our passion for them and 'their looseness and easy transition from one person to another' (Hume 2000: 314, 3.2.2). But humankind is 'an inventive species' and in time (and largely through a mixture of experiment and experience), men find a way to deal with the turbulence occasioned by the instability of external goods and thus secure more fully the advantages of social life. To this end, they establish: 'A convention enter'd into by all the members of the society to bestow stability on the possession of those external goods, and leave every one in the peaceable enjoyment of what he may acquire by his fortune and industry' (Hume 2000: 314, 3.2.2).

This convention for 'stability of possession' is not a surrender of our interests nor does it require a transformation in our natures. Hume insists that the passion for acquiring goods and possessions for ourselves and our friends is 'insatiable, perpetual, universal, and directly destructive of society'. But the convention that secures respect for justice (which, in Hume's account, is in substance a respect for the property of others) is, in fact, a better means of securing our selfish interests while coincidentally providing the same assurance (and benefits) to all others. The passion for possession is: 'much better satisfy'd by its restraint, than by its liberty ... by preserving society, we make much greater advances in the acquiring possessions, than in the solitary and forlorn condition, which must follow upon violence and universal licence' (Hume 2000: 316, 3.2.2).

It is of the essence of the rules of justice that possession should be *stable*. Our over-riding concern with stability of possession means that we shall sometimes be obliged to make decisions in individual cases that are the opposite of those which benevolence or indeed immediate utility would suggest (for example, transferring the resources of the impoverished but worthy head of household to the feckless but wealthy bachelor or the mean-spirited and childless miser where this is what the rules of ownership dictate). In these circumstances, the greater utility of maintaining expectations of stability of possession trumps the wish to secure what utility and decency would seem to require in the particular case.

In one sense, Hume's approach is profoundly radical. He makes all property claims conventional. There is no question of an original donation from God (or anyone else). No one has, by nature, any more claim to the earth's resources than any other. Natural law (of any more traditional kind) does not ground anyone's claims to property. Hume is aware of this radical conventionalism – but he is not much worried by it. The crucial thing is that property should be stable (however it is first allocated). What, then, should this first (and potentially crucial) allocation be? Again, Hume is sanguine. His catalogue of property-creating actions draws very heavily on the categories of the Roman Law, but always with a recognition that it is the existence of reliable rules rather than the content of these rules that matters – and that while certain rules suggest themselves to the human imagination, and in this sense they are 'natural', there are no rules in nature for the allocation of property titles to particular individuals. Imagining a society in which people had landed upon the idea of property but had yet to allocate its possessions, Hume insists that 'this difficulty will not long detain them': 'It must immediately occur, as the most natural expedient, that every one continue to enjoy what he is at present master of, and that property or constant possession be conjoin'd to the immediate possession' (Hume 2000: 323, 3.2.3).

This general rule for the 'assignment of property to the present possessor' is described as 'natural' but, as the extensive footnotes which fill up the rest of this chapter of the *Treatise* would suggest, determining what actually counts as possession is very far from straightforward. And Hume himself suggests that the rules which determine who gets what are 'principally fixed by the imagination, or the more frivolous properties of our thought and conception'. In the end, for Hume, it does not very much matter what this distribution is, since what is really important about justice is that property is stable and that the property regime secures the greater public interest.

Hume's position is conservative because he takes as his key distributive principle that things should remain distributed as they are since, he supposes, the fact that eighteenth-century commercial life in Edinburgh goes on well enough shows that the existing property regime 'works'. Redistribution is pernicious, not because it takes away that to which property-holders are properly entitled (through labour or conquest or whatever; this is largely a matter of contingency) but because the property regime is underpinned by *stability of possession*. Lacking this, all the advantages of a private property regime are vulnerable to change.

At face value, this is a profoundly conservative argument. No redistributive principle can have any purchase upon the present distribution of property because what justifies this distribution is not something about the distribution itself, or about its origins, but simply that it is the distribution which corresponds to a convention upholding the security and stability of property, in which we all have an interest (whether a present property-holder or not) and which proves its value just by being there. But its conservatism comes at a high price. Justice and the allocation of property are artificial and conventional. The rich do not deserve their wealth, nor the poor their penury. The sole defence of the present order ('warts and all') is that it works. But what if we judge that it does not work (say, it does not enable people to flourish?) And what if utility seems to point towards a quite different distribution?

Utility points to equality

This was the problem that Jeremy Bentham faced barely half a century later. Bentham's view of property is also strictly conventional. Property itself is entirely a product of the law: 'property and law are born together and must die together. Before the laws, there was no property: take away the laws, all property ceases' (Bentham 1962 [1838]: 309).

He also has no interest in the history of present property titles – since this has nothing to do with their justification. Bentham's benchmark is utility: 'the greatest good of the greatest number'. Bentham's account is future-focused and the utility to which he makes appeal is not so much the present value or usefulness of any property as it is the present enjoyment of the prospect of continuing (and secure) possession. This is the logic of 'pleasure and pain by anticipation'. Property is best understood as 'an established expectation', an expectation established by the body of laws, which only the laws can guarantee and which it is therefore the duty of the law-maker to respect. Bentham recognises that the principle of utility points towards equality of enjoyment. Thus: *'the more nearly the actual proportion* [of wealth] *approaches to equality, the greater will be the total mass of happiness'* and 'no reason can be assigned why the law should seek to give one man more than another' (Bentham, 1962: 305, 302).

Thus, 'equality may be fostered, both by protecting it where it exists, and by seeking to produce it where it does not exist' (Bentham, 1962: 302). All of which seems clear enough. But, for a whole series of countervailing reasons (grounded in the 'benevolent genius' of security), redistribution in favour of greater equality is almost never justified in Bentham's account (Bentham, 1962: 311). For one thing, it is only the spur of differential possession that has motivated men to labour and to graft and the overall improvement in the production of wealth which this has brought about is something which is shared (albeit unequally) by both rich and poor. Those at the bottom of the distribution are not discouraged by looking at the top (their focus is much closer to home) and they too can enjoy the pleasure that comes from *hoping* that their lot may improve. In this way, 'the laws contribute as much to the happiness of the cottage, as to the security of the palace' (Bentham, 1962: 309).

Equality is, in any case, radically unstable and, as soon as it is secured, it is in the process of being unseated:

> If all property were to be equally divided, the certain and immediate con-
> sequence would be, that there would soon be nothing more to divide.
> Everything would be speedily destroyed. Those who had hoped to be
> favoured by the division, would not suffer less than those at whose expense it
> would be made. If the condition of the industrious were not better than the
> condition of the idle, there would be no reason for being industrious.
>
> (Bentham, 1962: 303)

All attempts to equalise outcomes will have a deleterious impact way beyond the actual redistribution they may attain. Since the most important source of happiness is the *expectation* of the security of future possession, even the threat of future redistribution is damaging to present enjoyment. So to the 'pain of loss', we must add 'the fear of loss' (Bentham, 1962: 310). Even the mildest redistribution will raise the prospect of further intervention and thus undermine both the pleasure and the incentive effects of current property inequalities. And this effect is amplified by Bentham's insistence that we all feel a loss much more keenly than we value a gain – so that whatever is reallocated will always bring less pleasure than it occasions pain (though this is, of course, countermanded by the argument from marginal utility, which makes the pound gained by the poor worth 'more' than the pound lost by the rich). Bentham's conclusion is clear: 'when security and equality are in opposition, there should be no hesitation: equality should give way' (Bentham, 1962: 311).

In practice, this means that we should normally leave the property order just the way it is, however it came to be the way it is and irrespective of how unequal this may be. Indeed, even if it institutionalises slavery!

Both Hume and Bentham end up endorsing the status quo (although Bentham does allow for some element of redistribution at the point of inheritance, when the property-holder's expectations can no longer be disappointed). But we are not required to go with them the extra mile that carries them from contingency and utility and/or equality towards the *status quo*. We may simply say, and surely with as much conviction as David Hume or Jeremy Bentham, *this* property order does *not* work. If utility points towards equality and the justification of the property regime is conventional (rather than historical or rights-based), it might well appear that we have a lot of space to re-design our property order in a way which prioritises equality, subject only to whatever practical constraints our own agreed version of the maximin principle requires (see, for example, Rawls, 1971 or van Parijs, 1995).

A 'progressive property'

To give some substance to this claim, I turn finally to a contemporary source. In 2009, four senior law professors in the US published in the *Cornell Law Review* what was in effect a manifesto calling for a commitment to 'progressive property'. Amongst those signing up was Laura Underkuffler, law professor at Cornell. She insists: 'We are compelled to consider the distributive consequences of property laws not because they are some kind of supplementary afterthought, but because they are inseparable from the core idea of property' (Underkuffler, 2014: 152).

A similar argument is made by another signatory, Joseph Singer, law professor at Harvard. Singer has a long track record of taking a 'social relations' approach to property law. That is he rejects all those accounts which hold that we are property-holders prior to our engagement with society or that people have a right to inherit or that first possession or our labour-power gives us some incontestable claim to possess (in the face of the need of others). In a recent paper, he writes:

> Property is more than the law of things; property is the law of democracy.
> Property law shapes social relations, and because we live in a free and demo-
> cratic society that aspires to treat each person with equal concern and respect,
> a crucial function of property law is to interpret what that means.
>
> (Singer, 2014: 1291)

'Property is a *system* and not just an individual entitlement', he insists. If we live in
a democracy that claims that all are to be treated with 'equal concern and respect',
this 'requires property to be distributed in a manner that gives each and every
person a place where she is entitled to be and sufficient resources so that she is able
to sustain life and to pursue happiness' (Singer, 2014: 1326).

This commitment is rehearsed in the 'progressive property' manifesto:

> 4. Property confers power. It allocates scarce resources that are necessary
>   for human life, development, and dignity. Because of the equal value
>   of each human being, property laws should promote the ability of each
>   person to obtain the material resources necessary for full social and polit-
>   ical participation.
> 5. Property enables and shapes community life. Property law can render
>   relationships within communities either exploitative and humiliating or
>   liberating and ennobling. Property law should establish the framework
>   for a kind of social life appropriate to a free and democratic society.
>
> (Alexander et al., 2009: 72–73)

Conclusion

Our very short survey of the very long history of property thinking in the Latin
West reveals some quite surprising claims: that the right to live is prior to the right
to property (the latter is only there to secure the former); that our claims to (superfluous) private property must yield in the face of the needs of others; that the allocation of property in societies like ours is contingent, and in its origins grounded in
'force and fraud'; that our needs and natures suggest that the best property regime
is one in which all are regarded as equal. All of these historical claims are potentially
important for those who are seeking to make out the case for a very different sort
of income distribution now.

But I want to finish by focusing more specifically on the support that a 'progressive property' approach may give to the kind of CBI that Ailsa wanted to
promote. Recall the formulation from the 'Progressive Property Manifesto' that
our property arrangements should 'give each and every person a place where she is
entitled to be and sufficient resources so that she is able to sustain life and to pursue
happiness'. The point is that, upon such an account, a Citizen's Basic Income is
not an 'add-on' to (or for some critics, a subtraction from) our legitimately held
private property (including income from labour or investment). It is part of what it
means to live in a liberal democracy that can claim to be legitimate. It is a part of a

property order which we all choose, as we must, since there is no 'given' property order. For Singer, property is 'the law of democracy'. In the end, how we choose and how much we choose to allocate, and to whom, are questions that are open to democratic contest and collective determination.

I hope that Ailsa McKay might have liked that democratic argument too!

References

Alexander, G.S., Penalver, E.M., Singer, J.W. and Underkuffler, L.S. (2009). 'A statement of progressive property'. *Cornell Law Review*, 94: 742–743.

Aquinas (2006 [1265–1274]). *Summa Theologiae*. Cambridge: Cambridge University Press.

Ambrose (1927 [c387]). *De Nabuthae* (trans. M.R.P. McGuire). Washington D.C.: Catholic University of America.

Bentham, J. (1962 [1838]). 'Principles of the civil code'. *Complete Works (Volume One)*. Edinburgh: Tait.

Clement of Alexandria (1994 [c180–210CE]). 'Who is the rich man that shall be saved?' In P. Schaff (ed.) *Ante-Nicene Fathers: Volume 2: Fathers of the Second Century*. Grand Rapids, Michigan: CCEL, pp. 1239–1263.

Habig, M.A. (ed.) (1973). *St Francis of Assisi: Writings and Early Biographies*. London: SPCK.

Hume, D. (2000 [1739/1740]). *A Treatise of Human Nature*. Oxford: Oxford University Press.

McKay, A. (2005). *Future of Social Security Policy: Women, Work and a Citizens' Basic Income*. Abingdon: Routledge.

Paine, T. (1899 [1797]). 'Agrarian justice'. In Conway M.D. (ed.) *The Writings of Thomas Paine: Volume 3*. London: Putnam, pp. 322–344.

Peter (2005 [100–150CE]). 'The preaching of Peter'. In Elliot, J.K. (ed.) *The Apochryphal New Testament* (trans. M.R. James). Oxford: Oxford University Press, pp. 22–24.

Pierson, C. (2013). *Just Property: A History in the Latin West: Volume One*. Oxford: Oxford University Press.

Rawls, J. (1971). *A Theory of Justice*. Oxford: Oxford University Press.

Singer, J. (2014). 'Property as the law of democracy.' *Duke Law Journal*, 63: 1286–1335.

Underkuffler, L. (2014). 'A theoretical approach: the lens of progressive property'. *Property Law Review*, 3(3): 152–160.

Van Parijs, P. (1995). *Real Freedom for All: What (If Anything) Can Justify Capitalism?* Oxford: Oxford University Press.

Widerquist, K., Noguera, J.A., Vanderborght, Y. and De Wispelaere, J. (eds) (2009). *Basic Income: An Anthology of Contemporary Research*. London: Wiley-Blackwell.

15

A CITIZEN'S BASIC INCOME AND ITS IMPLICATIONS

Annie Miller

Introduction

On 15 January 2014, I had the privilege of sharing a platform with Ailsa McKay for a seminar and round-table discussion at the Scottish Parliament, hosted by Jim Eadie, Member of the Scottish Parliament. Ailsa's was the voice of Citizen's Basic Income (CBI) in Scotland until her untimely death. She spoke first, creating a vision of what a CBI could do to transform our society. She spoke inspiringly and with passion, drawing on the philosophical and political arguments about why we should explore the concept of, and eventually implement, a CBI in Scotland. I followed up with the more mundane, but equally necessary, facts and figures to demonstrate the economic feasibility of a CBI scheme.

One can make the case for a CBI, but Ailsa had a gift for making connections, and providing insights that gave people profound experiences and won new converts to the idea. For those who support a CBI, these may seem obvious, but on first hearing them, they help us to view the world in a different light. In her paper for the Scottish Parliament, she pointed out that 'The concept itself involves the acceptance of a whole new way of thinking about social security policy ... a CBI is more representative of a *radical idea* than a *welfare reform* proposal' (McKay, 2014: 7).

She emphasised the need to de-couple income and work and that CBI provided an opportunity 'to rethink our notions of work, income and citizenship rights within modern capitalist economies' (McKay, 2014: 7).

She argued for an awareness of the 'diverse roles of women as wives, mothers, carers and workers' (McKay, 2014: 7) and that gender concerns should be central to the debate on social security policy. She also noted that a CBI increases both efficiency and equity, thus appealing to both the right and the left of the political spectrum. I am committed to continuing her CBI project here in Scotland, but must admit that hers are big shoes to fill.

In this chapter, I note that the UK social security system has changed over the last seven decades and that changes in society have also occurred resulting in a social security system that no longer meets its original purpose of banishing want, so a new system fit for the twenty-first century is now required. It is not just that the benefit levels are below the European Union's (EU) official poverty benchmark as calculated by the Department for Work and Pensions (DWP, 2015), but the system is complex and beset by structural faults.

The main purpose of this chapter is to demonstrate how the set of options defining the current means-tested Social Assistance system in the UK can be identified as the cause of many current problems, often failing those who depend on it, especially women. They are contrasted with alternative options, including those that define a CBI system and which can produce more attractive outcomes. The chapter concludes by summarising the ways in which a CBI could have beneficial outcomes for women.

Why we need change

Beveridge (1942) identified five giant social evils: want, ignorance, squalor, idleness and disease. His solutions were a social security system, the 1944 Education Act, an extensive house-building programme, full employment policy and the NHS respectively. These together became the 'Welfare State' as part of the post-World War II consensus in the UK.

Society has changed markedly since the end of the war. Manufacturing has declined and many people are now on low wages, in part-time work, on zero or small hours contracts, in temporary work or insecure jobs. A much higher proportion of women are in the labour force now than in 1948. Marriage breakdown occurs more frequently, more couples cohabit without being married and there are more lone parent families (Donabie et al., 2010). The value of women's unpaid work in the home and caring for children and elders is still unacknowledged.

In addition, for income inequality has increased in the UK over the last four decades. The Gini coefficient is a measure of inequality of income or wealth, the values of which lie between 0 and 1, where 0 indicates complete equality, and 1 indicates complete inequality where everything is owned by one person. In 1979 it was 0.24, but it rose to 0.34 by 1991. Since then, it has stayed around 0.35 ± 0.02, including under the New Labour government between 1997 and 2010 (Belfield et al., 2015: 32). This was partly due to a steady reduction in real gross wages, as a result of globalisation and automation, but it has been exacerbated by the fiscal policies carried out by all UK governments since 1979 that have resulted in a distribution of income and wealth towards the rich (Bell, 2013).

Wren-Lewis (2015) makes a convincing case for claiming that the 2010-15 UK coalition government used the reduction of the deficit as an excuse for imposing its austerity policy for ideological reasons, causing an avoidable delay in the UK's economic recovery. Although the absolute poverty rate in the UK was already substantial at 21.6 per cent in 2013–2014 (13.6 million people): 'Looking further ahead, planned benefit cuts over this parliament will hit low-income working-age households hardest, and will therefore tend to put upwards pressure on absolute income poverty – including in-work poverty' (Belfield et al., 2015: 63).

The Social Security system in the UK was set up in 1948 and was designed for a very different society. It comprises a complex range of benefits with different bases of entitlement, but there are three main types: a contributory National Insurance (NI) scheme; a means-tested, Social Assistance (SA) safety net; and categorical benefits that are paid to those who meet specific conditions, for example, disability benefits (Millar, 2009). The NI scheme was designed for a full employment economy and comprised payments to replace earnings during periods of maternity, invalidity, sickness and unemployment, together with a retirement pension. The Social Security system has been undermined by many marginal changes over the decades. The value of NI benefits has eroded, so that these are less now than the safety net SA benefits, which themselves have been eroded (Spicker, 2015). It is not just that benefit levels are low today – few SA benefits meet the government's own poverty benchmark of 0.6 of median equivalised household income (DWP, 2015) – but also the design of the system causes problems for its recipients (Timmins, 2001).

The structure of income maintenance systems

Any income maintenance system must firstly specify its unit for the assessment and delivery of its benefits, and secondly define who is eligible to receive the benefits. Thirdly, it must decide whether everyone who is eligible receives the same level of benefit or whether there is differential entitlement, and lastly, it must stipulate whether entitlement is conditional or unconditional. These four design features, *the benefit unit, eligibility, selectivity* and *contingency*, together create the internal structure of income maintenance systems. A similar internal structure can be identified for employees' National Insurance Contributions and for the income tax system in the UK.

The **unit for assessment and delivery of benefits** can be based on the individual man, woman and child, or on a group of individuals (such as a couple, a family or a household).

Eligibility defines *who* is eligible to receive a benefit. It can be universal or targeted. Universality in this context means that everyone in a defined population is eligible. Targeting, as the term implies, designates a part of the defined population as being eligible, and this could be based on, for example, need, means or contribution record, among other things.

Selectivity refers to *differential levels of entitlement* for people who are otherwise equally eligible. Selectivity can have different bases or categories, including personal characteristics, such as age, gender, sexual orientation, race, chronic illness and disability. Selectivity implies that different levels of benefit would be paid according to someone's status within a particular basis. Selectivity could also be applied to situations which can be loosely grouped together as household relationships, including the number of adults in the household, marital status, number of dependent children, unpaid caring relationships or householder status. Non-selectivity means that differential entitlement is not applied.

Means-testing of benefits is a mixture of targeting based on low means, and also of selectivity because the entitlement decreases as incomes increase.

Contingency refers to whether conditions are imposed or not. Conditionality introduces further requirements that claimants must meet in order to qualify, imposing pre-conditions in order to affect the recipient's behaviour, for example through proof of availability for work, 'actively seeking work' or doing voluntary work. Sanctions may be imposed if the conditions are not fulfilled. This usually involves discretion in decision-making about entitlement.

Contributory benefits are usually based on the individual and eligibility is based on previous contributions, together with not being able or required to work, for example on account of maternity, sickness, unemployment or age (e.g. retirement). For unemployment benefit, selectivity would be based on being of working age, and meeting the kind of conditionality requirements outlined above.

Social Assistance benefits are among some of the most complex of all benefits. Cohabiting couples are assessed jointly and cannot make separate claims. Eligibility is based on low incomes. A complex selectivity is imposed. The newly introduced, means-tested Universal Credit in the UK, for example, is a working age benefit for people regardless of whether or not they are in employment. However, a range of selective criteria can apply including: age, whether the claimant is single or in a couple, the number of children, disability, childcare costs and housing costs (Miller, 2011).

Citizen's Basic Income structure

A CBI scheme is a program of cash transfer payments. It is based on the individual, and is universal, not means-tested, non-selective except by age, and is unconditional. It is: 'an unconditional, automatic and non-withdrawable payment to each individual as a right of citizenship … subject to a minimum period of legal residency in the UK' (Citizen's Income Trust, 2013: 3, 5).

A CBI can be full or partial. A full CBI would be paid at a high enough level for a single person to enjoy a dignified, if modest, standard of living, enabling participation in society, for example as indicated by the EU's official poverty benchmark of 0.6 of median equivalised household income (DWP, 2015). A partial CBI would require a means-tested safety net for those unable to top-up their partial CBI through earnings. Whilst a CBI is designed as an individual benefit, the primary care-giver would receive the Child CBI to administer on behalf of the child, as is the case for Child Benefit in the UK at present. A CBI would be tax-exempt.

If a CBI was implemented in the UK, it is assumed that it would replace the main income-replacement means-tested benefits, and contributory benefits, the State Retirement Pension and Child Benefit. It would also be accompanied by the phasing out of the Personal Allowance and other tax reliefs and allowances in the income tax system. More generous schemes would require more comprehensive changes to the income tax system. A CBI by itself could not redistribute income from rich to poor; for that to happen a progressive income tax system is needed.

The next section examines and compares the key features of the social security system in the UK with those of a CBI.

The unit for assessment and delivery of benefits

Helena Kennedy, the well-known barrister and broadcaster, wrote:

> Until the late nineteenth century, under the Common Law a husband and wife were treated as one person and marriage meant the surrender of separate legal rights for a woman. From this unity of husband and wife sprang all the disabilities of the married woman.
>
> (Kennedy, 1993: 25)

Indeed, many of these disabilities survive to this day. It was only as recently as 1990-91 that married women in the UK became entitled to independent taxation of their income and chargeable gains (HMRC, 2015).

Under the current SA system in the UK, all couples – married, in a civil partnership or otherwise cohabiting – have to make joint applications for benefits. In effect, the result of this is that most married or cohabiting women with no source of personal income are expected to be financially dependent on their husbands or partners. A married woman can have no recourse to an independent income except by termination of the marriage by divorce or widowhood (Thomson, 2002: 47). She is not legally entitled to any of her husband's income. This is not a gendered provision, and in theory it could also apply to a male partner, but it is gendered in its effect, since more women than men are likely to be affected in this way. Mothers, in the period after their maternity benefits come to an end and before they return to work, may find themselves in a position where they are not entitled to any social assistance in their own right and so become financial dependants. With nearly 57,000 births in Scotland in 2014 (National Records of Scotland, 2015: T2), a large number of women may be subject to this experience at any one time. In the current system, an adult offspring who lives with his or her parents is entitled to apply for benefits on his or her own account, while his or her financially dependent parent is not so entitled.

In contrast, a CBI scheme would entitle every man, woman and child to a cash payment in his or her own right. Those adults, mainly women, who would otherwise have been financial dependants can become emancipated, and through that, potentially empowered within the household, to negotiate fairer sharing of caring responsibilities and domestic tasks. In a recent basic income pilot project in India, everyone in the pilot communities had bank accounts into which their CBI could be paid and women's status was reported to be enhanced by their new financial independence (Davala et al., 2015). The tax/benefit unit for assessment and delivery being based on the individual is a necessary, but not sufficient, condition for full empowerment; it also requires universality and unconditionality.

Household economies of scale

Estimates for Minimum Income Standards (Centre for Research in Social Policy, 2015) confirm that households with two adults require less than twice that required by a comparable single-adult household, due to household economies of scale (HES) (Hirsch, 2015). If all adults receive the same level of CBI, then two adults sharing accommodation would be able to manage financially more easily compared with a singleton. In the current SA system in UK, HES are limited by the use of the cohabiting couple as assessment unit, but it is not applied to other adult couples, sharing accommodation such as two siblings or a parent and an adult offspring.

Under the current UK system, claimant couples can receive more between them apart than together. HES could provide an incentive for adults to share accommodation, both for two individuals to form a household together or, for example, for parents to stay together with their dependent children. The important point is that the financial disincentive effects of assessment based on the couple or family can affect household formation (Torry, 2013: 102– 103). Individual assessment implies that everyone's entitlement is the same whether single, married or otherwise cohabiting. The choice is between: joint assessment, avoiding HES, but maintaining the status of 'financial dependant', which affects more women than men; and individual assessment contributing to greater financial independence, while accepting HES for couples.

Eligibility: targeted or universal

Eligibility defines *who* is eligible to receive a benefit. It can be universal or targeted. Universal eligibility requires the population to be defined. Targeting excludes some members of the population from eligibility. Social Assistance benefits in the UK are targeted.

People on low incomes in the UK can apply for means-tested benefits. The targeting of benefits can divide society. It facilitates the stigmatisation of claimants, who feel the humiliation and rejection by their peers even more painfully than the problem of living on below poverty-level benefits. The stigma leads to low take-up of the benefits to which vulnerable people are entitled (Bamberg et al., 2013).

Universality means that everyone is included and, by avoiding the division that is created by targeting, it could lead to a more united and harmonious society. If those who were formerly excluded from state benefits are included, then it could help to reduce the *incidence* of financial poverty, depending on the generosity of the CBI. This is especially important for working-age adults, for whom there is no universal provision at the moment.

Although a CBI is universal, the population or geographical area to which it applies must be defined. Thus, some eligibility criteria are required. CBI could be paid as a right of citizenship, based on the legal right to reside in the country. However, this applies to many who have relocated abroad, so tighter criteria are required – both a residency condition of having lived in the country for a given period prior to payments commencing, and that they must continue in residence in the country for most of each year. This is not without its administrative problems (De Wispelaere et al., 2007). However, these issues arise with any income maintenance system, and are not explored further here. Criteria would also need to address specific residence criteria to stipulate the conditions under which asylum seekers and refugees are included.

Another potential criticism of CBI is that its universal eligibility includes rich people, who do not need it. However, universal services, such as the NHS in the UK, are inclusive, popular and redistributive. It is much more efficient to give a CBI to everyone, and to assess individuals for their means only once each year for income tax purposes. Building progressivity into the income tax system could ensure that the wealthy are no better off as a result of the introduction of a CBI.

Eligibility offers a choice between targeting, which can be divisive, stigmatising and leads to low take-up, and universality, which can help to create a more united and inclusive society, and helps to reduce the *incidence* of income poverty.

Targeting based on means-tested benefits (MTBs)

MTBs can introduce disincentives to work-for-pay into the system. Low-paid workers in the UK not only face deductions of income tax and employees' National Insurance Contributions (NICs) from their earnings, but the tapers (withdrawal rates) of their various MTBs are aggregated and also deducted, creating a Marginal Deduction Rate (MDR) which can be nearly 96 per cent (DWP, 2010: 8, para. 14). The MDR acts like a tax rate, and the high MDR rates facing low-income people introduced by the withdrawal of MTBs are greater than those facing higher-income taxpayers, whose MDRs are 42 per cent or 47 per cent at the most. These resultant effective tax rates are very regressive. A 96 per cent MDR would mean that a £10 pay rise was worth only 40p to the recipient once all deductions and benefits entitlements had been adjusted. The high MDRs inherent in MTBs depress the net incomes of low- and middle-income families, who would be obvious beneficiaries of the replacement of means-tested benefits by a CBI. Those not in the workplace would not necessarily gain unless the level of the CBIs was greater than their current benefit levels. Unemployed workers contemplating a return to the workplace in low-paid jobs also face this problem. Coupled with the erosion of the National Minimum Wage in real terms over time, it is now more difficult though not impossible for low-paid workers to earn their way out of poverty in the UK. The introduction of Universal Credit as the new working age benefit will improve this aspect slightly (Miller, 2011).

Entitlement to CBI will not be means-tested, either on the income or wealth of the recipient, or on that of another family or household member. Not means-testing benefits restores the incentive to work provided by the gross wage rates, even for individuals on low earnings, increasing labour market efficiency and it avoids making the income tax system regressive.

Selectivity

Selectivity refers to the practice of granting *differential levels of entitlement* to people who are otherwise equally eligible. The amounts of benefits may vary according to personal attributes (age, gender, disability) or circumstances. The administration of selective schemes can become much more complex where attributes change along a continuum rather than according to categories, or where they are based on circumstances that can change frequently.

A CBI scheme is non-selective, except that it could be age-related, with different amounts for a child, young adult, other working-age adult and for those over pension-entitlement age, with a child usually receiving less than an adult. Non-selectivity reduces administration and compliance errors by both recipients and staff. It is simpler and cheaper to administer and monitor and this should make it more transparent and accountable. It would also reduce the current time-consuming personal effort required for claimants to apply for benefits.

Can some selectivity be justified? The people most at risk of income poverty are:

- those over pension-entitlement age;
- the responsible parent of a dependent child, (parent with care);
- dependent children, aged 0–15;
- people with disabilities or chronic illnesses;
- unpaid carers.

A compassionate society would not compel a financially vulnerable adult to top up his or her partial CBI from earnings, which implies payment of a full CBI.

Disabled people

If introduced in the UK, disabled people would receive a CBI on the same basis as others. In addition, they should continue to receive tax-exempt, non-means-tested, disability benefits based on need, as now. This would comprise a parallel, but separate, system from the CBI scheme. Retaining all of the current disability benefits, with new automatic gateways to these benefits where necessary, would ensure that no disabled person is worse off under the new system. Ideally, each disabled person should receive a package of payments that would cover the extra cost of disability, for example for care, mobility, special equipment, special diets, extra heating and laundry costs. It could be argued on the ground of equity that disabled people who are able to undertake paid work should not have to use their earnings to cover the costs of disability (that are necessities to them), while other people can use theirs for luxuries (Spicker, 2015).

A full CBI, or reasonably generous partial CBI, for working-age adults would enable some unpaid carers to choose to take on the role voluntarily, without having to be nominated or approved officially. If costs are incurred on account of a caring role, such as fares to accompany the disabled person on a hospital visit, then ideally this should be part of his or her 'costs of disability' package. This would avoid the bureaucracy required to associate a particular unpaid carer with the disabled person.

Contingency: conditionality or unconditionality

Contingency refers to the practice of imposing pre-conditions on potential recipients which affect their entitlement to benefits, such as work tests, being involved in voluntary service or behaving according to traditional gender roles. In the UK, SA benefits used to be conditional on 'being available for work', but this has been replaced by the more stringent condition of the claimant having to provide evidence of having actively sought work (Watts et al., 2014). The implementation and enforcement of conditionality requires extra monitoring and administration, compared with a system without conditions, leading to an increased risk of error and fraud.

A relic from earlier times is the conditionality imposed on lone parents that, in theory, is gender-neutral, but in practice affects many more women than men. Their single status entitles them to an enhanced entitlement, but this is conditional on not living together as husband and wife, also known as 'the cohabitation rule'. Evidence of a regular, overnight, male visitor can lead to the withdrawal of benefit on the assumption that the regular visitor is supporting the single resident financially, even if he is not, casting him into the role of breadwinner and her into that of dependent home-maker (Kelly, 2011).

In contrast, unconditionality could help to reduce the inequality of power relationships. Together with the assessment unit being based on the individual and universal eligibility, unconditionality can emancipate and empower individuals. It grants the unconditional right not to be destitute, and contributes to financial security. Unconditionality gives people more choices and flexibility in life, helping them to develop to their full potential.

'The feminist version of the liberal egalitarian tradition that has as its foundation a universal, unconditional basic income at a level to meet basic needs ... prioritises the emerging norm of combined care work and paid employment throughout adulthood' (Zelleke, 2011: 39).

There are two main problems associated with unconditionality: firstly that everyone will give up working for pay and the economy will then plunge into a downward spiral; and secondly the idea of giving people 'something for nothing' which encourages 'free riders'. Atkinson (2015: 221), for example, would exclude from his Participation Income those who devoted their lives to pure leisure, while Van Parijs (1991) makes the opposite case for 'why surfers should be fed'. Perhaps society should celebrate the fact that some would willingly embrace a minimal consumption life-style, gaining enjoyment from living on a very modest, unconditional income. It may well be cheaper to tolerate free riders, rather than try to foist reluctant workers onto otherwise efficient companies, so long as they cause no harm, and their critics can choose to do likewise.

Labour market effects of unconditionality

Economic theory recognises two incentives that influence the number of hours that individuals are willing to offer in the labour market (their labour supply): one is the amount of unearned income, including a CBI, and the other is the real wage rate net of all deductions (such as income tax and NICs), that they face (Borgas, 2009). However, there is also a reservation wage below which a worker is unwilling to offer labour. In these circumstances, conditionality is used to over-ride the natural incentives of the market.

The evidence from labour supply economics is mixed, but the introduction of even a full CBI is unlikely to be sufficient to allow people to abandon their jobs. Layard (2006: 67–68) reports that work is the third most important factor affecting happiness after family relationships and financial situation. Thus it would appear that most people want to work for pay, not just for the earnings, but for the social and health advantages also (Pasma, 2009). Further, the replacement of MTBs by universal benefits would lower the Marginal Deduction Rates facing many low-waged workers, and the resultant increased real net wage rate could rise above their reservation wage rates and could increase their paid work hours markedly. Redistribution between unpaid and paid work could also occur. Unconditionality coupled with a full CBI would mean that no individual could be forced into the labour market to carry out unfulfilling drudge-work on low wages and parents could choose whether to take up paid work or look after their families at home (Mason, 2015).

Indexing the levels of the CBI to mean income per head, for the term of a parliament, would provide a self-stabilising mechanism for the economy. If people worked fewer hours on account of the CBI and mean income per head fell, then the level of the CBI in the following time period (as the same proportion of a lower mean income per head) would be lower, which in turn might provide an incentive for people to increase their work effort and earnings. However, a CBI also gives people the opportunity to make their contribution to society in a way that is important to them (Geoghegan, 2015).

Conclusion

The key strengths of a CBI system derive from its definition. It is a program of tax-exempt cash-transfer payments that are: based on the individual, universal, not means-tested, non-selective except by age and unconditional. Each of these features provides a major benefit for women. The benefit unit being the individual banishes the status of 'financial dependant' that traps many women, and offers them financial autonomy and the opportunity to rebalance power relationships. The benefit unit is likely to lead to household economies of scale, but this will also reduce disincentives for adults to share accommodation (including the parents of dependent children) and should help to reduce the demand for single person housing.

Universality avoids stigmatisation and division, helping to heal and unite society. The fact that fewer benefits will be means-tested restores incentives to work for pay, avoiding the poverty and unemployment traps, and making it more advantageous to be in the labour market.

Non-selectivity will end the practice of giving differential amounts based on household composition, which could vary relatively frequently, instead providing a CBI for each person in his or her own right.

Finally, unconditionality would end the cohabitation rule that can intrude into the lives of many single women claimants. It can help to reduce income poverty and provide financial security and contribute to the emancipation of women, giving them more life choices. It gives both men and women more control over their work-life balance and choice about how much time to spend on unpaid caring work and other domestic responsibilities. Even a partial CBI could provide many of these advantages to some degree, but the greater the generosity of the CBI, the greater its impact on the population.

A CBI provides a foundation for a very different type of society, which values the individual, helping him or her to meet material needs and offering choices and the opportunity to develop and flourish. It is designed to provide a floor to protect the poorest and most vulnerable in our society.

CBI is not a panacea for all society's ills. It cannot repair the damage caused by a housing policy that encourages speculative investment in homes and relies on means-tested benefits to make housing affordable for low-income groups. It would not replace public services such as education, health, social care and childcare, which are needed to complement the CBI system. It is not a sufficient condition on its own for a better society, but it is a necessary one.

References

All references to the *Citizen's Income Newsletter* are freely available to be read, printed, or downloaded, from the Citizen's Income Trust website, www.citizensincome.org (accessed 26 June 2015).

Atkinson, A. (2015). *Inequality: What Can Be Done?* Massachusetts: Harvard University Press.
Bamberg, B., Bell, K. and Gaffney, D. (2013). *Benefits Stigma in Britain*. Canterbury: University of Kent.
Belfield, C., Cribb, J., Hood, A. and Joyce, R. (2015). *Living Standards, Poverty and Inequality in the UK: 2015*. London: Institute for Fiscal Studies.
Bell, K. (2013). *Abolishing Want in a Social State*. London: Centre for Labour and Social Studies. [Online] Available from: http://classonline.org.uk/pubs/item/abolishing-want-in-a-social-state (accessed 9 September 2015).
Beveridge, William (1942). *Report on Social Insurance and Allied Services*. Cmnd. 6404. London: HMSO.
Borgas, G.J. (2009). *Labor Economics*. Boston, MA.; London: Irvin/McGraw-Hill, 5th edition.

Centre for Research in Social Policy (2015). *A Minimum Income Standard for the UK: Latest Minimum Income Standard Results*. [Online] Available from: www.lboro.ac.uk/research/crsp/mis/results (accessed 18 August 2015).

Citizen's Income Trust (2013). *Citizen's Income: A Brief Introduction*. London: CIT.

Davala, S., Jhabvala, R., Mehta, S. and Standing, G. (2015). *Basic Income: A Transformative Policy for India*. London: Bloomsbury.

De Wispelaere, J. and Stirton, L. (2007). 'The public administration case against participation income'. *Social Service Review*, 81(3): 523–549.

Donabie, A., Hughes, M. and Randall, C. (2010). 'Social trends through the decades'. *Social Trends*, 40: xxviii–xxxviii.

DWP (2010). *Universal Credit: Welfare That Works*. Cmnd. 7957. London: DWP.

DWP (2015). *Households Below Average Incomes (HBAI) Statistics: Data to 2013/14*. [Online] Available from: www.gov.uk/government/collections/households-below-average-incomes-hbai—2 (accessed 18 August 2015).

Geoghegan, P. (2015). 'Why money for nothing is good for all'. *The National*, 13 July: 10–11.

Hirsch, D. (2015). *Could a 'Citizen's Income' Work?* York: Joseph Rowntree Foundation. [Online] Available from: www.jrf.org.uk/Publications/could-citizens-income-work (accessed 24 June 2015).

HMRC (2015). *RE1000 – Married Couples: How to Treat Their Incomes for Tax Purposes*. [Online] Available from: http://webarchive.nationalarchives.gov.uk/+/http://www.hmrc.gov.uk/manuals/remanual/re1000.htm (accessed 18 September 2015).

Kelly, S. (2011). 'The truth about cohabitation'. Paper presented to *Social Policy Association conference*. Lincoln. [Online] Available from: www.social-policy.org.uk/lincoln/Kelly.pdf (accessed 9 September 2015).

Kennedy, H. (1993). *Eve Was Framed: Women and British Justice*. London: Vintage Books.

Layard, R. (2006). *Happiness: Lessons from a New Science*. London: Penguin.

McKay, A. (2014). 'Arguing for a Citizens Basic Income in a new Scotland'. *Citizen's Income Newsletter*, issue 2: 7–8.

Mason, P. (2015). 'Paying everyone a basic income would kill off low-paid menial jobs'. *The Guardian*, 1 February. [Online] Available from: www.theguardian.com/comment-isfree/2015/feb/01/paying-everyone-a-basic-income-would-kill-off-low-paid-menial-jobs/ (accessed 18 August 2015).

Millar, J. (2009). 'Introduction: the role of social security in society'. In Millar, J. (ed.) *Understanding Social Security*, 2nd edn., Bristol: Policy Press, pp. 1–10.

Miller, A. (2011). 'Universal Credit: welfare that works: a review'. *Citizen's Income Newsletter*, issue 1: 4–10.

National Records of Scotland (2015). *The Registrar General's Annual Review of Demographic Trends 2014*, 160th edition. [Online] Available from: www.nrscotland.gov.uk/files//statistics/rgar2014/table/rgar-14-appendix-table2.pdf (accessed 7 September 2015).

Pasma, C. (2009). *Working Through the Work Disincentive*. Ottawa: Citizens for Public Justice. [Online] Available from: www.cpj.ca/files/docs/orking_Through_the_Work_Disincentive_-_Final.pdf (accessed 18 September 2015).

Spicker, P. (2015). *An Introduction to Social Policy*. [Online] Available from: www.spicker.uk/social-policy/socialsecurity.htm (accessed 9 September 2015).

Thomson, J.M. (2002). *Family Law in Scotland*. London: LexisNexis Butterworths Law (Scotland).

Timmins, N. (2001). *The Five Giants: A Biography of the Welfare State*. 2nd edn. London: HarperCollins.

Torry, M. (2013). *Money for Everyone: Why We Need a Citizen's Income*. Bristol: Policy Press.

Van Parijs, P. (1991). 'Why surfers should be fed: the liberal case for an unconditional basic income'. *Philosophy and Public Affairs*, 20: 101–131.

Watts, B., Fitzpatrick, S., Bramley, G. and Watkins, D. (2014). *Welfare Sanctions and Conditionality in the UK*. York: Joseph Rowntree Foundation. [Online] Available from: www.jrf.org.uk/sites/files/jrf/Welfare-conditionality-UK-Summary.pdf (accessed 9 September 2015).

Wren-Lewis, S. (2015). 'The austerity con'. *London Review of Books*. 19 February. 37(4): 9–11.

Zelleke, A. (2011). 'Feminist political theory and the argument for an unconditional basic income'. *Policy and Politics*, 39(1): 27–42.

16

DEBATING A CITIZEN'S BASIC INCOME

An interdisciplinary and cross-national perspective

Caitlin McLean

Introduction

A Citizen's Basic Income (CBI) as it is known in the UK, also known as a Basic Income Guarantee (US), a Guaranteed Annual Income (Canada), or more generally as a Universal Basic Income (UBI), has gained renewed interest cross-nationally in both academic and policy circles in recent decades. For example, a European organisation for the advocacy of a basic income (the Basic Income European Network) was launched in 1986, and changed its name to the Basic Income Earth Network in 2004 in order to better reflect its international scope. In the UK a CBI has been advocated by the non-partisan Citizen's Income Trust as well as the Green Party as part of its 2015 election manifesto.

A CBI can be defined as 'an income paid by a political community to all its members on an individual basis, without means test or work requirement' (Van Parijs, 2004: 8). However, this leaves open to debate the particulars of any given basic income proposal including the extent of universality, the level of the payment and more (De Wispelaere and Stirton, 2004). In practice discussion of basic income often includes related proposals such as a Negative Income Tax (Friedman, 1962), Participation Income (Atkinson, 1996) and/or a Basic Capital Grant (White, 2011). This chapter, however, will refer specifically to a basic income, that is, an income which is:

- universal – paid to everyone in the population;
- individual – paid to each adult rather than as a single household payment;
- unconditional – without means-test or conditions regarding family or employment status;
- a cash benefit – delivered as a continual rather than one-off cash grant.

Although the core idea of a basic income is an old one, most commonly linked to Thomas Paine in 'Agrarian justice' (1796), the academic literature on the subject has only really begun to expand in the past few decades. Most of this literature has focused on the normative and theoretical arguments for basic income, also known as the 'ethics and economics' (Widerquist, 2005). Indeed, until relatively recently the two core questions of CBI research have been: 'Is it just?' (political philosophy) and 'Is it efficient?' (economic). New research has turned toward academic exploration of practicalities, or 'Could it work?' This has involved economic modelling and experimentation to ascertain the financial feasibility and sustainability of a CBI (Haigner et al., 2012) as well as political analyses concerning the role of the political process in shaping advocacy and possibilities for reform (Caputo, 2012; Murray and Pateman, 2012) and the challenges of implementation and administration (De Wispelaere and Stirton, 2012).

This turn towards feasibility questions has also led to increased attention to relevant empirical evidence and discussions on how to build the evidence base for a CBI. At present this consists of: an examination of a handful of real-world examples such as the programmes in Alaska and Iran; analyses of experiments and/or pilot programmes; and social scientific studies, especially surveys of likely responses to economic security and comparative-historical analyses of reform movements worldwide.

This chapter presents an overview of both the theoretical debates and the evidence base to date, with attention to both the interdisciplinary and cross-national nature of this rich and growing literature.

Theoretical and normative debates

Ethics

Political philosophers have long discussed whether and how a CBI could contribute to the ideals of a good society. The proposal has attracted support and criticism from a wide range of perspectives, including libertarianism, egalitarianism and communitarianism.

For libertarians, the principle benefit of a CBI is its individual and unconditional nature which promotes individual freedom and autonomy. Left libertarians such as Van Parijs (1995) argue that 'real freedom' *requires* a basic income in order to go beyond the formal processes of justice toward ensuring the means to carry out individual choice. Other libertarian advocates take a more pragmatic view, viewing a CBI as permissible rather than necessary, or the 'least worst' redistributionist policy which is most compatible with free markets and individual autonomy (e.g. Munger, 2011). This especially relates to the lack of conditionality requirements attached to a basic income: a CBI, particularly compared to most contemporary forms of social security, includes a lower degree of paternalism and intrusiveness regarding claimants' personal lives and a higher degree of neutrality regarding different lifestyle choices. Libertarian critiques tend to reflect broader normative commitments regarding the extent to which state coercion is justified rather than critiques of a CBI itself, although some have raised specific objections such as the possibility of increased immigration controls (Zwolinski, 2012).

Egalitarians promote a basic income on the basis of reducing social and economic inequalities via a universal minimum income floor. This includes class inequalities and redistributions of power between capital and labour (Wright, 2005), but also gender equality and increasing economic autonomy for women (see Gillespie, 2016). The principle of universality is especially key for increasing social solidarity and decreasing the stigmatisation of the poor. Nevertheless, some egalitarians have argued that a CBI is too blunt a policy instrument which does not go far enough in achieving equality of outcomes, as it emphasises formal equality in the face of difference (e.g. of capabilities – see Anderson, 2001).

From a communitarian perspective, the core benefit of a CBI is its emphasis on citizenship as the basis of entitlement and the potential for social inclusion which extends beyond the realm of remunerated employment (Jordan, 1992), a point which is also crucial for gender equality advocates, of whom Ailsa McKay (2005) has been a leading example. However, a key concern for communitarians is the extent to which a CBI, due to its unconditional nature, facilitates individualism at the expense of a sense of reciprocity and social obligation (Gorz, 1992). Indeed the question of reciprocity has sparked a substantial debate among political philosophers (see White, 2006), with detractors concerned about potential 'free riding' on the system (Van Donselaar, 2008).

Economics

The question of 'free riding' has also been particularly pervasive among economic discussions of a CBI. Economic perspectives on CBI proposals are diverse and have included neoclassical frameworks (e.g. Atkinson, 1995; Parker, 1989) as well as analyses from other economic schools of thought such as behavioural economics (Pech, 2010), Austrian economics (Nell, 2013) and feminist economics (McKay, 2005). In general, however, economists have focused largely on the potential effects of a CBI on economic growth and labour market efficiency, including employment incentives.

A core concern for economists has been the financial feasibility of a CBI, including the costs of the programme and any related behavioural effects – specifically whether implementing the policy would lead to a decreased incentive to be employed or to earn additional income, which would threaten the sustainability of the policy over the long run (for a detailed overview of this issue, see Pasma, 2010). Detractors working from standard economic models argue that giving people money unconditionally decreases their incentive to go out and earn it themselves and further creates incentives to 'free ride' on others' contributions to the economy. However, the net effects of a CBI on labour market participation are unclear, as a CBI is also likely to raise work incentives for many individuals, particularly those who face poverty and unemployment traps created by current systems of social security, in which low-income households face severe reductions in benefits for every pound they earn (see Miller, 2016). Further, financial incentives are not the only factors which determine an individual's propensity to engage in paid labour – non-monetary benefits of working such as status as well as intrinsic motivation from enjoyment of a task also motivate people to seek and undertake employment (see Pech, 2010).

CBI advocates have also challenged a narrow concern with employment incentives, arguing for a more nuanced appreciation of the complexity of economic life. In particular, from a macroeconomic perspective a CBI could smooth labour market transitions in a post-industrial society by providing security of income in a world of flexible, but insecure employment (Standing, 2002). Similarly, the ability to consider and potentially turn down offers of employment which are not suitably attractive to any given individual is important partially for normative reasons such as individual choice and freedom but also, from an economic perspective, because it increases the efficiency of the sorting mechanism of the labour market, better matching employees with employers and thus increasing their productive capacity (Van Parijs, 1992).

Ailsa McKay (2005) is amongst those feminist economists who have questioned whether some reduction in paid employment would be entirely detrimental if it leads to a redistribution of time between remunerated and (potentially) unremunerated but productive activity such as care work, volunteer work and entrepreneurial risk-taking, all of which could stimulate the economy indirectly.

Politics

More recently there has been a turn toward questions of political as well as economic feasibility. This has included practical discussion of implementation (De Wispelaere and Stirton, 2012) as well as detailed analyses of existing political contexts and prospects for reform, including the extent of support from political parties and other organisations (see Caputo, 2012; Murray and Pateman, 2012).

De Wispelaere and Stirton (2004) stress that basic income proposals are frequently advocated at a highly abstract level and therefore leave open for debate several dimensions which are crucial for policy design and implementation. Setting aside debate on a CBI versus similar alternatives, some of the most pivotal of these issues for a CBI are universality, uniformity and adequacy.

Universality refers to the extent of the population covered by a CBI, or who counts as a 'citizen' for the purposes of receiving a 'citizen's income'. Most proposals have been formulated at the level of the nation-state. Within this context, while some favour limiting the benefit to those who are citizens in the strict legal sense, many advocates, including Van Parijs, argue for a wider basis for inclusion, for example, on the basis of a certain period of residency, in order to limit reinforcement of inequalities between migrants and non-migrants. However, as Van Parijs (2004) notes, a CBI conceivably could be set at various levels of government and political communities, including at the supranational level, in order to sidestep economic objections about countries as 'welfare magnets' (Boso and Vancea, 2012) as well as normative objections to limiting eligibility to citizens of particular countries (Howard, 2006).

Uniformity refers to whether or not all eligible claimants receive a similar level of benefit. Many proposals advocate age differentiation in the level of benefit with smaller amounts for children and larger amounts for pensioners. There is also the question of whether payments should be allowed to vary to account for geographical price differences (see De Wispelaere and Stirton 2004: 269).

Lastly, and perhaps most controversially, is the question of adequacy, or at what level of payment a CBI should be set. In principle, a CBI could be set at, below or above subsistence level. While Van Parijs (1995) advocates for a basic income to be paid at the 'highest sustainable' level, he leaves open the possibility that political feasibility would necessitate a lower amount. Yet this is a crucial question. In particular, the level of income is key for debate regarding whether or not a CBI could feasibly be considered a substitute for current systems of social security (Murray, 2008) rather than a complement (Anderson, 2001).

However, policy design and administration are inherently political – they are shaped and constrained by existing political institutions and the vagaries of the political process; thus whether and how a CBI could be effectively implemented depends crucially on an understanding of how political processes work on a theoretical level (Boettke and Martin, 2011) as well as the relevant political context (De Wispelaere and Stirton, 2013).

At its most basic the political feasibility (and sustainability) of CBI depends on the perceived legitimacy of such a proposal. For example, regardless of the actual behavioural effects on employment, perceptions and expectations of 'free rider' behaviour have been acknowledged as a key barrier to the political feasibility of a CBI, especially within the contemporary context of increasing conditionality for income support and concerns about giving 'something for nothing' (Pasma, 2010).

On a more practical level, the successful implementation of a CBI also depends on strategies for reform. This includes plans for making the transition from the current set-up of social security arrangements in any given context as well as which political factions to court for support (De Wispelaere and Noguera, 2012). Healy and Reynolds (2012) suggest three possible approaches to reform:

1. all at once, or comprehensive reform;
2. by selective groups (e.g. children, elderly);
3. gradual reform via a piecemeal dismantling of the current system while building in steps toward a basic income.

Advocates are mixed on the best way to proceed. Jordan (2011) argues that partial steps (e.g. tax/benefit integration, reforms akin to negative income tax) are necessary because the political will and necessary advocacy for a full justice-based CBI is lacking. However, partial steps risk sacrificing some of the main benefits of a CBI, such as administrative simplicity.

In practice the choice of strategy will depend on the political context of the CBI proposal and the potential for support among various political and social organisations. For example, environmentalist and Green parties have been a key source of political advocacy for a basic income in many countries, yet their power to enact reform has to date been limited (De Wispelaere and Noguera, 2012).

Evidence

Real-world examples

A key limiting factor in the CBI debate is a lack of robust evidence on potential effects and outcomes due to the fact that there are few real world examples to study. The closest and most famous example is the Permanent Fund Dividend in Alaska (see Widerquist and Howard, 2012). Since 1982, each individual Alaskan has received an unconditional annual grant funded from state oil revenue. The amount varies by year and is very modest (usually between $1000–1500 per person, including children) and as such may be considered at best a partial basic income. The Alaska Permanent Fund has attracted a fair amount of attention, with advocates of CBI pointing to the programme's popularity among Alaskan citizens and Alaska's status as the US state with the least poverty and lowest income inequality. However, there has been little systematic analysis of the effects of the dividend on the Alaskan population (for an overview of available evidence, see Goldsmith, 2012).

A similar type of basic income was recently implemented in Iran, where all Iranians have been entitled to a small monthly cash benefit since 2010 (although the payment is not individualised, but instead goes to the head of the household) (Tabatabai, 2012). Like Alaska, it is financed from oil revenue.

In both cases, the successful implementation of a CBI relied on special circumstances: its introduction was relatively politically uncontroversial due to the method of funding (coming out of perceived common resources rather than as a tax on labour). Thus the question remains about the extent to which similar reforms would work elsewhere, for example by taxing other types of natural resources (see Widerquist and Howard, 2012).

Experiments and pilot programmes

In the absence of much real-world evidence on the effects of a CBI, many scholars have turned to evidence provided by a few experiments and pilot programmes of a basic income as well as related alternatives, such as the Negative Income Tax (NIT).

Although not technically a CBI as such (see Tondani, 2009 for a detailed overview of the key differences), the most widely analysed evidence comes from the NIT experiments in the US and Canada (see Widerquist, 2005 for an extensive review and analysis). Five experiments (four in the US and one in Canada) were conducted between 1968 and 1980. The experiments were designed to assess the effects on work incentives and they demonstrated, as expected, that those receiving unconditional cash transfers worked less than those who did not.

However, interpretation of this variation has produced widely differing conclusions about the merits of the programme. For one, the extent of work disincentive is complex. Few, if any, participants withdrew from the labour market entirely and the greatest reductions were primarily from secondary labour market participants who exchanged one productive activity for another (e.g. wives and mothers). Further, there was no evidence of a reduction in work effort sufficient to threaten the financial sustainability of the programme. Additionally, effects in other areas were largely positive (e.g. health, school performance). Nevertheless, concerns about any reductions in labour market participation and increases in divorce rates, as well as lay misunderstanding of the complexity of the findings and the limitations of the experiments, created strong political reservations about the proposals and they were abandoned in both the US and Canada.

More recently there have been pilots in developing countries which have aimed to test the effectiveness of unconditional cash transfers on alleviating poverty and other social goals. The first universal, unconditional basic cash transfer pilot in the world took place in Namibia in 2008. All residents (under 60, as a more generous pension scheme for older residents was already in place) of a small village received a small basic income of 100 Namibian dollars (roughly equivalent to 9 Euro) per month for two years. Results were reported as positive and included: reduction in crime (despite high degree of in-migration); reduction in food poverty and child malnutrition; higher school attendance and participation; and a rise in employment, especially self-employment due to entrepreneurial activities (see Haarman and Haarman, 2012).

However, the validity of these claims has been challenged in part due to methodological design (e.g. lack of a control group) as well as a lack of transparency for the data (Osterkamp, 2013). Like the NIT experiments, the pilot was not taken forward as it was plagued by controversy regarding the veracity of reported figures and the financial feasibility of the project.

Social science research

There has also been a push to increase social scientific analysis of the potential effects of a CBI using methods such as laboratory experiments, attitudinal surveys, parallels with related policy proposals and studies of political movements and attempts at reform.

Laboratory experiments (rather than those conducted in the field such as the US and Canadian NIT experiments) have been advocated as a potentially key source of evidence on how a CBI might work in practice (see Noguera and De Wispelaere, 2006), although to date there has been little advancement in this area (for an exception, see Haigner et al., 2012).

There has been comparatively greater use of survey research. Within this group, lottery winners have been a key population of interest, given the question of whether individuals would continue to be employed in the context of income security. For example, Marx and Peeters (2008) surveyed lottery winners in Belgium who received a lifelong stream of income rather than a one-off grant. The authors found little effect on labour market participation, but note that further research is needed given the low sample size of the pilot survey. Looking at hypothetical lottery winners rather than actual winners, Paulsen (2008) reviewed surveys which employ the 'lottery question' to gauge potential lifestyle changes if one unexpectedly received a substantial sum of money. The evidence suggests, as might be expected, that individuals with income security seem less willing to engage in labour they find wholly unsatisfying, although they nevertheless intend to pursue productive activity, including in some cases paid employment.

However, this is somewhat removed from the context of a CBI which under the vast majority of proposals would not provide a high standard of living on its own. Employing a more realistic level of income security with a hypothetical CBI proposal, Gamel et al. (2006) surveyed a sample of young adults in France, noting that few expected to withdraw from the labour market. Nevertheless, the hypothetical nature of the evidence militates against drawing anything more than tentative conclusions.

Another key method which has seen increased use is comparative-historical analysis (Caputo, 2012; Murray and Pateman, 2012; Widerquist and Howard, 2012). These edited volumes have charted political movements and attempts at reform toward basic income in countries as diverse as the US, Canada, Ireland, Germany, Brazil, South Africa and Mexico. Beyond documenting the increased interest in basic income proposals cross-nationally, these volumes have begun to unpick the factors at work in shaping support for or opposition to a CBI as well as the constraints on political action. For example, De Wispelaere and Noguera (2012) suggest four key aspects of political feasibility: strategic (the search for a robust coalition of advocates); institutional (state capacity for implementation); psychological (legitimation of the policy via broad social acceptance); and behavioural (policy sustainability in the face of possible behavioural change in line with incentives).

It has also not been particularly common for scholars to draw parallels between CBI proposals and similar or related social security measures, and as such the academic social policy literature remains a largely untapped resource. In particular, there has been remarkably little analysis by proxy of evidence on universal child benefits and/or conditional cash transfers (for exceptions, see Standing, 2008; Torry, 2012).

Conclusion

Although basic income proposals have a long history, academic research and policy debate about the subject have gained momentum in recent decades. This might well be a response to broad economic and social changes in the face of globalisation and a shift toward post-industrial economies, or due to increased political emphasis on questions of social inequality and the proper response of the state in the wake of the Great Recession.

Over the years, theoretical and normative arguments, especially the 'ethics and economics' of a CBI, have been particularly well developed. Only recently has there been a push to understand the political feasibility and practicalities of implementation, perhaps as a result of increased popular and policy interest spurred by organisations such as the international Basic Income Earth Network and the UK-based Citizen's Income Trust.

In line with this turn toward the practicalities of a CBI, researchers have begun to build the evidence base for basic income proposals. This has included descriptive accounts of real-world examples such as the Alaskan fund as well as analyses of pilot programmes. Increasingly, social scientific methods have been applied to the topic, such as comparative-historical analyses of reform movements in various countries and attempts to use survey or experimental methods to understand the likely effects of a basic income on labour market incentives.

Nevertheless, there remains much work to be done for academics and advocates of a Citizen's Basic Income. In particular, two challenges remain. The first is over-coming disciplinary divides in order to build a comprehensive understanding of the arguments for and likely outcomes of a CBI. The ethics, economics *and* politics of a CBI are each important but they are also interdependent.

Second, more effort should be directed toward building the evidence base for a CBI. This should include developing innovative uses for existing social scientific methods, such as recent studies which have applied survey and experimental methods. However, it should also include broadening the research questions. To date, most of these empirical analyses have focussed on the question of labour market incentives, but there is more to understand about a CBI. Future research should examine likely effects on other types of outcomes as well, such as poverty, individual wellbeing and gender inequalities, perhaps drawing parallels from other types of cash transfers. It could also include using attitudinal surveys and qualitative interviews to gauge understanding or support for a CBI, both from the public and from relevant stakeholders.

A movement in this direction would bolster the currently limited evidence base and help to parse arguments within a rich and lively theoretical debate on Citizen's Basic Income. For example, recent advances within feminist economics on issues such as women's labour market participation and intra-household inequalities of power and resources between men and women could help to illuminate debates about the role of a CBI in facilitating gender equality.

References

Anderson, E. (2001). 'Optional freedoms'. In Van Parijs, P., Cohen J. and Rogers J. (eds) *What's Wrong with a Free Lunch?* Boston, MA: Beacon Press, pp. 70–74.

Atkinson, A.B. (1995). *Public Economics in Action: The Basic Income/Flat Tax Proposal*. Oxford: Oxford University Press.

Atkinson, A.B. (1996). 'The case for a participation income'. *Political Quarterly*, 67(1): 67–70.

Boettke, P.J. and Martin, A. (2011). 'Taking the "G" out of BIG: a comparative political economy perspective on Basic Income'. *Basic Income Studies*, 6(2): 1–18.

Boso, À., and Vancea, M. (2012). 'Basic Income for immigrants? The pull effect of social benefits on migration'. *Basic Income Studies*, 7(1): 1–24.

Caputo, R.K. (ed.) (2012). *Basic Income Guarantee and Politics: International Experiences and Perspectives on the Viability of Income Guarantee*. New York: Palgrave Macmillan.

De Wispelaere, J. and Noguera, J.A. (2012). 'On the political feasibility of Universal Basic Income'. In Caputo, R. (ed.) *Basic Income Guarantee and Politics: International Experiences and Perspectives on the Viability of Income Guarantees*. New York: Palgrave, pp. 17–38.

De Wispelaere, J. and Stirton, L. (2004). 'The many faces of Universal Basic Income'. *The Political Quarterly*, 75(3): 266–274.

De Wispelaere, J. and Stirton, L. (2012). 'A disarmingly simple idea? Practical bottlenecks in the implementation of a Universal Basic Income'. *International Social Security Review*, 65(2): 103–121.

De Wispelaere, J. and Stirton, L. (2013). 'The politics of Unconditional Basic Income: bringing bureaucracy back in'. *Political Studies*, 61(4): 915–932.

Friedman, M. (1962). *Capitalism and Freedom*. Chicago: University of Chicago Press.

Gamel, C., Balsan, D. and Vero, J. (2006). 'The impact of basic income on the propensity to work. Theoretical issues and micro-econometric results'. *Journal of Socio-Economics*, 35(3): 476–497.

Gillespie, M. (2016). 'Citizen's Basic Income: a radical and transformative idea for gender equality?' In Campbell, J. and Gillespie, M. (eds) *Feminist Economics and Public Policy: Reflections on the Work and Impact of Ailsa McKay*. Abingdon: Routledge, pp. 189–197.

Goldsmith, S. (2012). 'The economic and social impacts of the Permanent Fund Dividend on Alaska'. In Widerquist, K. and Howard, M.W. (eds) *Alaska's Permanent Fund Dividend: Examining Its Suitability as a Model*. New York: Palgrave Macmillan, pp. 49–63.

Gorz, A. (1992). 'On the difference between society and community, and why Basic Income cannot by itself confer full membership of either'. In Van Parijs, P. (ed.) *Arguing for Basic Income: Ethical Foundations for a Radical Reform*. London: Verso, pp. 178–184.

Haarman, C. and Haarman, D. (2012). 'Namibia: seeing the sun rise – the realities and hopes of the Basic Income Grant Pilot Project'. In Murray, M.C. and Pateman, C. (eds) *Basic Income Worldwide: Horizons of Reform*. New York: Palgrave Macmillan, pp. 33–58.

Haigner, S., Höchtl, W., Schneider, F.G., Wakolbinger, F. and Jenewein, S. (2012). 'Keep on working: Unconditional Basic Income in the lab'. *Basic Income Studies*, 7(1): 1–19.

Healy, S. and Reynolds, B. (2012). 'Ireland: pathways to a Basic Income in Ireland'. In Caputo, R.K. (ed.) *Basic Income Guarantee and Politics: International Experiences and Perspectives on the Viability of Income Guarantee*. New York: Palgrave Macmillan, pp. 107–124.

Howard, M. W. (2006). 'Basic Income and migration policy: a moral dilemma?' *Basic Income Studies*, 1(1), 1–22.

Jordan, B. (1992). 'Basic Income and the common good'. In Van Parijs, P. (ed.) *Arguing for Basic Income: Ethical Foundations for a Radical Reform*. London: Verso, pp. 155–177.

Jordan, B. (2011). 'The perils of Basic Income: ambiguous opportunities for the implementation of a utopian proposal'. *Policy and Politics*, 39(1): 101–114.

Marx, A. and Peeters, H. (2008). 'An unconditional Basic Income and labor supply: results from a pilot study of lottery winners'. *Journal of Socio-Economics*, 37(4): 1636–1659.

McKay, A. (2005). *The Future of Social Security Policy: Women, Work and a Citizens' Basic Income*. Abingdon: Routledge.

Miller, A. (2016). 'A Citizen's Basic Income and its implications'. In Campbell, J. and Gillespie, M. (eds) *Feminist Economics and Public Policy: Reflections on the Work and Impact of Ailsa McKay*. Abingdon: Routledge, pp. 164–176.

Munger, M. (2011). 'Basic income is not an obligation, but it might be a legitimate choice'. *Basic Income Studies*, 6(2): 1–13.

Murray, C. (2008). 'Guaranteed income as a replacement for the welfare state'. *Basic Income Studies*, 3(2): 1–12.

Murray, M.C. and Pateman, C. (eds) (2012). *Basic Income Worldwide: Horizons of Reform*. New York: Palgrave Macmillan.

Nell, G.L. (ed.) (2013). *Basic Income and the Free Market Austrian Economics and the Potential for Efficient Redistribution*. New York: Palgrave Macmillan.

Noguera, J.A. and De Wispelaere, J. (2006). 'A plea for the use of laboratory experiments in Basic Income research'. *Basic Income Studies*, 1(2): 1–8.

Osterkamp, R. (2013). 'The Basic Income Grant Pilot Project in Namibia: a critical assessment'. *Basic Income Studies*, 8(1): 71–91.

Paine, T. (1899 [1797]). 'Agrarian justice'. In Conway M. D. (ed.), *The Writings of Thomas Paine: Volume 3*. London: Putnam, pp. 322–344.

Parker, H. (1989). *Instead of the Dole: An Enquiry into Integration of the Tax and Benefit Systems*. London: Routledge.

Pasma, C. (2010). 'Working through the work disincentive'. *Basic Income Studies*, 5(2): 1–20.

Paulsen, R. (2008). 'Economically forced to work: a critical reconsideration of the Lottery Question'. *Basic Income Studies*, 3(2): 1–20.

Pech, W.J. (2010). 'Behavioral economics and the Basic Income Guarantee'. *Basic Income Studies*, 5(2): 1–17.

Standing, G. (2002). *Beyond the New Paternalism: Basic Security as Equality*. London: Verso.

Standing, G. (2008). 'How cash transfers promote the case for Basic Income'. *Basic Income Studies*, 3(1): 1–30.

Tabatabai, H. (2012). 'Iran: a bumpy road toward Basic Income'. In Caputo, R.K. (ed.) *Basic Income Guarantee and Politics: International Experiences and Perspectives on the Viability of Income Guarantee*. New York: Palgrave Macmillan, pp. 285–300.

Tondani, D. (2009). 'Universal Basic Income and Negative Income Tax: two different ways of thinking redistribution'. *Journal of Socio-Economics*, 38(2): 246–255.

Torry, M. (2012). 'The United Kingdom: only for children?'. In Caputo, R.K. (ed.) *Basic Income Guarantee and Politics: International Experiences and Perspectives on the Viability of Income Guarantee*. New York: Palgrave Macmillan, pp. 235–264.

Van Donselaar, G. (2008). *The Right to Exploit: Parasitism, Scarcity, and Basic Income*. Oxford: Oxford University Press.

Van Parijs, P. (1992). 'The second marriage of justice and efficiency'. In Van Parijs, P. (ed.) *Arguing for Basic Income: Ethical foundations for a Radical Reform*. London: Verso, pp. 215–240.

Van Parijs, P. (1995). *Real Freedom for All: What (if Anything) Can Justify Capitalism?* Oxford: Oxford University Press.

Van Parijs, P. (2004). 'Basic Income: a simple and powerful idea for the twenty-first century'. *Politics & Society*, 32(1): 7–39.

White, S. (2006). 'Reconsidering the exploitation objection to Basic Income'. *Basic Income Studies* 1(2): 1–17.

White, S. (2011). 'Basic Income versus basic capital: can we resolve the disagreement?' *Policy and Politics*, 39(1): 67–81.

Widerquist, K. (2005). 'A failure to communicate: what (if anything) can we learn from the negative income tax experiments?' *Journal of Socio-Economics*, 34(1): 49–81.

Widerquist, K. and Howard, M. (2012). *Exporting the Alaska Model: Adapting the Permanent Fund Dividend for Reform around the World*. New York: Palgrave Macmillan.

Wright, E.O. (2005). 'Basic Income as a socialist project'. *Rutgers Journal of Law & Urban Policy*, 2(1): 196–203.

Zwolinski, M. (2012). 'Classical Liberalism and the Basic Income'. *Basic Income Studies*, 6(2): 1–13.

17

CITIZEN'S BASIC INCOME

A radical and transformative idea for gender equality?

Morag Gillespie

> A CBI explicitly incorporates the notion that income *should* be derived from rights of citizenship. Such an approach to policy provides for an account of the different social experiences of men and women in a market-based economy. A CBI therefore has the potential to shift the focus away from a 'gender blind' approach to social security provision and to promote more gender equitable outcomes.
>
> (McKay, 2005: 248)

As a feminist economist Ailsa McKay wanted to change how people think about key issues that affect women and men differently but are often gender blind in their planning and delivery. We first met when Ailsa came to work with me in a welfare rights service and it was during her time doing advice and advocacy work that Ailsa developed her long-standing interest in social security. As she helped people experiencing poverty to negotiate major social security reforms in the UK, the inefficiencies of the existing system became clear. She thought the terms of the debate on social security were flawed and began to explore alternative approaches that might address the realities of people's lives more effectively. She was drawn to the idea of Citizen's Basic Income (CBI), a universal income guarantee, but found that many proponents, as well as detractors, focused on issues around income maintenance and paid employment and did not take sufficient account of women's diverse roles.

Unpacking the issues concerning women, work and a CBI became the focus for her doctoral thesis and monograph, with a central concern that: 'social security policy designed and delivered with specific reference to the goal of promoting work incentives which fails to incorporate gender as an influencing variable will ultimately act in reinforcing traditional gender inequalities' (McKay, 2005: 35).

The global financial crisis and the recession and austerity measures that followed reignited debates about social security systems. In addition, the independence referendum in Scotland in 2014 provided a rare opportunity for people engaging in the debate to think 'outside the box' and challenge long-standing assumptions about social security. Ailsa was amongst those who dared to think about how Scotland might do things differently – and radically so – in a newly independent country, or one with far greater autonomy than existed at the time (for example, see McKay, 2013a). The remainder of this chapter outlines the key and developing arguments in her work on CBI as a radical idea and an emancipatory measure for women.

CBI – more than income maintenance?

The CBI is a form of minimum income guarantee that has generated interest and support across a broad political spectrum (McLean, 2016) and from within a range of academic disciplines. It differs from other forms of minimum income guarantee

> by virtue of the fact that it is paid:
> 1. to individuals rather than households;
> 2. irrespective of any income from other sources; and
> 3. without referring to any present or past work performance, or the willingness to accept a job if offered.
>
> (Van Parijs, 1992: 3)

Although the idea of a basic income has a long history (McKay, 2005; Pierson, 2016), the CBI presents as a radical approach to state-supported income maintenance policy in modern times and offers an alternative to existing policies and systems, particularly in terms of justifying principles, design and delivery mechanisms. As a form of social security, the aim of a CBI would be to replace all income maintenance benefits, including all reliefs set against tax liability, and the amount paid would be tax free. It would involve integration of the tax and benefits systems, reducing administrative costs. A CBI would ensure the financial gains from work were always positive (McKay, 2005). This contrasts with current arrangements, particularly in countries like the UK, where social security benefits (and the interaction of tax and benefits structures) are very complex and can result in poverty and unemployment traps that mean people are worse off, or no better off, when their income increases or they enter paid work (see for example: Miller, 2009; Spicker, 2011).

Key criticisms of CBI (see McLean, 2016) include: its perceived negative effects on the labour market; and the cost of providing a universal entitlement, particularly if it is implemented at a level that would act as a replacement for income maintenance benefits. Estimating the potential costs of a CBI is complex, involving a wide range of factors including funding sources (Torry, 2013). However, Ailsa McKay (2013a) argued that a focus on the perceived prohibitive cost of a universal individual entitlement is premature because funding sources and actual costs would depend on decisions made at the point of implementation, including the level of payment and how social security benefits and tax reliefs are defined and treated within national accounting frameworks.

Although some local and partial examples exist, the lack of any country-wide scheme means that a CBI is a reform proposal that thus far has not translated into reality at a national level (McKay, 2013a). Critics have argued that a CBI would create distortions and disincentives to engage in the labour market (see Pasma, 2010). However, supporters argue that a CBI promotes greater choice and enhances rather than restricts labour market flexibility, removes poverty traps and increases flexibility. Further, for people who are disadvantaged in the labour market, a CBI would provide a more secure basis for decisions about employment, making it possible to 'spread bargaining power so as to enable (as much as is sustainable) the less advantaged to discriminate between attractive or promising and lousy jobs' (Van Parijs, 2005: 15). Taking account of the value that modern society attaches to work, the notion of paying people 'something for nothing' presents as particularly challenging. In the UK attitudes towards recipients of social security have hardened considerably in recent years (Taylor-Gooby and Taylor, 2015), even though the value of working age benefits has fallen in comparison to average incomes (Rutherford, 2013). However, supporters of a CBI argue that it can contribute to improving social cohesion because of its universal nature, at the same time as reducing perverse incentives that discourage work and savings (Torry, 2013).

Beyond the market: a question of values

A key limiting factor for a comprehensive understanding of the potential of a CBI arises in the sphere of economic analysis. Economics as an academic discipline continues to be 'socially constructed and dominated by a particular, and limited, conception of human interactions.' (McKay, 2005: 8). In particular, mainstream economic policy and analysis tends to be gender blind so that gender justice issues are subordinated to concerns of economic efficiency. Activities that do not fit neatly into the model are not treated as 'productive' and consequently become undervalued by society in general. This type of work is largely invisible and has 'resulted in many labels including provisioning activity, affiliation and caring work. Whatever we refer to it as – it is work' (McKay, 2013b: 9–10) and it is mainly done by women.

Many supporters of CBI have tended to conform to this dominant approach and make their arguments within the confines of debate on income maintenance policy linked with the goals of preserving traditional work and pay relationships, with an implicit acceptance that formal labour market participation is the desired end result, leaving hidden the unpaid work of caring, affiliation and provisioning that supports the market economy to function. However the reality of people's lives is not reflected in a simple dichotomy so such advocates of CBI miss a key argument in their favour (McKay, 2007) in that a CBI, unlike most systems of social security, is more than compensation for non-access to the labour market and would provide the freedom to make choices. Whilst not standing in opposition to paid work it has the potential to 'act in promoting *gender neutral* rights of citizenship' (McKay, 2005: 247, original emphasis) with the potential to be an emancipatory measure for women. It can highlight the gender bias in current state welfare arrangements and account for the different social experiences of men and women in a market economy (McKay, 2007).

There is debate between feminists on the idea of a CBI including its potential impact on women's position within the household. Some feminists have argued that a CBI would institutionalise women's position in the home rather than emancipating them (for example, Orloff, 1990), serving only to alter the balance between staying at home to undertake unpaid caring activities and engaging in poorly paid work. However, Ailsa McKay (2005, 2007) questioned assumptions that alternatives, such as measures to support women into paid work, would address patterns of work allocation within households.

Women's attachment to the labour market today is stronger than in the past. However, while women have moved into the labour market in ever increasing numbers, the shift in roles within households has been much more limited. Despite women's increasing participation in the formal labour market, gender roles within households are shifting much more slowly so that women bear a continuing double burden of labour market and domestic work in the UK (Ben-Galim and Thompson, 2013) and across Europe (Mills et al., 2014). This would appear to be the case regardless of the nature of household employment arrangements.

Whilst many women may manage this through undertaking part-time and insecure forms of employment, the problem of women's double shift at work and at home persists. How sustainable is it for women to continue to support both the current and future labour markets? Carol Pateman (2004) highlights that, in the criticism of a CBI as encouraging free riding, images tend to envisage a man avoiding paid employment and some commentators have argued that, in the domestic sphere, women who are full-time housewives are also free riders. However, unpaid work in the home falls well short of the idea of idleness and fun and Pateman (2004: 99) argues that: 'The mutual reinforcement of marriage and employment explains why husbands can take advantage of the unpaid work of wives and avoid doing their fair share of the caring work. That is why there is massive free riding in the household – by husbands.'

Taking account of social *as well as* economic wellbeing means there is a need to recognise that work is not necessarily liberating or welfare enhancing and that the labour market is part of the solution but too narrow a focus on its own. It is possible for CBI to displace work for some people or support some who might struggle to access the paid labour market and, given their greater risk of poverty and inequality and their concentration in low-paid jobs and insecure forms of work, a CBI would help women to exercise some discrimination against 'lousy' jobs and improve their bargaining power. Crucially, according to Ailsa McKay (2013b), a CBI could promote individual autonomy and allow for the development of social and economic relationships beyond the confines of traditional market-oriented transactions.

Crisis, cuts and recession

One of the consequences of the global financial crisis and subsequent economic recession was that most governments in Europe embarked upon a programme of economic austerity involving substantial reductions in public spending. One result of these cuts, combined with a decline in labour market activity, is that the nature of the public sector in modern welfare states has been transformed. This unprecedented situation provided 'the opportunity and the challenge to sculpt new policies and institutions that will re-embed the economy in society' (Standing, 2011: 11). However, for feminist economists it is crucial that such debate reflects gender inequalities. The crises arose from processes that were gendered and:

> women were virtually absent from key sites of decision making in the financial sector; and in which neither private nor public finance was equitably distributed, and failed adequately to address the requirements of women as producers and as carers. The impact of these crises is gendered, too.
>
> (Elson, 2010: 202)

Campbell et al. (2016) show that women have been particularly disadvantaged by public spending cuts in terms of job losses in the public sector where women predominate, their greater likelihood of being underemployed and in insecure forms of work and their greater use of public services. Although the global recession presented initially as an opportunity to rethink our values, the opportunities for alternative political economy trajectories 'gave way to a strategy that involved effectively "rewarding" our revered financial institutions for what can only be described as reckless and irresponsible behaviour' (McKay, 2013c: 95).

Given the nature of poverty, inequality and exclusion, the recession and public spending cuts have heightened concerns about how sustainable and meaningful employment opportunities are for women. This reinforces the argument that the labour market can only provide part of the solution. Gendered economic processes fail to address the requirements of women as producers and carers and, particularly given the nature of poverty and inequality today, call into question the sustainability of the double burden of work and care on women, however much it is ignored in the formal accounts of work and the economy. Although it may present challenges, there is a need to consider how we can build new analytic frameworks, reconceptualise work, manage the social costs of increasingly unequal societies and deal with the problem of free riders. For Ailsa McKay, a CBI should be viewed as a radical rather than a reform proposal since it can provide the basis for creating space to rethink notions of work, income and citizenship rights within modern capitalist economies, whereas a continued exclusive focus on promoting work will 'fail to account for the experience of that work for many vulnerable individuals, including most significantly women' (McKay 2013c: 114).

Scotland's Independence Referendum – reassessing values at home

The run-up to the Scottish independence referendum in September 2014 created the space for people to reimagine policies unfettered by the constraints of existing arrangements. Thinking big about social security afforded the opportunity to shape a distinctively Scottish approach to social security rather than reform what already exists. For Ailsa McKay (2013a), this should meet the challenges of the dynamics of modern labour markets and the need to secure equality as well as efficiency objectives, moving towards a more proactive approach. A more inclusive starting point for debate raises key questions about the values and principles that inform investment in state welfare support: what kind of society we want; who and what do we value in that society; and how can the way we account for progress reflect those values (McKay, 2013a)? Such questions reflect the desire to respond to the perceived crisis in capitalism, the economic recession, austerity and growing inequalities and exclusion.

The momentum for thinking big about social security in a new Scotland was bolstered to an extent by some positive indicators in the political environment, with scope to build on core principles of equality enshrined in high-level strategy and processes. This included the founding principles of the Scottish Parliament itself (McKay 2013a), and a Scottish government economic strategy that had the twin goals of sustainable economic growth and promotion of equality (Scottish Government, 2011). The Scottish Government recognised the particular importance of women's position in Scotland's economy, for example in the first Women's Employment Summit in 2012, hosted jointly by the First Minister and the Scottish Trades Union Congress in 2012, which:

> highlighted the importance of women's role in Scotland's labour market and in the economy. It flagged the current pressures on women's employment and the limitations of economic models which fail to reflect the contribution of women's paid and unpaid employment.
>
> (Scottish Government, 2012: 6)

It must be noted that the challenges facing women in Scotland are similar in scale and nature to women elsewhere in the UK and Europe. In addition to the impact of the recession on the nature and quality of women's work in Scotland (Campbell et al., 2016), Engender (2013) summarise some key issues for women in Scotland as compared with men, including: their greater financial dependence on social security; their lower access to occupational pensions; the gender pay gap and women's over-representation amongst the lowest income groups. Women across the UK would also appear disproportionately to be bearing the brunt of changes to taxes and benefits in the UK, impacting on individual welfare as well as economic performance: 'According to the House of Commons library, some 80 per cent of the revenue raised and expenditure saved through changes to personal taxes and social security since 2010 will come from women' (WBG, 2014: 2).

All these factors led Ailsa McKay to argue, with renewed vigour, that CBI can provide the basis for creating space to rethink our notions of work, income and citizenship rights within modern capitalist economies (McKay, 2013b). Crucially, this needs to involve a clearer understanding of how the structures and processes associated with our economic system can better serve the needs of all citizens across all of our communities, making the relationship between society and the economy more explicit so that the opportunities and challenges can be identified and addressed.

Conclusions

The no-vote in the 2014 independence referendum meant that the potential for full autonomy over social security arrangements and for radical changes in Scotland has receded. We do not know how things might have developed in an independent Scotland, whether gender equality would have been sustained as a priority, with women's contribution to the economy and Scottish society reflected through the introduction of a CBI. Although she would have been disappointed with the result of the referendum, Ailsa would have continued to engage with political and policy actors (as well as students and women activists) to promote CBI as a radical idea. She would have pressed home her arguments to move beyond the confining parameters of the present analysis of the labour market and income maintenance policy and the work/non-work dichotomy and to decouple work and income, the better to understand and take account of women's roles in the economy.

In refining the debate about CBI as an emancipatory measure for women, it is important to recognise that it is not a panacea and the wider policy context is crucial. A more inclusive analysis, however, can help decision makers understand and address some key policy concerns that, if developed differently and in harmony within a wider social security strategy that includes a CBI, could address poverty and exclusion. Key examples in Scotland and the UK today include addressing the burgeoning problem of the lack of affordable housing, meeting the cost of disability, tackling the need for and costs of care and ensuring that the 'citizen' in CBI – or any other system of social security – is defined in a way that is inclusive, humane and non-racist.

Ailsa McKay would have taken every opportunity to argue that gender should be at the heart of social and economic policy analysis to understand how structures and processes could serve the needs of all citizens better and that a CBI provides the platform on which to build our understanding of what we mean by a 'good society'. She was a force for good who left a rich legacy that she built with passion, commitment, engagement and a wicked sense of humour.

References

Ben-Galim, D. and Thompson, S. (2013). *Who's Breadwinning? Working Mothers and the New Face of Family Support.* London: IPPR.
Campbell, J., McKay A. and Ross S. (2016). 'Scotland and the great recession: an analysis

of the gender impact'. In Campbell, J. and Gillespie, M. (eds) *Feminist Economics and Public Policy: Reflections on the Work and Impact of Ailsa McKay*. Abingdon: Routledge, pp. 112–123.

Elson, D. (2010). 'Gender and the global economic crisis in developing countries: a framework for analysis'. *Gender & Development*, 18, 2: 201–212.

Engender (2013). *Gender and Welfare Reform in Scotland: A Joint Position Paper*. Edinburgh: Engender.

McKay, A. (2005). *The Future of Social Security Policy: Women, Work and a Citizens' Basic Income*. Abingdon: Routledge.

McKay, A. (2007). 'Why a citizens basic income? A question of gender equality or gender bias'. *Work, Employment and Society*, 21: 337–348.

McKay, A. (2013a). 'Arguing for a Citizen's Basic Income in a new Scotland'. In Hassan, G. and Mitchell, J. (eds) *After Independence: An Informed Guide to Scotland's Possible Futures for Anyone Who is Pro or Anti Independence, Unsure or Just Generally Curious*. Edinburgh: Luath Press Ltd.

McKay, A. (2013b). *Welfare to Work or a Welfare System that Works? Arguing for a Citizens Basic Income in a New Scotland*. Research Paper no. 5/2013. Edinburgh: David Hume Institute

McKay, A, (2013c). 'Crisis, cuts, citizenship and a basic income: a wicked solution to a wicked problem'. *Basic Income Studies*, 8(1): 93–104.

McLean C. (2016). 'Debating a Citizen's Basic Income: an interdisciplinary and cross-national perspective'. In Campbell, J. and Gillespie, M. (eds) *Feminist Economics and Public Policy: Reflections on the Work and Impact of Ailsa McKay*. Abingdon: Routledge, pp. 177–188.

Miller, J, (2009). *Understanding Social Security: Issues for Policy and Practice*. Second edition. Bristol: Policy Press.

Mills, M., Tsang, F., Präg, P., Ruggeri, K., Miani, C. and Hoorens, S. (2014). *Gender Equality in the Workforce: Reconciling Work, Private and Family Life in Europe*. RR-462-EC. Report for the European Commission. Brussels: Rand Europe.

Orloff, A. (1990). *Comments on Ann Withorn, 'Is One Man's Ceiling Another Woman's Floor? Women and BIG'*, Paper presented at the 3rd international conference on basic income, Florence.

Pateman, C. (2004). 'Democratizing citizenship: some advantages of a basic income'. Politics and Society, 32 (1): 89–105.

Pasma, C. (2010). 'Working through the work disincentive'. *Basic Income Studies*, 5(2): 1–20.

Pierson, C. (2016). 'On justifying a Citizen's Basic Income'. In Campbell, J. and Gillespie, M. (eds) *Feminist Economics and Public Policy: Reflections on the Work and Impact of Ailsa McKay*. Abingdon: Routledge, pp. 153–163.

Rutherford, T. (2013). *Historical Rates of Social Security Benefits*. Standard note SN/ SG 6762. London: House of Commons Library.

Scottish Government (2011). *The Government Economic Strategy*. Edinburgh: Scottish Government.

Scottish Government (2012). *Equality Statement: Scottish Draft Budget 2013–14*. Edinburgh: Scottish Government.

Spicker, P. (2011). *How Social Security Works: An Introduction to Benefits in Britain*. Bristol: Policy Press.

Standing, G. (2011). 'Responding to the crisis: economic stabilisation grants'. *Policy and Politics*, 39(1): 9–25.

Taylor-Gooby, P. and Taylor, E. (2015). 'Benefits and welfare'. In Ormston, R. and Curtice, J. (eds) *British Social Attitudes: The 32nd Report*. London: NatCen Social Research. [Online] Available from: www.bsa.natcen.ac.uk (accessed 17 August 2015).

Torry, M. (2013). *Money for Everyone: Why We Need a Citizen's Income*. Bristol: Policy Press.

Van Parijs, P. (1992). *Arguing for a Basic Income: Ethical Foundations for a Radical Reform*. London: Verso.

Van Parijs, P. (2005). 'Basic income: a simple and powerful idea for the twenty-first century'. In Ackerman, B., Alstott, A. and Van Parijs, P. (eds) *Redesigning Distribution: Basic Income and Stakeholder Grants as Alternative Cornerstones for a More Egalitarian Capitalism*. London: Verso, pp. 3–42.

WBG (2014). *The Impact on Women of Budget 2014: No Recovery for Women*. London: Women's Budget Group.

Conclusions

18

CONCLUDING THOUGHTS

Building on Ailsa's legacy

Jim Campbell and Morag Gillespie

The chapters in this book have reflected on the issues that most concerned Ailsa McKay and the influences she has had on peers and policy makers in shaping theoretical perspectives and approaches to policy and practice in relation to women and the economy. In this final chapter we discuss how those interested in improving the position of women might build on her legacy, particularly in Scotland where her impact was most profound.

Despite her premature death, Ailsa achieved a huge amount both academically and politically for a 'daft wee lassie fae Falkirk' which was how she described herself in a radio interview in 2013 (Stark Talk, 2013). She was the first woman to head the Economics Department at Glasgow Caledonian University. Her work was appreciated by feminist economists globally and she was widely known as someone who challenged the status quo. In one of her last published works she called for a reshaping of the economy, economic theory and the economics profession:

> what is required is a more useful framework for understanding the complexities of human activity, the life experiences of all individuals, women in particular, and a widening of the debate to include the whole range of factors that contribute to human well-being.
>
> (Bjørnholt and McKay, 2014: 11–12)

The three themes explored in this book – gender budgeting; Citizen's Basic Income (CBI); and women, work and childcare – represented Ailsa's main research interests. However her writing and advocacy of these issues were not just as ends in themselves but to help us build a different and a better world. Whether in the lecture room, conference hall or in her writing, Ailsa always sought to demystify economics and to warn her audience against the sleight of hand, trickery and discombobulation that neo-classical economics promoted. Although she often set them in a Scottish context they are all global issues. This book celebrates Ailsa's success and impact in pushing these issues forward. However they are all very much 'work in progress' and this final chapter considers the next steps.

Despite the fact that mainstream economic models failed to predict the global financial crisis, it is these models which continue to inform the macroeconomic policies adopted by most governments. As Diane Elson eloquently demonstrates in Chapter 3, such policies in the UK have had a disproportionately negative impact on women. So clearly the starting point is to challenge the mainstream approach to macroeconomic policy and engender a paradigm shift in economic theory and policy towards alternatives that are relevant to women's lives and roles. This may seem a tall order but, to a large extent, progress on gender budgeting, a CBI and measures to address women's unequal access to and position in the labour market, including access to high quality childcare, are dependent upon just such a shift in thinking. Ailsa suggested that in order achieve this paradigm shift:

> it is necessary to draw on multiple approaches, acknowledging the overlap, inter-connection and cross-fertilisation between feminist economics, feminist legal theory, theorizations of care, care-work and dependency, in philosophy as well as in comparative welfare state research, and the reinvigoration and new theorizations of human rights.
>
> (Bjørnholt and McKay, 2014: 11–12)

Gender budgeting

In this spirit, the Women's Budget Group (WBG) and Scottish Women's Budget Group (SWBG) plan for a caring and sustainable economy – called Plan F – argues for a different economic strategy for a recovery that benefits the majority of people and reverses the damage cause by austerity measures in the UK since 2010. Amongst other things, they propose reversing cuts, reforms to harsh social security changes, new protections for carers and investment in social infrastructure. They do not shrink from addressing how to pay for it either, pointing out that: 'Deciding not to commission a replacement for the Trident nuclear submarine system would save £100 bn. over the next 30 years' (WBG and SWBG, 2015: 2).

In Scotland the evidence suggests that the arguments for the utility of gender budgeting has had some impact on the thinking of government ministers and policy makers. In particular, the refreshed Government Economic Strategy launched in 2015 is framed around the twin pillars of growth and equality (Scottish Government, 2015a). However while the shift in rhetoric is positive and is to be welcomed it remains to be seen whether this will translate into specific actions. In order to ensure that it does, organisations like SWBG and the Women in Scotland's Economy Research Centre (WiSE) need to keep pushing at the door Ailsa managed to prise open.

As a relatively new area of study and practice, gender budgeting and methods of analysis are continuing to evolve. In this book, case studies from Italy and Turkey highlight the potential of a capabilities approach for developing wellbeing analysis. But all the gender budgeting chapters remind us of the need to find ways to make the theory and analysis 'stick' not just in the rhetoric of equality, but in the planning and decision making processes concerning budgets and the economy.

How do we persuade governments to adopt gender budgeting? The country case studies in this book highlight that, even where there is political engagement, gender budgeting needs to get beyond political rhetoric and penetrate public finance practice. However, to our knowledge, gender analysis throughout the public budgeting processes is not yet a reality anywhere. Scotland, where the focus is on the (wider) equality impact of the budget, is no different and gender budgeting is still some way off. However, Ailsa's argument for the principles of gender analysis of budget setting and planning to be applied to economic strategy and policy in Scotland did generate more positive responses.

Women, work and childcare

Perhaps the area where Ailsa's efforts had the greatest impact is in helping to shape the Scottish government's childcare policy. The Scottish government is committed to increasing the amount of free childcare for all 3- and 4-year-olds in Scotland from 600 hours a year in 2014 to 1140 hours per year by 2021, the equivalent of 30 hours per week (Scottish Government, 2015b). The aim of providing 1140 hours free childcare featured in the Scottish Government's White Paper on Independence (Scottish Government, 2013); in other words this was something which they were committed to doing if Scotland had voted in favour of independence in 2014: 'we will put into action our independence plan to transform childcare – a plan put to me first by the late Professor Ailsa McKay of Glasgow Caledonian University' (Salmond, 2014).

Subsequently the government decided to implement the policy even though Scotland remains part of the UK. Indeed the former First Minister, in an interview shortly after he stepped down, indicated that his worst mistake during his time as First Minister was that he had not realised sooner the potential gains from the expansion of childcare as Ailsa had proposed (Sunday Herald, 2014: 9). He later elaborated on this:

> My passion for nursery education and the reason it appears so prominently in the YES campaign stems from the work of a wonderful feminist economist, the late Ailsa McKay. It was Ailsa who convinced me that affordable and universal nursery provision was not just a good idea (which just about everyone supports) but one of the essential economic strategies for developed democracies.
>
> (Salmond, 2015: 177)

So how did the 'wee lassie fae Falkirk' get to influence and shape Scotland's childcare policy? In part it was opportunistic: through her work with SWBG, her attendance at meetings of the Equality and Budgets Advisory Group (EBAG) and her role as special advisor to the Equal Opportunities Committee of the Scottish Parliament, she had access to senior government ministers and officials from the establishment of the Scottish parliament in 1999. The Scottish National Party was keen to demonstrate how things could be different and better in an independent Scotland and childcare presented as a good example. Furthermore, in the 2015 refreshed economic Strategy (Scottish Government, 2015a), increased free childcare provision can be seen as both a measure which delivers greater equality and also contributes to improved economic growth.

Occupational gender segregation in the Modern Apprenticeship programme remains an enduring issue, despite commitments from successive administrations in Scotland to tackle the problem. Scotland's flagship training programme continues to reflect and reinforce segregation in the wider labour market. Although women's participation in the formal labour market has improved significantly, despite the impact of the great recession, Campbell et al. in Chapter 11 remind us of the need to take care to look beyond the headline figures. Women are more likely than men to work part-time, be underemployed or subject to zero hours contracts. So the gender pay gap sustains as women continue to be concentrated in low paid, often precarious jobs and care and caring roles remain invisible in the analysis that informs policies and decision making.

In relation to childcare and modern apprenticeships in particular, Ailsa was able to convince the government that a more gender aware policy was a more effective policy in terms of delivering the policy objectives: 'Unless we can adapt the theory, policy will remain static and thus ineffective … if the way we interpret and understand the world remains driven by an attachment to neo-classical economic theory, we will never fully understand the nature of deprivation' (McKay, 2005: 245).

Ailsa would have used opportunities such as those presented by the revised Scottish Government Economic Strategy (Scottish Government, 2015a) to push for the analytic framework to reflect the lives and roles of all people in communities and not just formal labour market participation. Of course, this demands challenging but necessary investigative work to be done, including within household analysis, to inform policy and decision making. For example, investigating the impact of deflationary fiscal policy should include an examination of patterns of distribution within and across households; an assessment of the impact of a lack of affordable care services, on access to paid employment for men and women and an evaluation of how patterns of social reproduction are affected by economic restructuring that transfers costs from the formal paid economy to the unpaid household economy. Time use studies could provide interesting results in this respect (Olsen et al., 2009). Clearly, standard market-based indicators are not sufficient to provide a comprehensive analysis which accounts for gender.

Citizen's Basic Income

These issues were key concerns in Ailsa's thesis that a CBI had the potential to be an emancipatory measure for women. For her, the attraction was not just that it offered the possibility of a more efficient and effective system of income mainte-nance. Rather it offered the opportunity to reshape our thinking on what makes a good society and what and who we value in that society. A CBI offered the poten-tial to build a welfare system that recognises the totality of women's contributions to the economy and wider society. In particular, it would involve taking account of the provisioning role that women play which our current economic models do not acknowledge since they do not acknowledge the relevance of gender.

Therein lies the problem and the solution. In the current climate with the con-tinued dominance of the neo-classical economic orthodoxy, a CBI is not a realistic possibility, certainly in the UK. In order for it to become an acceptable policy the economic orthodoxy needs to change to one which recognises gender and that women and men have different lives, roles and relationships with the welfare state and that public spending can have differential impacts on men and women.

Although the potential for a radical change to social security receded follow-ing the referendum in Scotland, Ailsa would have continued to argue the case for CBI as the platform on which to build a welfare state that addresses poverty and exclusion and works towards a different vision for a 'good' society. There remains much work to do and some key questions to address in Scotland and more widely. How can we achieve affordable and accessible housing, with less reliance on large scale means-testing as in the UK today? How can the complex issues facing disabled people be tackled, in less intrusive ways than now, such as the extra cost of disability and the provision, access to and cost of the care and support they need? Policy makers need to rethink the nature and significance of care and the relationships between care, work and the wider economy – how do we address care and caring to ensure that carers are not exploited and put at risk of poverty and that care and its costs are more evenly shared? How can we ensure that the 'citizen' in CBI is defined in an inclusive, humane and non-racist way that does not leave people at risk of destitution and exclusion?

Conclusions

Ailsa's work shows that building gender awareness amongst policy makers takes time and acting on that awareness can take even longer. Advocates for change need to be in it for the long term, but a good starting point is to address how decisions about public spending are determined, in other words the budget. This means gender budgeting has a key role in challenging the way in which policies and spending decisions are made. Whatever remains to be done, it is clear that policy makers in Scotland are more gender aware and that is, in part, because of the lobbying and persuasive arguments of Ailsa McKay. Her impact is reflected in the words of John Swinney, MSP Finance Minister and Deputy First Minister, at Ailsa's commemorative conference in January 2015:

> Economic orthodoxy has always been that a strong economy is essential to building a fair and wealthy society. When I came to office as Finance

Minister in 2007 that probably captured my view of the world. But Ailsa was not an orthodox economist. She challenged us to consider that the reverse might also be true, that a society that is fair and equitable underpins a strong economy. And she certainly had an effect on my thinking because my thinking no longer subscribes to the economic orthodox view ... My view is that a society which is fair and equitable underpins a strong economy. Essentially that thinking is now underpinning the approach the government is taking to the formulation of the next iteration of its economic strategy.

Ailsa McKay: mother, wife, sister, feminist legend and disruptive force for good.

References

Bjørnholt, M. and McKay, A. (2014). 'Advances in feminist economics in times of economic crisis'. In Bjørnholt, M. and McKay, A (eds) *Counting on Marilyn Waring: New Advances in Feminist Economics*. Toronto: Demeter Press.

McKay, A. (2005). *The Future of Social Security Policy: Women, Work and a Citizens' Basic Income*. Abingdon: Routledge.

Olsen, W., Purdam K. and Afkhami R. (2009). 'Gender equality? Approaches and quantitative evidence sources for understanding the circumstances of men and women in the UK'. *Radical Statistics*, 99: 12–33.

Salmond, A. (2015). *The Dream shall Never Die: 100 days that Changed Scotland Forever*. London: William Collins.

Salmond, A (2014). *Speech by Alex Salmond to SNP Conference 12/4/14*. Available from: www.snp.org/media-centre/news/2014/apr/first-minister-alex-salmond-snp-conference-address (accessed 28 August 2015).

Scottish Government (2013). *Scotland's Future: Your Guide to an Independent Scotland*. Edinburgh: Scottish Government.

Scottish Government (2015a). *Scotland's Economic Strategy*. Edinburgh: Scottish Government.

Scottish Government (2015b). *Early Learning and Childcare Funds to Double*. Edinburgh: Scottish Government. Available from: http://news.scotland.gov.uk/News/Early-learning-and-childcare-funding-to-double-1667.aspx (accessed 28 August 2015).

Stark Talk (2013). *Stark Talk: Professor Ailsa McKay*. Radio Scotland, 26 November, 13.30.

Sunday Herald (2014). *Salmond: My Biggest Mistake*. 16 November, p. 9.

UK Women's Budget Group and Scottish Women's Budget Group (2015). *Plan F: A Feminist Economic Strategy for a Caring and Sustainable Economy*. [Online] Available from: http://wbg.org.uk/wp-content/uploads/2015/02/PLAN-F-2015.pdf (accessed 18 July 2015).

INDEX

Note: 'n' after a page number indicates a note; a **bold** page number indicates a figure; 't' indicates a table.

Addabbo, T. 54, 56, 57, 64
adequacy 181
Adiego, M. 72–3
Alaska 182
Alexander, G.S. 162
Ambrose 154
apprenticeships *see* Modern Apprenticeship
    (MA) programme
Aquinas, Thomas 155–7
Aristotle 155
Armstrong, P. 19
Atkinson, A. 172
Augustine 155
austerity policies 120, 144, 165–6, 193, 202

Basic Income Earth Network 177
Belfield, C. 166
Bell, D. N. F. 117
Bentham, Jeremy 160–1
Beveridge, F. 48, 165
Bevin, Ernie 143
Bjørnhølt, M. 68, 201
Black, Clementina 142
Blanchflower, D. G. 117
Bonvin, J.M. 58
Brown-Acton, P. 14
budgets, 'golden rule' for 30–1

Budlender, D. 41
Bunch, C. 50

Campbell, J. 84, 193
capabilities: defined 54, 64; Gaziantep
    Municipality budget allocation 68t
capabilities approach: to gender budgeting
    54–8; methodology 56–7; to wellbeing
    gender audit 64–5, 68t
care economy 19–20
care work: and occupational segregation
    17; as public service 91; terminology 17,
    18; unequal gender distribution of 56; as
    unpaid 18
CBI *see* Citizen's Basic Income (CBI)
childcare: costs of 101–2, **101**; economic
    case for 106; effect of, on women's
    employment 98–102, 108, 119; effects
    of expanding provision of 102–6, **105**;
    and gender equality 96, 98, 101; as
    infrastructure investment 83–92, 139–40;
    as investment spending 57, 96; McKay's
    support for 8, 94, 203–4; public benefits
    of 87–8, 105–6; public spending on
    106; in Scotland 8, 97, 203–4; as social
    infrastructure 85–6; as undervalued
    labour 141; and wellbeing 89

Citizen's Basic Income (CBI): advantages of, for women 10, 153, 168, 172, 173, 192, 195, 204–5; criticisms of 190–1; defined 10, 177; and disabilities 171–2; economic views of 179–80; ethics of 178–9; examples of 182–3; feasibility of 178, 179, 181, 184; and household economics of scale (HES) 169; in Iran 182; justifications for 153–63; McKay's support for 10, 13–14, 153–4, 164, 180, 189–95, 204–5; in Namibia 183; and Negative Income Tax (NIT) 182–3; as non-selective 171; overview of 190; Permanent Fund Dividend (Alaska) 182; political views of 180–2; and progressive property 162–3; research on 183–4; and Scottish independence referendum 194–5; structure of 167–8; and tax system 170; as unconditional 172–3; universal eligibility under 169–70, 180–1; *see also* social security system (UK)
Clement of Alexandria 155
Close the Gap (2014) 143
cohabitation 168, 169, 172, 174
conditionality 172–3
Constance, A. 132, 139–40
contingency 167, 172–3
Cooper, Selina 145

dementia 90
democracy 162–3
De Wispelaere, J. 180, 184
disability benefits 171–2
double shift 192, 193

E4E *see* Economics for Equality (E4E) programme
EBAG *see* Equality Budgets Advisory Group (EBAG)
economic policy, and gender budgeting 48–9
economics, feminist: actions for policy change 40–1, 40t; theories of occupational segregation 126; *see also* gender budgeting
economics, mainstream: 'golden rule' concept 30–1; limitations of 5; McKay on 191, 201; theories of occupational segregation 125–6

Economics for Equality (E4E) programme 51
economy: and CBI 179–80; impact of great recession on sectors of 119–21; Nelson's definition of 6
education: as investment spending 57; spending for, as excluded from public investment 32–3
EGBN *see* European Gender Budgeting Network (EGBN)
eligibility 166, 169–71
Elson, D. 38, 55, 84, 146, 193, 202
EMAKUNDE 41–2
employment: childcare's effect on, for women 87–8, 98–102, 104–6, **105**, 108; impact of great recession on 112–21, 113t, 114t, 138–9; motives for engaging in 173, 180; part-time 114–15, 115t, 116, 117, 119, 139; public vs. private sector 119–21; rate of, for men vs. women 98, **99**, 100t, **100**, 113t, 114t; self-employment 115–16, 116t, 118; short hours contracts 116–17; underemployment 117–19, 118t; women's aspirations for **103**; Women's Employment Summit (2012) 139–41; zero hours contracts 116–17
Equality Act (2006) 133n2
Equality Budgets Advisory Group (EBAG) 47, 49
ESA *see* European System of National Accounts (ESA)
ethics 178–9
European Gender Budgeting Network (EGBN) 41
European System of National Accounts (ESA) 32–3
European Union: social security system in 165; tax rates in 72

feminist economics *see* economics, feminist
fertility rates 88
financial crisis (2008-2009) *see* great recession (2008-2009)
Fitzgerald, R. 41, 72
Folbre, N. 17, 126
Francis 155
functionings, defined 54–5

Gamel, C. 184

gender: defined 14–15; occupational segregation by 9–10; *see also* third gender

gender audits: McKay on 68; of wellbeing, in Turkey 64–5, 66–8t

gender budgeting: analysis tool for 50; capabilities approach to 54–8; defined 6, 39; and economic policy 48–9; favourable conditions required for 42–4, **43**; as feminist policy change 38–44; and information sharing 50–1; in Italy 58; and macroeconomic policy 27–36; McKay's support for 202–3; overview of 38–9; in Scotland 41, 42–4, 46–52; in South Africa 39; in Spain 41–4, 58, 71–2; and taxation in Spain 71–8, 75t; in Turkey 62–9; and wellbeing 57–8

gender equality: and childcare 88, 96, 98, 101; policies for 40–1, 40t

gender inequality 15; in employment 113–14, 113t, 114t, 117–18, 118t, 120–1; of social vs. physical infrastructure investments 84; *see also* income inequality; occupational segregation

Gillespie, Morag 146

'golden rule' 30–1

Govender, P. 39

great recession (2008-2009): gender impact of, in Scotland 112–21, 138–9, 144; impact of, on economy 98, 119–21; impact of, on employment 112–21, 113t, 114t; overview of 112–15

Gunluk-Senesen, G. 57, 64

Hamilton, Cicely 141

Happy Planet Index 21

Harding, S. 13

health care 33

Healy, S. 181

HES *see* household economics of scale (HES)

Hewitt, G. 41

Himmelweit, S. 55

Hirschman, A. O. 84

household economics of scale (HES) 169

Htun, M. 40

human capital 84

Hume, David 157–9

income inequality: causes of 125–6; Close the Gap (2014) 143; by gender 75, **76**, 124; historical overview of 142–4; increase in 165; and Modern Apprenticeship (MA) programme 129, 133; and occupational segregation 141; in Scotland 194

income maintenance systems 166–7 *see also* Citizen's Basic Income (CBI); social security system (UK)

infrastructure: childcare as investment in 83–92, 139–40; defined 84–5; economic 85; as investments 31; social 34; social vs. physical 84, 85; spending on 16; *see also* public services

investment, defined 84

Iran 182

Irwin, Margaret 142

Italy 58

Jordan, B. 181

Kaul, N. 17

Kennedy, H. 168

Kingston, D. 140

labour force surveys 22

labour market: effects of great recession on 115–17; participation in, and CBI 183; participation in, for lottery winners 184; and unconditionality 173

Lagarde, C. 104

Layard, R. 173

Long-Term Care Insurance (LTCI) 19–20

lottery winners 184

Mackay, F. 47, 51

Macpherson, S. 131

macroeconomic policy: gender bias in 27–9; and gender budgeting 27–36; in United Kingdom (UK) 28–9

'mancession' 113

Marx, A. 184

Mazur, A. 40

McKay, Ailsa: biographical overview 4–5; and CBI 10, 13–14, 153–4, 164, 180, 189–95, 204–5; and childcare 203–4; on economics 191, 201; on gender auditing 68; and gender budget analysis 6–7, 39, 41, 46–7, 48, 49, 50–2, 71, 202–3; on gender budget initiatives 61, 62; influence of 13; research on occupational segregation 129–33; and Scotland's childcare policy 94; on stories' value 3; and trade union movement 146–7; and women's employment 140

Meagher, G. 8

means-tested benefits (MTBs) 167, 169, 170–1

Meikle, Anne 51

men: employment rate of **99**, 100t, **100**, 113t, 114t, 139; impact of great recession on 113–20, 113t, 114t; and part-time employment 114–15, 115t, 139; as self-employed 116t

menstruation 145

military systems 32

Modern Apprenticeship (MA) programme: female participation in 127–8t, 127–30; and income inequality 129, 133; male bias of 124–5; occupational segregation in 124–33, 204; overview of 126–7

MTBs see means-tested benefits (MTBs)

Mukherjee, A. 15

Namibia 183

National Health Service (NHS) 90

National Institute for Health and Care Excellence (NICE) 90

National Insurance (NI) 166

Negative Income Tax (NIT) 182–3

Neil, Alex 143–4

Nelson, J. 6, 8

Nelson, J. A. 13, 17

Netto, G. 133

NHS see National Health Service (NHS)

NICE see National Institute for Health and Care Excellence (NICE)

NIT see Negative Income Tax (NIT)

Noguera, J.A. 184

Nott, S. 48

Nussbaum, M. 54, 55, 56

occupational segregation: and care work 17; causes of 125–6; by gender 9–10; horizontal vs. vertical 125; impact of McKay's research 129–33; and income inequality 141; in Modern Apprenticeship (MA) programme 124–33, 204; see also gender inequality

O'Hagan, Angela 146

O'Hara, S. 20

Ostrom, E. 20

Paine, T. 178

parental leave 56

Pasma, C. 181

Pateman, C. 192

Paulsen, R. 184

pay gap see income inequality

Peeters, H. 184

Permanent Fund Dividend (Alaska) 182

Personal Social Services (PPS) 90

Peter 154

Peter, F. 22

Picchio, A. 55

politics 180–2

poverty rates 88

PPS see Personal Social Services (PPS)

property, private: Aquinas on 155–7; Bentham on 160–1; early Christians on 154–5; Hume on 157–9

property, progressive 161–2

provisioning, as concept 5–6

public services: and care work 91; defined 84–5; women's use of 28, 144, 193 see also infrastructure

public spending: capital vs. current 84; cutbacks in, and women 55, 193; on family benefits, by country 106, **107**, 108, **108**; as investments 31, 57; issues of defining, as investments 32–4, 89–91; UK policy 29–30; see also gender budgeting

Reed, H. 29

revenue see taxation

Reynolds, B. 181

Robeyns, I. 56

Robinson, Joan 5

Rubery, J. 39

Salmond, Alex 139, 203
Saltini, S. 57
Scotland: austerity policies 120; and CBI 13; childcare in 8, 203–4; economic strategy of 95–6, **95–6**; gender budgeting in 41, 42–4, 46–52; gender impact of great recession in 112–21, 144; independence referendum 194–5; McKay's influence on childcare policy in 94; public vs. private sector employment 119–21, 144; rationale for childcare provision in 97
Scottish Trades Union Congress (STUC) 138, 139, 140
Scottish Women's Budget Group (SWBG) 41, 42, 47, 48, 50, 51, 130
segregation, occupational *see* occupational segregation
selectivity 166–7, 171, 174, 181
self-employment 115–16, 116t, 118
Sen, A. 30, 54–5
Sharp, R. 40, 42, 50
short hours contracts 116–17
Singer, J. 161–2, 163
Siraj, I. 140
Smith, Grahame 145
SNA *see* System of National Accounts (SNA)
Social Assistance (SA) 166
social infrastructure *see* infrastructure
social security system (UK): benefit levels 165, 166; as conditional 172–3; and household economics of scale (HES) 169; justifications for changes to 165–6; and means-tested benefits (MTBs) 170; targeted eligibility under 169–70; women as financial dependents under 168; *see also* Citizen's Basic Income (CBI)
Sosenko, F. 133
South Africa 39
South Korea 19–20
Spain: gender budgeting in 41–4, 58, 71–2; taxation in 71–8, 75t
Standing, G. 193
Starr, Mark 143
Stirton, L. 180
STUC *see* Scottish Trades Union Congress (STUC)
Sturgeon, N. 34, 83, 109, 132, 139

SWBG *see* Scottish Women's Budget Group (SWBG)
Swinney, J. 205–6
System of National Accounts (SNA) 84

taxation: and CBI 170; in European Union 72; in Spain 71–8, 75t
third gender 14–16
Tolmie, Agnes 139
Trade Union Act (1927) 143
trade union movement: McKay's alliance with 146–7; women's participation in 144–5
transportation 57
Truger, A. 33
Turkey: Gaziantep Municipality budget allocations 66–8t; gender budgeting in 62–9; wellbeing gender audit in 64–5

UK Equality Act (2006) 29
UK Women's Budget Group 29
unconditionality 172–3, 174
underemployment 117–19, 118t, 121
Underkuffler, L. 161
unemployment 113–14, 113t, 114t *see also* employment
uniformity *see* selectivity
United Kingdom (UK): Fiscal Charter 34–5; macroeconomic policy in 28–9; public expenditure 29–30; social security system in 165
Universal Basic Income (UBI) *see* Citizen's Basic Income (CBI)
universality 169–70, 174, 180–1
utility 160

Vanautu 21
Van Parijs, P. 153, 172, 177, 178, 180, 181, 190, 191
Vas Dev, S. 40

Walker, I. 129
Waring, Marilyn 147
Weldon, S.L. 40
wellbeing: and childcare 89; defined 54; and gender budgeting 57–8; as investment return on spending 34; women's role in, for families 55

Widerquist, K. 178
WiSE *see* Women in Scotland's Economy Research Centre (WiSE)
women: advantages of CBI for 10, 153, 168, 172, 173, 192, 195, 204–5; childcare's effect on employment of 98–102, 104–6, **105**, 108; and double shift 192, 193; employment aspirations of **103**; employment of 87–8; employment rate, vs. men 98, **99**, 100t, **100**, 113t, 114t; financial dependence of 168, 194; Fiscal Charter (UK) impact on 35; impact of great recession on employment 112–21, 113t, 114t, 138–9; in Modern Apprenticeship (MA) programme 127–8t, 127–30; and part-time employment 114–15, 115t, 116, 117, 119, 139; and public sector employment 120–1, 144; as public services users 28, 144, 193; and public spending cutbacks 55, 193; as self-employed 116, 116t; and trade union movement 144–5; underemployment of 117–19, 118t, 121; and unpaid work 28, 55–6; and wellbeing 55; work of, as undervalued 141–4, 191

Women in Scotland's Economy Research Centre (WiSE) 50, 84
Women's Employment Summit (2012) 139–41, 194
work *see* care work; employment
work, unpaid: in care economy 18; performed by women 28, 191; and women's household labour 55–6; *see also* care work
World War I 141–2
World War II 143
Wren-Lewis, S. 165
Wright, Val 146

Zelleke, A. 172
zero hours contracts 116–17
Zhu, Y. 129